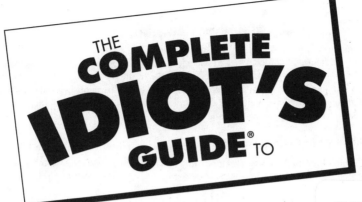

THE
COMPLETE
IDIOT'S
GUIDE® TO

Edible
Gardening

by Daria Price Bowman and Carl A. Price

ALPHA

A Pearson Education Company

This is a CWL Publishing Enterprises Book, developed for Alpha Books by CWL Publishing Enterprises, Inc., Madison, WI, www.cwlpub.com.

International Standard Book Number: 0-02-864411-5
Library of Congress Catalog Card Number: 2002113243

04 03 02   8 7 6 5 4 3 2 1

Interpretation of the printing code: The rightmost number of the first series of numbers is the year of the book's printing; the rightmost number of the second series of numbers is the number of the book's printing. For example, a printing code of 02-1 shows that the first printing occurred in 2002.

Printed in the United States of America

For marketing and publicity, please call: 317-581-3722

The publisher offers discounts on this book when ordered in quantity for bulk purchases and special sales.

For sales within the United States, please contact: Corporate and Government Sales, 1-800-382-3419 or corpsales@pearsontechgroup.com

Outside the United States, please contact: International Sales, 317-581-3793 or international@pearsontechgroup.com

Publisher: *Marie Butler-Knight*
Product Manager: *Phil Kitchel*
Managing Editor: *Jennifer Chisholm*
Senior Acquisitions Editor: *Renee Wilmeth*
Development Editor: *Ginny Bess Munroe*
Senior Production Editor: *Christy Wagner*
Copy Editor: *Michael Dietsch*
Illustrator: *Chris Eliopoulos*
Cover/Book Designer: *Trina Wurst*
Indexer: *Julie Bess*
Proofreader: *Megan Douglass*

Contents at a Glance

Appendixes

Contents

17 Exotic, Unusual, and Esoteric Edibles   171

Foreword

I am certain that more people would garden if they felt confident in succeeding. And I don't mean throwing a few marigold or zinnia seeds onto a patch of bare soil, and seeing them compete with a jungle of weeds to produce a splash of color, regardless of rainfall or soil fertility. I mean the deeply more satisfying form of gardening that produces edible results—luscious cantaloupes with chin-dripping flavor, meaty tomatoes where one slice can cover an entire slice of bread, raspberries the size of strawberries, strawberries the size of peaches, and bell peppers up to ten inches long—crunchy, nutritious, and delicious. Surely, there are few gardening accomplishments in life more satisfying than planting an Early Cascade variety of tomato in your garden and harvesting a hundred or more red, ripe billiard ball–size fruits in a single season, or serving to a guest a dinner the blemish-free Buttercrunch head lettuce they just admired on a tour of your garden.

That is why I recommend this book. It inspires confidence, assures success, and explains clearly and convincingly how to enjoy a bountiful harvest of not only the most worthwhile vegetables to grow, but also fruits, berries, and herbs.

Daria Price Bowman and Dr. Carl A. Price are a daughter-and-father partnership I greatly admire, for in this collaboration Daria brings to bear a practical approach, a lively writing style, and organizing ability, while her father is a wealth of information about the science of gardening. As a retired professor of plant biochemistry at Rutgers University for 40 years, he knows the scientific reasons why certain basic gardening practices (like composting and disease treatments) work, even if the remedy itself is simple. Both are life-long gardeners, and though they advocate an organic remedy as the first line of defense, they know when to turn to science when all else fails.

There have been many garden books aimed at beginners, but these are largely focused on flower gardening, and many are "gimmick" books, advocating some sensational method of gardening with exaggerated claims like "weed free" and "no work." The information in this book, on the contrary, offers choices and clearly explains how to succeed whether you want to garden in traditional straight rows, plant in blocks, or harvest abundant produce from raised beds or containers. It's all here—clearly explained with special helpful sidebars such as Prof. Price's Pointers and others.

Every dietary study, it seems, confirms the wisdom of eating more fruits and vegetables and using herbs for seasoning, for a healthy, long life. Broccoli is known to have anti-cancer properties; we are told that blueberries can reverse the process of aging; carrots can improve eyesight; garlic is associated with a healthy bloodstream; and vegetable fiber will cleanse the colon of impurities.

Of course, fruits and vegetables, and even herbs, can be obtained in quantity from the grocery section of every supermarket, but the longer a vegetable stays on the shelf, or travels in transit from field to point-of-purchase, the more it will lose freshness, crispness, and flavor. Moreover, flavor in many fruits and vegetables can be adversely affected by being picked too early so as to survive long journeys, even if they are flavorful varieties to begin with. But more often they are not those special home garden varieties with a reputation for top flavor; rather they are commercial grower varieties, bred mainly for appearance and the ability to ship safely, without bruising. Indeed, few home garden varieties ever make it to the local produce counter simply because flavor is fairly far down on the list of priorities for commercial growers.

So here is a book written for the home gardener in mind, impartial in its advice, with step-by-step instructions to guide you every step of the way, whether you are keen to have a small garden the first year, or a plot big enough to feed a family of four from the last frosts of spring through the first frosts of autumn, and even until snow covers the ground. Follow its advice, and I believe you can be a successful gardener the very first season.

Derek Fell

Derek Fell is an award-winning author of gardening books and magazine articles, with more than 60 books to his credit, including *Vegetable Gardening with Derek Fell* (Friedman/Fairfax) and *Herb Gardening for Beginners* (Friedman/Fairfax). He has won more awards from the Garden Writers Association than any other person.

Introduction

Home gardening takes many forms. There are gardeners whose joy in life comes from raising dwarf conifers. Others find pleasure in planting peonies. Growing an edible garden is probably the most popular of all gardening styles and it's not difficult to understand why. After all, when we till the earth, plant seeds, and harvest food to feed our family and friends, we are repeating tasks that humans have done for thousands of years.

In this book, you will find everything you need to know to create a garden of edible plants. There is very basic information that may be new to the novice, along with plenty of in-depth advice for those who are more experienced. While there are no guarantees, after reading this book and following the techniques and procedures outlined in these pages, along with plenty of sunshine, adequate rainfall, and a sprinkling of good luck, you should be able to enjoy a bountiful harvest of home-grown edibles.

How This Book Is Organized

The Complete Idiot's Guide to Edible Gardening is written in six parts. Each one addresses a different aspect of growing vegetables, herbs, and fruits in the home garden.

Part 1, "Why Grow Food When the Grocery Store Is So Close By?" takes a broad look at why, when grocery stores are so convenient, we would want to grow our own fruits and vegetables. Of course it all has to do with things like health, quality, and freshness, not to mention saving money, having a steady source of hard-to-find foods, the fun of it, and the sense of accomplishment that it brings.

This part of the book will also help you decide what kind of garden you want to make, how big it will be, what it will look like, and even how much help you might need. There are also sections on gardening with kids, growing organically, and making the most of small spaces.

In **Part 2, "Essential Planning,"** we'll get into some of the really important basics of gardening including an overview of what tools you will most likely need to have, where you are going to put this garden, how to do proper planning on graph paper and then translating a plan to a plot, and exploring some design schemes that may appeal to you.

We'll also have a chance to look at some of the smaller, but no less important, details like fencing options, paths and walkways, environmental factors, and architectural elements of your property.

Part 3, "Get Ready to Plant," gets down and dirty. It's in these five chapters that you'll learn all about the science of gardening including an entire chapter on soil and another on the biology of plants. It's fairly complicated stuff, but we have broken it down into easy-to-understand tidbits.

This part also takes you step-by-step through creating garden beds where plants will thrive, and the process for sowing seeds both indoors and directly in the garden, as well as how to transplant tender new seedlings.

Part 4, "What to Plant," is essentially a catalog of dozens of different edible plants, and is chock full of what you need to know to grow them. One chapter is on basic things like lettuce, tomatoes, corn, and beans. Another focuses on melons, peppers, peas, eggplants, leafy greens, and the *Brassica* family (cabbages and their relatives). Farther into Part 4, you'll "get back to your roots" with information on root vegetables like turnips and parsnips and other vegetables like onions and potatoes whose edible parts also grow underground. There is also a full chapter on herbs, another one on unusual and exotic edibles, and one on small fruits.

Part 5, "Keeping It Going," is all about maintenance: how and why to weed, the essentials of irrigation, pests and diseases, pruning and trimming, and a section on troubleshooting.

Finally, in **Part 6, "Reaping the Rewards,"** you'll learn how and when to harvest the edibles you have grown, and then what to do with them once they are in your harvest basket. Canning, freezing, drying, and making jams, jellies, and pickles are some of the options you'll learn about. There is also a section on sharing the bounty of your garden with those who are less fortunate. Part 6 ends with a look at the world of seed saving, taking care of tools, keeping records, and planning for the next gardening season.

Some Other Important Stuff

With the hope of making this book easy to read and conveniently organized for finding what you need to grow your edible garden, there are four different types of sidebars that provide additional information. These are explained here.

 Garden Guru Says

In these sidebars, you'll find bits and pieces of horticultural information, techniques, and cultural practice that will, I hope, improve your expertise in the garden.

Food for Thought

You'll find advice, tips, anecdotes, and even a little gardening lore in these sidebars.

Compost Pile

These sidebars contain a collection of warnings about gardening pitfalls and potentially serious or even dangerous situations that will require your special attention.

Prof. Price's Pointers

Sprinkled throughout each chapter are a few of these sidebars in which Prof. Price explains scientific, technical, historic, or academic aspects of gardening, and gives definitions of terms.

Acknowledgments

The authors would like to thank a few folks who made this book possible. First, there is John Woods of CWL Publishing Enterprises, the packager of this book, who was able to get past his previous experiences with my writing habits and invited me to write this book. He and his editor Bob Magnan have been encouraging and supportive throughout. Thanks also go to developmental editor Ginny Bess who was able to make sense of my work, who didn't fuss when I took so long to get it all done, and made this into something I am very proud of. I owe so much to my wonderful husband Ernie Bowman, who keeps everything running smoothly when I am deep into a project, and loves me no matter how cranky I get; and to Cassie who manages so well when her mom is on the computer for 12 hours straight; and to Sam for her encouraging daily e-mails. I am grateful to my colleagues at Coldwell Banker Hearthside Realtors, where I make my living, for graciously putting up with my whining about deadlines, and my hogging the computers for so many weeks. It is, however, my amazing father, Carl A. Price, the Prof. Price of this book, to whom I am most grateful. I am forever indebted to him for his good counsel and endless consultations; his research and rewrites. His contributions to this book were huge and essential. Thank you for everything, Daddy.

Daria Price Bowman
New Hope, PA
August 2002

Trademarks

All terms mentioned in this book that are known to be or are suspected of being trademarks or service marks have been appropriately capitalized. Alpha Books and Pearson Education, Inc., cannot attest to the accuracy of this information. Use of a term in this book should not be regarded as affecting the validity of any trademark or service mark.

Part 1

Why Grow Food When the Grocery Store Is So Close By?

Not everyone needs or cares to know the history or the science behind what we do, but we find that kind of stuff fascinating. While researching this book, we were able to fill in some rather large gaps in our own knowledge banks, especially about the origins of agriculture that we are hoping you'll find interesting. (And Prof. Price has provided us with some really essential information about fruits and vegetables, and the science of why foods make it possible for us to live. But there's really only a little academic stuff here, so don't worry.)

I USED THESE TIRES TO PROTECT MY TOMATO PLANTS. NOT ONLY DO THE TOMATOES TASTE GREAT, BUT THEY ALSO GET GREAT MILEAGE!

Chapter 1

Growing Food

In This Chapter

- A look at the growth (if you'll pardon the pun) of agriculture from ancient times
- Learn why fresh produce is so satisfying
- Discover what organic gardening really means
- See why you might want to grow specialty and hard-to-find items
- Learn how to save money on fruits and vegetables

There is nothing more basic than food. The earliest humans learned this the hard way, as they chased after bison and bears with nothing but a big rock to kill them with. It didn't take long—only a few thousand years—for our ancient ancestors to figure out that life is easier when there is a steady source of food, and the only way to have a truly reliable supply is to *grow* it. Thus agriculture was born.

From agriculture came farming and gardening, and the rest is history. In this chapter, we look at how our long-ago relatives tamed plants and carried them from continent to continent, developing new ways to garden along the way. And we see why growing vegetables and *fruit*s has become one of America's favorite pastimes.

A Little History

About 12,000 years ago, human beings had had enough of their primitive hunting and gathering existence. They had, by that time, discovered fire and had come to the realization that cooked food was a lot tastier than raw food. These early men and women had also learned how to craft quaint cooking vessels out of bark, seashells, tortoise shells, and eventually from clay. Some of the smarter members of the human clan had cleverly devised food combinations that met their bodies' nutritional needs, and had begun to mix meat and fish with collected fruits, roots, leaves, and seeds in their new cookware, making tasty soups and stews.

Because the hunting and gathering lifestyle was difficult and unpredictable, the very smartest folks developed ways to make plants grow in convenient places. (They also domesticated animals, but that's another book.) So around 10000 B.C.E. in what is now the Middle East, agriculture was born and soon spread to the Western Mediterranean and points north and east.

Prof. Price's Pointers

The word **fruit** actually refers to the ripened ovary of a plant's flower. Therefore, most vegetables are actually fruits. Tomatoes, zucchini, and corn are all fruits of the plants on which they grow.

Over the next 10,000 years, farmers began to cultivate new food plants all over the world. In 7000 B.C.E., walnuts and beans were first planted. The year 6000 B.C.E. was a big one for corn. Grapes, oranges, and watermelons got their cultivation start around 4000 B.C.E. By 3000 B.C.E., barley, peas, carrots, onions, fava beans, and apples became part of the farmer's repertoire.

The vegetables and fruits we grow and eat today are either Old World or New World plants. From a historical perspective, Christopher Columbus gets the credit for introducing most of the New World plants to Europe.

New World foods include the following:

- Beans
- Corn
- Peanut
- Pepper
- Pineapple
- Potato
- Pumpkin
- Squash
- Strawberry
- Sunflower
- Tomato

Old World foods include the following:

- Beet
- Broccoli
- Carrot
- Eggplant
- Lettuce

- Okra
- Onion
- Pea
- Radish
- Yam

Prof. Price's Pointers

In order to sustain life, a human being must consume foods that contain sugars (carbohydrates), proteins (nitrogen components), lipids (fats), micronutrients (minerals and vitamins), and fibers. All of these essential nutritional elements are available by consuming a variety of plant species.

It's hard to believe that at one time, lettuce, peas, and radishes were rare and exotic. Today, we take even some of the most exotic foods we eat for granted. When I was growing up, in the 1950s and 1960s, lemongrass might have been available in San Francisco, but the produce manager at the A & P in Arlington, Massachusetts, probably never heard of it. In the late 1970s, when I taught a class in Mexican cooking at the YMCA, I had to order cilantro by mail from a specialty house in New York. Now it's carried in most grocery stores.

With modern commerce, we are able to enjoy foods from every corner of the globe. And with the huge number of seed and plant growers and vendors, there's just about nothing you can't find to grow yourself.

Fresh Is Best

If you have never picked a tomato right from the vine and taken a bite out of it right there in the garden, you don't really know what fresh food is. Harvesting edible plants and consuming them immediately is one of life's most sensual pleasures.

When I was a very young child, my family had a favorite summertime ritual—while Mom started a big pot of water on the stove, Dad and the kids would drive a short distance to a neighborhood farm where the farmer would let us pick our own corn. We would shuck the ears while Dad drove and by the time we got home, the water would be boiling on the stove. In went the corn and, a few minutes later, we sat down to feast. That's as fresh as it gets.

With recent nutrition research proving that canned, frozen, and otherwise processed fruits and vegetables might be just as good, or even better, for us than their raw counterparts, should we be less interested in growing our own? Absolutely not! While most of us might assume that our home-grown foods might be more healthful, the real reason we are willing to do all the work that goes into producing produce is because fresh fruits and vegetables taste so much better.

Prof. Price's Pointers

Fresh fruits and vegetables are undeniably wholesome and healthful. But eating them raw isn't necessarily the healthiest approach. According to a study published by the American Chemical Society, the antioxidant levels of carrots increased dramatically immediately after being cooked to the point of mushiness. Research done at Cornell University showed that the antioxidant value of tomatoes is increased significantly when the tomatoes are cooked. In fact, many canned or frozen vegetables and fruits have more nutritional or disease-prevention value than their raw counterparts.

A Matter of Taste

While there are many reasons people garden, one of the primary motivating factors is a matter of taste. Homegrown vegetables and fruits taste far superior to anything you can buy in a store. Sure, roadside stands and farmers markets sell great stuff, but nothing is as fresh as right out of your own garden.

Edible gardening gives us the opportunity to experience foods in a different way than we are used to. We know where the fruits and vegetables come from, what went into growing them, how they have been handled, and how fresh they are. We can plan meals based on what is ripe. And we can choose to grow those things that we savor most without being at the mercy of a produce manager's whim.

Of course, there are limitations. The grocery store can offer us asparagus and artichokes most of the spring and summer as it comes in from various places around the world. The home gardener has one season—often all too brief. But the joys of some other vegetable whose time has come might be enough consolation.

Specialties of the House

One of the best rewards of edible gardening is the opportunity it gives you to grow something special, something different from the ho-hum veggies found in every grocery store. For just a few dollars you can become a specialist in Asian or Mexican vegetables. With a handful of herb plants and a little research, suddenly you are an expert on subtle seasonings or herbal remedies.

Growing your own food plants is so versatile, too. With successive plantings you can add new things mid-season or stop planting something that didn't work out that well. You can change your approach from year to year.

Here are some specializations you might want to consider:

- A wide variety of one type of plant (beans, corn, carrots, etc.)
- Baby and dwarf vegetables
- Produce for pickling
- Salad fixings (including 10 types of lettuce)
- Asian stir-fry foods
- Onions and their relatives
- Peppers (from hot to sweet)
- Heirloom vegetables
- Bramble fruits
- Pumpkins or melons
- Fancy potatoes
- Tomatoes
- Latino cooking ingredients
- Herbs for French cuisine
- Medicinal herbs

Prof. Price's Pointers

The natural sugars in fruits and vegetables are what give them the flavors we like so much. After harvest, that is, when the fruit is removed from the plant, those sugars are quickly converted to starch that has a different and less stimulating taste. The longer the fruit sits before consumption, the less sugar is available to produce the flavors we crave.

One of the great things about gardening is the flexibility it gives us. Each new season offers the opportunity to redefine what kind of gardener we are.

To Be Organic or Not to Be

There are organic gardeners and then there are Organic Gardeners. Those truly committed to creating and maintaining a completely organic garden should understand that it requires more than simply forgoing pesticides and herbicides. Having an organic garden means that one has embraced an entire set of standards.

Earth-Friendly

David Benner, a gardening friend of mine who lectures and writes about his gardening practices, has one of the most earth-friendly gardens you can imagine. While he specializes in shade plants, moss, and native flowering shrubs, his techniques would translate well to edible gardens.

David removed every last square inch of grass from his property so he would no longer have to use a (noise and air) polluting lawn mower. He composts all his garbage and garden debris and uses the rich results to amend the soil and feed the plants. He faithfully conserves water and encourages native plants that require less than exotic imports. David grows only those plants that are appropriate to the climate and conditions in his garden.

Food for Thought

Here are some basic organic gardening rules:

- Select a location that is appropriate for the plants you will grow.
- Prepare the soil with organic material.
- Choose disease-resistant varieties of plants.
- Rotate crops to avoid infestations and soil depletion.
- Compost your plant material and debris.
- Use compost and other organic material to enhance soil.
- Use nonchemical approaches to disease and insect control.
- Conserve water.
- Avoid use of power equipment.

Protecting the Hyper-Allergic

Allergies are a problem for millions of people. For some, an allergy might be little more than an annoyance, but for others, an allergy to a food or environmental factor can be life threatening. For those who have serious environmental allergies, especially allergies to insecticides, pesticides, and herbicides, growing foods organically might be one of the few ways to have some control over the quality of their lives.

Protecting the Environment

Whether or not you are planning to garden organically, it's a good idea to understand why so many people are interested in this concept.

A major source of water pollution in the United States is fertilizer residues in storm water runoff. A great deal of that fertilizer comes from lawn and garden applications by homeowners. In addition, research indicates that most homeowners use far more than the recommended amounts of herbicides and pesticides when they treat their gardens and lawns. Careless watering is another problem in many parts of the country where several years of drought have strained supplies.

Careful use of resources and products is an intelligent way to approach gardening, whether or not you buy into the organic way of life.

Saving Money

Fussy consumers will spend considerable time picking through the snap peas, fennel, frying peppers, and bok choy at supermarkets, specialty stores, roadside stands, and farm markets. And they will pay hefty prices for the best stuff. Artichokes go for $2 apiece. A tiny sprig of rosemary is $1.99. And the mesclun, try $9 a pound—if you can find it. Even plain old no-frill vegetables can be as costly as chicken or beef.

Garden Guru Says

Consider this equation: You buy 10 young tomato plants for $1 a piece and each plant yields about 20 pounds of tomatoes. Calculated at $1.99 per pound (the price at the grocery store for yucky, hot-house tomatoes), your $10 investment gives you about $398 in fresh, delicious tomatoes—enough to eat fresh all summer long with a few left over for canning or drying.

There is a better way. Growing your own produce can save money. A friend of mine raises fancy mixed lettuces in a flat on her terrace. Her $9 investment in seeds, the seed tray, and potting mix rewards her with gourmet salad for two for most of the summer.

In addition to growing your favorite vegetables and fruits, why not grow the most expensive ones? Most won't cost any more to grow than the low-cost varieties.

Some of the more expensive types you might want to consider are the following:

- Fancy leaf lettuces
- Cherry and grape tomatoes
- White eggplant
- Fancy potatoes
- Herbs
- Radicchio
- Arugula
- Baby and dwarf vegetables

String beans are relatively inexpensive, but dainty French filet beans cost a fortune. The zucchini is practically given away by midsummer, so grow tiny, trendy, patty pan squash instead.

When you grow your own produce from seed, the savings become even greater. Take, for example, fancy mesclun salad mix. These beautiful little salad greens can be prohibitively expensive, especially for everyday salads. But for $3 to $4 you can buy 1,500 seeds of assorted lettuces, cresses, arugula, and mache, which will produce so much of the stuff, you'll be giving it away to grateful friends.

Garden Guru Says _____

There are some wonderful fruits and vegetables whose initial investment is relatively high, but that have a big payoff down the road. Asparagus, artichokes, raspberries, blueberries, and strawberries all should be started from plants rather than seed. It could cost $100 or more to start a raspberry patch. But 10 years later when you are picking those exquisite ripe berries, you'll know it was worth every penny.

The price of fresh vegetables can be astronomical, even higher sometimes than chicken or beef.

For those who regularly select organically grown produce at the grocery store, growing your own organic produce can be a real money saver.

CAUTION

Compost Pile _____

While it is possible to save money by growing your own foods, the investment in time is considerable. If you calculate the number of hours it takes to prepare the soil, sow the crops, weed, water, and protect the plants from insects, and then multiply those hours by what you earn in an hour ... Well, don't bother to do the math. You'd never break even!

The Least You Need to Know

- ◆ Grow your own vegetables and fruits to have a steady supply of your favorites. Or create a specialty garden to supply your passion for particular types of cooking.

- ◆ Realize that fresh vegetables taste best, but that their nutritional and disease-prevention qualities might not be as high as their canned or frozen counterparts.

- ◆ Really understand what organic gardening means before you give yourself that label.

- ◆ Remember that growing your own vegetables and fruits can be less expensive than buying them, as long as you don't add in the cost of your time.

Chapter 2

What Kind of Garden Will You Grow?

In This Chapter

- Calculating the time you need to grow the garden you want; knowing when and how to hire help
- Growing a little of this and a little of that
- Developing a garden of culinary delights, including grapes and other fruits
- Working with culinary and medicinal herbs
- Uncovering the benefits of square foot gardening

In this chapter, we look at what sort of garden you might want to create, with an emphasis on the time it will take to achieve the goals of each type of garden. Is your garden going to be one that gives you a smorgasbord of vegetables or just focus on just a few culinary favorites? Are the medicinal and curative powers of herbs your special interest? Or does the idea of growing your own grapes have enormous appeal? When considering these types of gardens, how much can you realistically handle? In addition to looking at the issues behind these questions, we also look at the highly specialized concept of square foot gardening.

Later chapters cover, in much more detail, the techniques for growing various fruits and vegetables. In this chapter, we focus on the general types of gardens you might want to grow.

Time Is of the Essence

Gardening is America's favorite pastime—with the emphasis on time. Unlike other great hobbies and avocations like golf, stamp collecting, or flea marketing, gardeners can only take time off in the off-season. And even then there is stuff to do. When you commit to growing plants, you have to tend to their needs, or they die. That's a basic fact of life!

So how much time does it take to grow edible plants?

The reality is, it takes as much as you are willing to give. I'm not being flip. You can grow a few edibles, such as herbs, in a couple of little pots on a windowsill or on the terrace and your time commitment will be minimal. Count on half an hour to put them in pots and a couple of minutes each week to keep them watered and fertilized. That's it. No fuss, no muss.

If on the other hand, your plan is to grow enough food to feed your family all year with some left over to sell at a little stand at the end of the driveway, you might want to consider quitting your day job.

These are the steps it takes to establish an extensive vegetable garden in a space that might have previously been your lawn.

1. Test the soil.
2. Remove sod.
3. Turn soil.
4. Remove rocks and roots.
5. Amend soil.
6. Install irrigation.
7. Install fencing.
8. Create furrows, rows, mounds, and so on.
9. Buy seeds and plants.
10. Plant seeds and plants.
11. Put in trellises, plant cages, or stakes.
12. Water seeded and planted areas.
13. Thin seeded areas.
14. Weed furrows, rows, mounds, and so on.

15. Mulch.

16. Continue to water.

17. Continue to weed.

18. Deal with bugs.

19. Harvest.

20. Remove dead plants.

21. Turn soil.

22. Plant cover crop.

The size and type of garden you decide on will dictate how much time you should spend on gardening and on how many of these steps you will need to take. Not every garden will require each one of these steps, but you get the picture.

Even if you have never gardened before (and you shouldn't be considering this type of gardening if you are a novice), you can estimate how much time it will take you to do some of these tasks. Then double the hours you have estimated because things always take much longer than you had planned. If you think you can afford that kind of time, go for it!

Square Foot Gardening

About 20 years ago, a fellow by the name of Mel Bartholomew created a method of gardening based on the traditional French-intensive way of growing edibles in backyards. The premise is that plants don't really need as much room as we tend to give them and they will do quite well when they are all crammed in together, as long as good preparations are made.

Mr. Bartholomew's methods were touted on public television and he wrote a book about it that was very popular in the 1980s. This is a terrific approach for people who like things neat and tidy and are willing to do a fair amount of preparation work in the beginning in order to not have to work so hard later on.

Square foot gardens are usually done in raised beds that take a bit of time and, of course, cash to construct. But once installed, maintenance is less time-consuming. We will look at this technique in more detail in Chapter 12.

Prof. Price's Pointers

The foundation for intensive French gardening, which was the inspiration for square foot gardening, is perfectly prepared soil. The long, narrow beds (to fit in the long, narrow backyards) were dug down at least two feet deep. Then the soil was amended with rich compost and humus and tilled to a light, fluffy consistency to allow for good root growth.

A Taster's Garden

I think this is the type of garden that appeals to most people. You plant a few basic things like tomatoes, green peppers, and basil. And maybe you add eggplant, onions, and kale. You might even try broccoli, watermelon, and butternut squash. A little of this and a little of that is the idea in choosing your garden varieties. You don't want too much of any one variety. It's a great way to get your hands dirty for the first time.

Even a small garden like this one will require many hours of preparation and maintenance. Once it is established (the initial preparation, fencing, irrigation, and other structural aspects), you can experiment with different plants each year, adding more of the vegetables you really like, eliminating those that don't work so well for you, and trying a few new things.

If you are a total beginner, try the taster's garden approach. And if you are a total foodie, try it with your favorite culinary delights.

> **Food for Thought**
>
> What I call the taster's garden can be achieved in a collection of pots if your space and time are very limited. You might have to leave out the watermelon and butternut squash, but you could add more herbs, and perhaps peas, beans, lettuce, and hot peppers.

Culinary Delights

Culinary delights make up the garden for those who love to cook and love to eat. In the garden of culinary delights, you'll grow your favorite gourmet treats. It's not that you can't find these special things at a green grocer's or in specialty markets. It's just that they are so much tastier when they are freshly picked just before being added to the pot.

These are the fruits and vegetables that I like best. Some of them, such as the specialty potatoes, fresh raspberries, and delicate leaf lettuces, cost a fortune. So I would grow lots of them to gorge on for the brief time they are in season.

The reality is that I don't have the time or space to grow all these things, so I have to select the things that make sense for the way I garden now. That pretty much limits me to a few of the herbs (basil, parsley, dill, and coriander), the lettuces, and a couple of tomato plants. That would about do it. If I'm feeling really ambitious, I would add arugula and sorrel. Then, I just have to rely on my more prolific gardening friends to include me in their dinner parties—I'll bring the salad. My point is that you have to consider both time and space when deciding what you'll choose to prioritize with your culinary gardens, or with any garden.

Food for Thought _____

Given unlimited garden space and time on my hands, my garden of culinary delights would include the following:

- Artichokes
- Asparagus
- Tomatoes (big juicy ones, tiny grape types, and Italian plum varieties)
- Shallots
- Leeks
- Eggplant
- Patty pan squash
- Herbs (basil, parsley, dill, rosemary, sage, thyme, chervil, cilantro, and chives)
- Tiny beets

- Lettuce (all the frilly, delicate leaf varieties)
- Sorrel
- Arugula
- Radicchio
- Snow peas
- Poblano chilies
- Specialty potatoes
- Tomatillo
- Jicama
- Strawberries
- Raspberries
- Blueberries

Remember: I said if space and time were not an issue!

Herbs and Medicinals

For many gardeners, especially those with limited time and space, a garden devoted to herbs is enormously satisfying. And for a few folks, an herb garden also allows them to explore the nuances of folk and herbal remedies. We will take a detailed look at herb gardening in Chapter 16.

Seasonal Treats

Gardeners who specialize in flowering perennials strive to have something in bloom throughout the growing season. It takes considerable horticultural skill to plan a successful succession of bloom. Gardeners who grow edibles might also have a succession of harvests in mind when they create their gardens.

A few examples are shown in the following table.

MS	LS	ES	MS	LS	F
	Corn	Corn	Corn		
Lettuce	Lettuce	Lettuce	Lettuce	Lettuce	Lettuce
	Zucchini	Zucchini			
Spinach	Spinach				
	Straw-berries	Straw-berries	Straw-berries	Rasp-berries	Rasp-berries
	Rasp-berries				
	Blueberries	Blueberries			
	Grapes	Grapes			
Oregano	Oregano	Oregano	Oregano	Oregano	Oregano
	Basil	Basil	Basil	Basil	Basil
Sage	Sage	Sage	Sage	Sage	Sage
	Dill	Dill	Dill	Dill	
	Beans	Beans	Beans		
	Beets	Beets	Beets		
Broccoli	Broccoli	Broccoli	Eggplant	Eggplant	Eggplant
	Garlic	Garlic	Kale	Kale	Radicchio
	Leeks	Leeks	Leeks		
	Potatoes	Potatoes			
	Pumpkins	Pumpkin			
	Tomato	Tomato	Tomato	Tomato	
Radish	Radish	Radish	Radish	Radish	Radish
	Scallions				
	Melon	Melon			
	Arugula	Arugula			
Thyme	Thyme	Thyme	Thyme	Thyme	Thyme

Note: This set of harvest times is approximate, and based on conditions in my Pennsylvania garden. Harvest seasons will be different in other parts of the country.

By starting seeds indoors, using a cold frame, buying established plants, and planting several varieties of the same vegetable or fruit, it is possible to stretch out the harvest and enjoy a wide variety of edibles for many months. Those who live in warm climates such as California or Florida will have nearly year-long growing seasons, though not all plants will thrive (or even grow at all) under those conditions.

Fruits of the Vine and Bush

Though we have saved the topic of fruit trees for another book, there are a number of fruits for us to consider for edible gardens. You'll find more detailed information about growing these grapes, rhubarb, and various berries in Chapter 18.

Grape Vines

Ever think about making your own wine from your own grapes? What a romantic notion! Be sure to look before you leap. Grapes are extremely labor-intensive plants to grow and will require a relatively large dollar and space investment. They need support so you will have to construct an arbor or fence for them. Insects are always an issue. And it can take several years before the vines produce a reliable harvest. If you can get past these hurdles, you'll find the effort very rewarding.

Garden Guru Says

If you're not looking for a large grape harvest but just want to give it a try, you might try growing a couple of vines on an arbor in your garden. Grape vines are highly decorative, with beautiful new growth in the spring, the rich color of the fruit, and gorgeous fall foliage.

Blueberries

A native of North America, blueberries are synonymous with summer. These shrubby plants will grow up to six feet tall and require from four to eight square feet of growing space each depending on the variety. You'll need at least three of them in order to produce fruit. Blueberries take a little while to get established; if you plant very young bushes, your first harvest might be a couple years off, but the succulent berries are worth waiting for. And established blueberries require very little maintenance (especially compared with bramble berries) outside of fertilizing, winter protection, and some occasional pruning.

Bramble Berries

Raspberries and blackberries, along with their hybrids and relatives, are known collectively as bramble fruits. The bramble refers to the thorny branches or canes that the original plants always had. (Some newer varieties have been bred to be thornless, a boon to growers and pickers.)

Other bramble berries include loganberry, boysenberry, marionberry, ollaberry, and tayberry.

Compost Pile

If you are unwilling or unable to devote time to weeding and pruning your bramble berries, it's better to just leave the growing to someone else. An untended bramble patch can turn into a nasty briar patch in just one season of neglect.

Bramble berries, like other fruits, will require an investment of space and time. They have specific soil needs; some varieties require support on trellises or frames. There is some major pruning that must be done every year without fail. And staying on top of weeding is absolutely essential. Being a bramble berry grower is a major commitment.

Strawberries

Can you imagine a summer without strawberry shortcake? It's one of my favorite desserts. Strawberries are relatively easy to grow, but they need plenty of space and a couple seasons to really get going. Then after a few years most varieties tend to peter out and you have to replant them. To grow your own strawberries, you'll need a fair amount of space, plenty of time to get them started, and the ability to irrigate in drought conditions.

> **CAUTION**
>
> **Compost Pile**
>
> Growing gooseberries and currants is illegal in some parts of the country. Before investing your time and money on these fruit plants, check with your state department of agriculture or your county extension.

If you can't live without really fresh strawberries (or if you need tons of them because you love to make jam like I do), then the only alternative to growing your own is to pick them in someone else's patch.

Bush Berries

Currants and gooseberries are perennial fruits that grow on bushes or shrubs. Though they are not among the most commonly grown fruits, they do have their fans. Gardeners who opt to cultivate bush fruits like these will have to make the same kind of investment in time (soil preparation, planting, pruning) and money (initial investment, irrigation cost, and so on) as those who grow bramble berries or blueberries. The payoff is pretty good however. These bush fruits can live up to 20 years. That's a lot of fruit. (More on growing these fruits in Chapter 18.)

Strictly Organic

Gardening organically is a lifestyle commitment. Whatever type of garden you decide to create can be done organically. We will look at the specifics of organic gardening throughout the book, especially in Chapters 19, 21, and 23.

Hiring Help

In the years that I was a partner in a garden design business, I found that many of our clients wanted to do much of the landscape work themselves. They would call on our design services, but then want to select the plants, lay them out according to the plan, dig the holes, and install the plants. Then a few months later, they would call us complaining that the garden didn't look the way they thought it would. The problem was that, although they had a design done by professionals, the installation was done by amateurs. And it showed.

Garden Guru Says

If you are pressed for time or just don't like heavy lifting, hire help. Is it really worth your time to clear sod, turn soil, and add a truckload of manure when a local landscaper, farmer, or handyman will do the job for you for a couple hundred dollars?

They had selected the wrong cultivars or poor quality plants; they hadn't amended the soil properly; or they placed plants too close together or not exactly according to the plan. Any one of these errors throws an entire plan off kilter, and the result is that the garden just doesn't look right. Although a garden of vegetables and fruits doesn't require the same kind of precision as does a landscape, some things are best left to people who do this work for a living.

CAUTION

Compost Pile

If you hire local kids or other inexperienced gardeners to help with weeding, watering, and other chores in your garden, be sure you instruct them carefully. It's disheartening for everyone when a new hired hand proudly shows off his hours of labor only to be told that the weeds he pulled out were actually the new asparagus patch you spent an entire day planting.

Some ideal jobs for hired hands include installing irrigation systems, putting up fences, pulling weeds, laying down mulch, and turning the garden at the end of the season.

The Least You Need to Know

- ◆ Carefully consider the time you need for the style of garden you plan.
- ◆ Be realistic in your approach when evaluating your commitment to the type of garden you choose.
- ◆ It's always a good idea to start small unless you are an experienced gardener.
- ◆ Decide what kind of garden suits your lifestyle and tastes.
- ◆ Hire help if you need it.
- ◆ Don't be afraid to explore another type of gardening; just be prepared for the time and money it might require.

Do It in Style

In This Chapter

- How to grow edible food on windowsills, balconies, or fire escapes
- Create a truck farm on a large property
- Grow basic veggies and essential herbs in a whiskey barrel
- Make space for vegetables in your suburban backyard
- Introduce kids to the joys of edible gardening
- How to use edible plants in a flower garden or ornamental landscape

You know you want to do edible gardening and you have come up with some lists of the kinds of plants you would like to grow. You have some idea of what type of garden it's going to be and whether you'll use organic methods. Now it's time to get really serious. How is it going to work? Who is going to do the work?

Do you want to just make a few horticultural attempts without a big commitment? Or is this something you're really drawn to in a big way? In this chapter, you review options that allow you to create gardens with style.

Windowsills, Balconies, and Fire Escapes

Not every gardener is blessed with an acre of ground. Millions of Americans live in apartments, condominiums, townhouses, and flats where the outdoor spaces might be strictly regulated or even nonexistent. Yet erstwhile gardeners who live in multi-unit dwellings (that's what they are called in the real-estate world) still yearn to get their hands dirty. And for many, there is no reason why they shouldn't have an opportunity to grow at least a little bit of their own food.

I've always marveled at the ingenuity of city gardeners. From my friends' eleventh-floor apartment on New York's Upper East Side, I can see a huge variety of plants growing in containers on windowsills and on rooftops. In other parts of the city, fire escapes become mini jungles of flowers and produce during the summer months. At the retirement community where my mother lived, the elderly residents use their balconies to re-create tiny versions of the gardens they left in their former homes.

If there is a balcony, rooftop, fire escape, or windowsill, there is room for a plant or two.

Life on the Ledge

Windowsill gardening is an indoor and an outdoor affair, but for the purposes of this chapter, we will concentrate on the great outdoors. That's because in order to produce produce, most plants require far more sun than is available to them indoors. (One exception is greenhouse gardening, which is another book entirely. Herbs are the other exception. They are relatively easy to grow on a windowsill.)

By necessity, most windowsill gardens will be home to small plants. Herbs are the most likely candidates, especially the more compact and lower growing types like parsley, basil, marjoram, coriander, and oregano. See Chapter 16 for more information on herbs.

Several types of window boxes are available to choose from, including those made of cedar or plastic. On very wide masonry sills, like the ones on apartment buildings, cast cement, or reconstituted stone planters are another option. You should select whichever size and material that works best for your windowsill.

An ample window box can provide enough space to grow things like leaf lettuces, sweet and hot peppers, eggplant, bush beans and peas, and strawberries. Look for dwarf varieties of other plants too. Plants to avoid include root vegetables and sprawling plants like melons, squash, and cucumbers.

Make sure your window boxes are securely attached to either the windowsill or the wall to protect passersby

> **Garden Guru Says**
>
> Window boxes, as with any garden container, must have excellent drainage. Select containers that have enough drainage holes to allow water to pass through quickly or add more holes. Cover the holes with pieces of broken terra cotta pots or use a handful of Styrofoam peanuts in the bottom of the pot over the holes to keep soil from leaking out.

> **Prof. Price's Pointers**
>
> Vegetables will require a minimum soil depth of nine inches in order to thrive in a window box or other planter.

(and your insurance carrier) from any disasters. And always be considerate when watering. No one wants to a take an unscheduled shower in window box drippings.

Fire Escapes

I love fire escape gardens. For some reason they are one of the most hopeful, life-affirming things I know. The people who grow plants in the gritty environment of the urban streetscape exhibit great creativity and optimism. It's not easy to make things grow under these conditions, but they keep trying.

Even the most ambitious fire escape garden will be limited in size. But with some careful planning, you can still grow some incredible edibles.

There is something about a fire escape garden that calls for found-object containers, especially giant olive oil cans (the kind used in restaurants), two-pound coffee cans, milk cartons, and plastic water jugs with the tops cut off. I once saw tomatoes growing in milk crates lined with black plastic garbage bags. How creative!

The biggest problem facing fire escape gardeners is sunlight, or lack thereof. If the space gets less than about five hours of full sunlight a day, you'll have a really hard time growing edible plants. Consider growing ferns and impatiens instead.

Food for Thought

There are several ways to attach window boxes securely. Where there is a wide sill, rest the box on the sill and fasten it with screws or bolts through the bottom of the box. When the sill is shallow, attach brackets to the wall and screw or bolt them to the bottom of the container.

CAUTION

Compost Pile

Never block access or passage along a fire escape. Before you set out plants in containers on your fire escape, be sure your building rules and regulations allow it.

CAUTION

Compost Pile

Use fresh soil in your planters every year to avoid having the lead from exhaust poison your produce. Also, wash your harvest thoroughly before you serve it.

Balcony Bounty

For many folks, the only outdoor space they can call their own is a bit of balcony. This is where they park the hibachi, a lounge chair, and if they have any horticultural leanings, a few plants in pots. There's no reason why a balcony can't become a mini farm for those so inclined.

Balcony gardeners can usually grow their plants in a combination of planters, hanging baskets, and window boxes attached to the railings. With a little ingenuity, even the smallest space can accommodate a wide variety of edible plants.

Plastic milk crates lined with garbage bags are an unusual but effective alternative to pots.

A Truck Farm on the Back Forty

My first vegetable garden was an enormous affair, at least the size of a football field. We prepared it completely by hand and planted it with every vegetable we could think of. That summer, we spent all our free time sowing, weeding, watering, and harvesting. I took a class on canning at the County Extension and filled hundreds of jars with tomatoes and pickles. We had enough frozen green peppers to last five years. And the zucchini bread—after a while friends stopped coming to the door if they saw me arrive with a little package wrapped in aluminum foil.

I could never tackle a garden that large again, but it was worth all that effort for the incredible sense of accomplishment.

If you have the time, the space, and the cash for start-up expenses, doing it up big can be very rewarding. But if you have never gardened before, this is not the best route to follow.

Food for Thought _____

Need some reasons to do it up big? Here's a top 10 list:

1. You belong to a survivalist group and don't want anything to do with outsiders, including grocers.

2. You are convinced that the food labeled organic at the grocery store actually isn't organic.

3. You are recently retired and your spouse wants you out of the house for at least eight hours a day.

4. You've just opened a restaurant and want to supply your own fresh vegetables and herbs.

5. You think there is big money in growing fresh vegetables for local restaurants and specialty stores.

6. The local prison makes day labor available for 50 cents an hour.

7. You have 14 children, all of them home schooled, and you need something constructive for them to do.

8. You took a class on preserving food at your County Extension and you found it really inspiring.

9. You just found out about the real-estate tax benefits of having your land designated agricultural.

10. You've always wanted to have a little vegetable stand at the end of the driveway.

Basics in a Barrel

Whether you are limited by space or not, sometimes smaller spaces are smarter choices, especially if you are an inexperienced gardener. It is possible to grow a nice variety of edible plants in an old whiskey barrel or two. You've probably seen these barrels. They are cut in half across the middle, making planters about 2.5 feet across and about 2 feet deep. Whiskey barrels are not water tight, but still drill two or three holes in them for good drainage.

What can you grow in a barrel? The following list provides a few good combinations:

◆ **Combination #1:** 1 tomato, 2 peppers, 1 eggplant, and 1 parsley

◆ **Combination #2:** 3 basil, 1 oregano, 3 bean plants with a teepee, leaf lettuces, and mini carrots or radishes

◆ **Combination #3:** 3 herb plants (parsley, basil, and cilantro for example), 1 hot pepper, 2 cilantro, 1 lemongrass, and 3 snow pea plants on a teepee

◆ **Combination #4:** 2 parsley, 2 basil, 1 dill, 1 cilantro, 1 thyme, 1 rosemary, 1 oregano, and 1 chive

- ◆ **Combination #5:** 6 dwarf strawberry plants
- ◆ **Combination #6:** 1 large variety tomato plant and 3 basil
- ◆ **Combination #7:** 1 cherry or grape tomato plant, leaf lettuces, and 15 scallion sets

These are just a few of the many combinations of vegetables and herbs that will grow well in a large container like a whiskey barrel. Once you've tried it, you'll figure out what plants work best for you.

Food for Thought

To grow climbing peas in a pot, you'll need to provide them with something to climb. The easiest thing to do is create a support with bamboo stakes. Use three tall bamboo or fiberglass stakes equally spaced around the inside of the pot. Make sure the stakes are pushed all the way to the bottom of the pot. Secure the tops of the stakes with twine or a rubber band forming a teepee. The peas will climb the stakes on their own. This technique will also work for beans.

Keep in mind that you can use several whiskey barrels without increasing your workload significantly. And there's no reason why you can't try some larger plants like pumpkin, cabbage, zucchini, or even cucumber. Just look for dwarf or bush varieties.

The key to success for whiskey barrel gardening is adequate irrigation. Irrigation, fertilizer applications, and succession planting are discussed later in the book.

A whiskey barrel planted with a compact cherry or grape tomato plant with a few basil plants around the perimeter will provide a summer-long harvest and require almost no effort.

Suburban Spaces

The vast majority of Americans live in the suburbs where properties range from small lots measured in feet to multiple acre spreads. It is in the backyards of these homes that most of us garden.

Suburban landscaping is probably the largest segment of the gardening industry, with vast quantities of consumer dollars spent on foundation plantings and lawn care. It is reasonable to expect to pay up to 15 percent of the price of a new home on a landscaping package. And real estate agents will tell you that a badly landscaped house will not command as a high a price as its well-done counterpart.

But where does the vegetable garden fit into this picture? In most cases, it's an afterthought. It doesn't need to be. A successful backyard garden of edibles should be carefully planned so it is integrated into the landscape. We'll talk about how to do this in Chapters 5 through 7.

Something for the Kiddies

My earliest experiences with gardening weren't quite hands-on. Instead, what I remember was watching my father dig holes in the garden and move plants from here to there. I can also remember him growing tomatoes in a large plot at the far end of our big suburban backyard. I can't recall many details except that he regularly pinched back some of the flowers on the tomatoes to force them to grow larger fruits. And I'm sure he explained the physiological reasons for doing that in great detail. I loved every minute of it, because it allowed us to be together.

One of the best reasons to involve your kids in gardening is that it does give you more of that precious time together. And if you make the experience fun rather than a chore, you might help your children develop a lifelong interest.

It doesn't take much to create a kid-friendly garden. The following ideas are just some of gardening themes you might use to interest kids:

- A spaghetti sauce or pizza garden with tomato, pepper, onion, basil, and oregano plants
- An alphabet or name garden (a plant for each or some letter(s) of the alphabet; or one that spells out the child's name (S = squash; A = arugula; M = mint)
- A giant teepee (8 to 10 feet bamboo poles in a circle attached at the top with twine) with peas and beans planted at the base of the poles (They grow up the poles and cover them making an enclosure.)
- Vegetable plants outside a playhouse or at the base of a climbing set
- A section of your vegetable garden just for the kids and planted with their favorite vegetables

- A series of pots and containers on the deck with favorites
- A collection of dwarf, miniature, and "baby" vegetables; or a "giant" garden featuring extra-large varieties of pumpkins, tomatoes, watermelons, and cabbages

Most children have relatively short attention spans so it's really important that their gardens are low maintenance. And don't expect the kiddies to get too excited about preparing the soil or weeding. They will be most interested in planting seeds and seedlings and harvesting. Watering can be fun too, especially if it's done in a bathing suit and everyone gets wet!

A teepee garden can be a magical place. Try planting dwarf sunflowers around the perimeter for color (you can also harvest the seeds). Put an inexpensive grass mat and old pillows inside. It makes a great hideout.

Garden Guru Says

Several companies including Burpee Seeds and Bountiful Gardens (bountiful@sonic.net) have special collections designed for children, with easy-to-grow, colorful, and fun plants. Some feature child-friendly instructions, too.

Children can learn so much from the experience of starting plants from seed. Try quick-to-germinate plants like radishes, carrots, peas, and beans to start from seed. For tomatoes, peppers, and eggplant, start out with young plants.

If you have the room, try some real kid-pleasing plants like corn, watermelon, and pumpkin. They need a lot of space, but are very easy to grow. A heavy mulch (see Chapter 19) will keep weeding at a minimum (there's nothing like weeding to take the fun out of gardening).

Fun with Foods or Produce Among the Posies

While most folks think of vegetables, herbs, and fruits as simply edibles, many gardeners, including me, like to use these plants as ornamental additions to beds, borders, and planters.

A friend of mine who gardens in a tiny yard mixes vegetables with flowers throughout his garden. One time he trained a strong vining tomato up a trellis and across an arbor. The tomatoes hung below the vine, just waiting to be picked. It was beautiful, if unusual.

I first saw extensive use of edibles in ornamental gardens when I visited England. At one small row house just outside London, the owner grew rhubarb in giant raised planters and chives in pots on top of a wall. At Tintinhull House, one of the great National Trust properties in the southwest, fennel was used as a decorative accent in a perennial border. I also saw artichokes used decoratively.

If you think a vegetable is pretty, then by all means add it to the flowerbeds. Or try some of these tucked among the blooms:

- Purple beans
- Hot pepper
- Kale
- Arugula
- Curly parsley
- Purple basil
- Okra
- Swiss chard
- Strawberry
- Leaf lettuce
- Sage
- Chives

Grapes look beautiful grown on an arbor, especially in the fall. And blueberry, gooseberry, currant, and fig bushes are easily incorporated into shrub borders.

The Least You Need to Know

- Guard against lead contamination in the soil in city gardens by using fresh soil each season.
- Don't try to grow vegetables if your space doesn't have at least five hours of sun a day.
- Don't attempt a really large garden until you know you can handle it.
- Be aware of weight limitations for rooftop and balcony gardens, and be sure window boxes are securely fastened.
- Keep kids interested in their gardens by planting quick-growing vegetables.
- Use edible plants as ornamentals in your flower beds.

Part 2

Essential Planning

This is a pretty long section because there is so much ground to cover (that wasn't meant to be a pun!). In the next several chapters we go over the basic information you need to start and maintain your garden. Chapter 4 is all about the tools of your new trade. After reading Chapter 5, you should have a pretty good idea of where you'll put the garden and how large a garden you can actually handle. Chapter 6 features the steps you might take to plot out a garden. The work itself can get kind of tedious, but you really should pay attention to this part, because in the end it will save you time and even money. Chapter 7 is a bit more fun because we look at some of the design options for edible gardening including cute cottage style, formal European-style vegetable designs, and even a bit on the Feng Shui of gardens.

Chapter 4

Essential Tools

In This Chapter

- How and why tools evolved
- When and why to choose a spade over a shovel
- Selecting essential hand, cultivating, and pruning tools
- Get the dirt on tillers
- Choosing the best gloves for the task at hand

The very earliest gardening tool was nothing more than a stick. An early woman decided that planting seeds was easier when she made a hole in the ground with the pointy end of stick than it was doing it with her hands. (Remember, at this point men were still out in the forest throwing rocks and spears at wild animals while women were growing crops and raising chickens at home.)

We've come a long way since that stick. Gardening tools are big business, and the choices are limitless. This chapter helps you determine the tools you simply can't do without and those that make gardening tasks just a little easier. And you'll learn about some of the frills and extras.

Note: Not all essential tools are covered in this chapter. Pruning tools are discussed in Chapter 22. Tools and equipment for irrigation are discussed in Chapter 19. Tool care and maintenance is in Chapter 25. And Chapter 9 looks at machinery for tilling.

Dig This

Starting around 9000 B.C.E., people began planting seeds rather than just gathering them. (Remember the evolution from hunter/gatherer to farmer that we learned about in Chapter 1?) First came that digging stick followed soon after by a rudimentary wooden hoe. That went on for about 5,000 years until a bright farmer figured out how to harness an ox to pull a plow fashioned from a wooden hoe attached to a stone-age cutting tool like an adze (keep that word handy for crossword puzzles).

Another few thousand years passed. Around 650 B.C.E., a precocious R&D-type developed iron tools, a major breakthrough. The Romans made more innovations and transformed the plow into a heavier, more versatile tool. The tool trade remained more or less stagnant for a thousand years or so until the steam engine was invented and adapted for farming. Not long after that, the gasoline engine was developed and power tools came on the scene.

> **Prof. Price's Pointers**
>
> A 60,000-year-old digging stick found in Africa might be the oldest surviving relic of its kind.

Wood and metal gardening tools became more refined in the seventeenth and eighteenth centuries, and by the nineteenth century they began to look much like the tools we use today. While the materials are now more sophisticated—cast aluminum and fiberglass, for example—the shapes are pretty much the same.

Let's Call a Spade a Spade

The uninitiated might use the words *spade* and *shovel* interchangeably. But just try doing spadework with a shovel and you'll soon learn the difference. Here's the scoop: Use the spade to dig deep and straight down; use the shovel for larger areas and to move the soil out of the hole.

The difference between a spade and a shovel isn't all that subtle. Shovels have a larger bowl in the blade to move more of whatever material you are moving. Spades usually have straight-sided blades and are designed to cut through turf and soil.

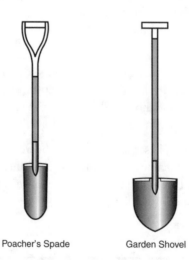

Poacher's Spade   Garden Shovel

The garden spade can be long-handled or short with a long blade or a short one. The blade end might be curved, slightly pointed, or cut straight. Although all kinds of spades might be used interchangeably, some shapes and styles work better for certain tasks. For example, a long-handled is useful for digging rocks or roots out of a bed. A spade with a rectangular blade is great for edging beds and making straight cuts through sod.

Food for Thought

If I had to restrict my tool collection to only one digging implement, I would choose my classic English poacher's spade from the *Smith & Hawken* catalog. This small, short-handled spade got its name from its early use by rabbit poachers on English estates. The long (5½ × 10½-inch) steel and powder-coated blade has a sharp, slightly curved end that makes it ideal for planting or transplanting large annuals, perennials, and small shrubs. It's great for cutting through sod, edging beds, and digging out tap-rooted weeds. And it's especially useful in tight, fully planted spaces or even large planters.

Shovels

In an Australian gardening book called *Tools for Gardeners*, author L. Dobbs says, "shovels are hopeless tools for digging." I think that's a pretty weird opinion. In fact, shovels are great for digging new beds after the sod has been removed, for creating planting holes for large shrubs, and for general digging in loose soil.

In addition to digging, shovels are good for shoveling—moving stuff like soil, compost, mulch, or manure from one spot to another. The best shovel for moving large quantities of material is one with a squared-off blade because it has a wider entry point for scooping.

Fork It Over

The garden or spading fork is another useful, and sometimes essential, digging tool. The fork is built like a spade or shovel except that it has tines instead of a blade. The fork is especially helpful when soil is hard or compacted. It's also easier to dig in clay soils with a garden fork than with a spade or shovel. Don't confuse pitchforks with spading forks. Pitchforks are used like shovels to move stuff, like hay or dried manure clumps, from one place to another.

You Can Handle It

Spades, shovels, and garden forks have either long or short handles. Generally, the shorter the handle, the easier the tool is to use, especially in confined spaces like established growing beds. But a longer handle gives you more leverage, which is helpful for moving heavy things like wet soil or a root ball.

Long-handled shovels, spades, and forks tend to have straight handles much like a broomstick. The shorter versions will frequently end in a D or a Y shape. These open handles create a spot to grip the tool and add an extra bit of leverage. In terms of efficiency and utility, there really isn't much difference between the D and the Y, so you might as well just select the one that feels best in your hand.

The Y- or D-shaped handles on these spades are typical of short-handled types. Choose the one you find most comfortable.

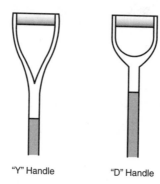

"Y" Handle   "D" Handle

The Material World

Shovel and spade blades and fork tines are made of metal, usually either stainless steel or carbon steel. Stainless doesn't rust, which means tools made of it don't need a lot of maintenance. Some of the carbon steel tools, like those sold by Smith & Hawken and Kinsman Garden Supply are made of carbon steel with an enamel coating. My poacher's spade is constructed that way and it hasn't rusted yet, after 10 years of heavy use and neglect.

I'm told that soil won't stick to stainless steel when you dig, but I've yet to find one that the soil doesn't stick to at least a little. But don't worry about this too much. I've never found having soil stick to my spade to be a problem.

Garden Guru Says

The very strongest shovels, spades, and forks are made from forged steel rather than sheet steel. Be sure to ask about the strength of the material before you purchase one of these tools, if you are looking for strength.

Some of the best digging tools have a powder coating over the steel (a kind of baked-on finish) that protects the steel and seems to prolong the life of the tools.

Spade, shovel, and fork handles are usually made of wood. Less expensive tools might be made with any one of several woods, but the best, most durable tools have handles made of ash, often with a metal strap. Some handles are made of fiberglass, which is a pretty sturdy material as well.

Hand Tools

No gardener could survive without a few hand tools. These essentials include a trowel, a hand fork, a cultivator, and a pronged weeder. Most hand tools are made of the same materials as their larger relatives. Look for similar construction too.

Trowels

When it comes to trowels, I break my own rule about only buying the best quality tools. I tend to lose at least one a year and sometimes more. I can't tell you how frustrated I get when I search for my trowel and can't find it. A trowel is absolutely indispensable, especially for people like me who do a lot of container gardening.

Trowel blades should be pointed enough to pierce the soil and break up clumps and wide enough to allow you to dig a hole pretty quickly. Transplanting trowels have long, narrow blades designed for making a deeper hole. I have one with depth markers that is handy for planting things like onion sets because you know exactly how deep you are going.

Hand Forks

The hand fork is a mini spading fork with wider tines. It's designed to turn over the top few inches of prepared planting beds or containers.

Cultivators

The hand cultivator has three bent prongs, usually with the center prong set higher than the other two. Use this handy tool to aerate surface soil and loosen soil around shallow-rooted weeds.

Food for Thought

The key to a good hand tools is the feel of the handle. Look for one with a nice smooth grip that won't splinter and isn't too big for your hand. Ash and beech are probably the top choice. They should also have sturdy steel blades or tines. The cast aluminum tools are a good choice for people who have trouble with heavy tools, because they weigh less. And hand tools with handles made of a soft, cushioned material, like Good Grips, are great for those with arthritis or other conditions that make gripping difficult.

Weeders

Not an essential tool in everyone's garden, the hand weeder is indispensable where tap-rooted weeds like dandelions and thistle are a problem. This tool is a long, thin metal rod with a V-shaped point on the end that lets you get down deep into the soil to root out these weed menaces.

Hoes, Rakes, and Other Infamous Characters

Hoes and rakes are the workhorses of the tool trade. Once the soil has been thoroughly dug and moved around, the hoes, rakes, cultivators, and weeders go into action. These are generally long-handled tools made of the same materials as spades and shovels.

Hoes

The hoe is the ancient tool that came into being right after the digging stick. No more than a sharp-edged blade of metal attached to a long handle, the hoe is primitive but essential. It is used to chop through the soil and push it around a bit.

Use your hoe to weed between individual plants or rows of vegetables and to break up the surface of the soil around plants so that water and fertilizers can penetrate into the roots.

The basic hoe has some specialized offspring:

- **Warren hoe.** This hoe has a heart- or arrow-shaped blade and it is used for making furrows or rows.
- **Eye hoe.** This has a circular hole at the top center of the blade. It is useful in hard packed soil or soil with lots of thick roots.
- **Circle hoe.** This hoe has a circle of metal instead of a blade. It can get in close to roots, and it is also useful in rocky soil. The blade comes in several sizes.
- **Dutch hoe.** This is also called the scuffle hoe; it has a flat blade with a horseshoe-shaped shank, and it is used to cut through weeds in a push-pull motion.
- **Collinear hoe.** This hoe has a small, very sharp, replaceable blade for weeding.
- **Grub hoe.** This is a very heavy-duty hoe with a sharply angled blade; it is used for tough digging like trenches.

Rakes

A garden rake is a classic tool. Think of Beatrix Potter's illustrations of Farmer McGregor chasing Peter Rabbit with a rake in his hand.

Rakes have long handles and a business end with short steel tines set perpendicular to the handle. This essential tool is used to move a thin layer of soil around the surface of beds, to separate stones, to loosen roots and light debris from prepared soil, and to pull soil up into mounds, hills, or furrows.

Gloves

Some gardeners consider gloves a necessity while others don't see the need to use them. For the first 20 years of my gardening life, I refused to use gloves except for the most brutal tasks like pulling out bullthorn or poison ivy. I liked getting my hands dirty and I didn't care much about the condition of my fingernails. On the flip side, a former neighbor, with impeccably manicured nails, would don a pair of flowered gardening gloves for *every* garden task including watering potted plants and deadheading perennials. To each her own.

Gloves are very handy for some gardening situations, particularly for the previously mentioned bullthorn and poison ivy removal. And they should always be worn when you handle chemicals like herbicides, insecticides, and fertilizers. Gloves are also useful when you're doing a lot of heavy digging or extensive planting, to help avoid painful blisters.

You will find almost as many garden glove designs as there are garden tasks to do. Here are a few types, their positive features, any drawbacks, and the jobs they are best for.

> **CAUTION**
>
> ## Compost Pile
>
> Any tool left lying on the ground unattended is potentially dangerous. This is especially true for rakes left tine-side up. Though it's hilarious when one of the Three Stooges gets clocked by the rake handle when he steps on a rake head, it's not a bit funny if it happens to you or an unsuspecting passerby. Always move your tools out of harm's way when you're not using them.

Glove	Job	Feature	Drawback
Cotton	General gardening	Washable	Doesn't hold up to heavy use; often too bulky for delicate work
Cotton/ polyester blend	General gardening	Washable	Often too bulky for delicate work; not always available in varying sizes
Knit cotton w/rubberized palms and fingers	General gardening	Washable; good dexterity; sturdy; comes in various sizes	

continues

continued

Glove	Job	Feature	Drawback
Calfskin or goatskin	General gardening	Comfortable and form-fitting; good dexterity	Fingertips tend to rip with heavy use; can be pierced by sharp thorns or rocks; becomes stiff after soaking; not washable
Pigskin	General gardening	Good dexterity; comfortable; stronger than calf or goatskin; better protection from thorns and sharp rocks	Becomes stiff after soaking; not washable
Cowhide	General gardening	Strong; durable; excellent protection from thorns, etc.	Not great dexterity; becomes stiff after soaking; not washable
Light-weight rubber	Chores with chemicals and water	Offers protection from water and noncaustic chemicals; some brands come in sizes	Little dexterity; rips easily
Latex	Chores with chemicals and water	Offers protection from water and noncaustic chemicals; some brands come in sizes; good dexterity	Rips easily; some people are allergic to latex
Heavy rubber	Chores with chemicals and water	Sturdy; offers good protection; some brands come in sizes	Often bulky; little dexterity
PVC	Chores with chemicals and water	Good protection; some brands come in sizes; less bulky than heavy rubber gloves	Can't be used with gasoline

It's probably a good idea to get into the habit of wearing gloves whenever you work in the garden. It's just a little bit of protection. I try to use them, though I often forget and I do tend to lose a few pairs every year. But when I do remember and when I can find them, my fingernails are a lot more attractive.

Garden Guru Says

Some other features to look for in a good gardening glove are ...

♦ Extra-long cuff to protect lower wrists and forearms from scratches, poison ivy, dirt, and so on.

♦ Small interior seams on cotton and leather gloves for comfort.

♦ Tight-fitting knit cuff on cotton gloves to prevent soil from slipping inside.

♦ Rubberized "gripper" dots on palms and fingertips for good dexterity.

♦ Good range of sizes for best fit.

♦ Thermal lining for work in cold weather.

♦ Cotton lining for absorbency.

♦ Seamless lining for comfort.

♦ Nitrile exterior for resistance to caustic chemicals.

Wheelbarrows and Carts

Only those who garden in tiny spaces can get away with not having a garden cart or wheelbarrow. There's always so much to haul around: bags of peat moss, mulch, or compost; flats of plants; ball-and-burlap fruit shrubs; tools; debris; or a big harvest of zucchini.

Wheelbarrows

Wheelbarrows are an ancient device dating to not long after the invention of the wheel. Though some wheelbarrows have two wheels, most have one wheel in front, and two handles with a tray or cargo box that together form a triangle.

Because the weight of the payload is carried on the wheel, the wheelbarrow allows the user to move heavy things with relative ease. They are highly maneuverable, but can be very tippy.

Garden Carts

A slightly newer invention, garden carts are more popular with home gardeners because they tend to have larger payloads and they are far more stable.

Usually shaped like a large box with a wheel on either side and a U- or T-shaped handle, garden carts are less maneuverable than wheelbarrows.

Features to Look For

The old-fashioned heavy steel wheelbarrow with wooden handles is more or less a thing of the past for most home gardeners. Today, sturdy polyurethane trays on lightweight aluminum frames are a better choice.

Carts are probably an even better choice. These range from the standard treated plywood with steel handles type to the rugged molded polyurethane varieties.

Other things to look for when choosing a cart include the following:

- Capacity from as small as 4 cubic feet to a whopping 12 cubic feet
- Flat bottom for carrying flats of plants
- An opening at the front for easy dumping
- Coated or galvanized finishes on metal for rust prevention and durability
- Good balance
- Light weight

The Least You Need to Know

- Use a spade to cut through sod and to dig straight, deep holes.
- Use a shovel to dig in large areas of loose soil and to move large quantities of soil, manure, compost, and so on.
- Use a spading fork to dig into hard, compacted, or clay soils.
- Always buy the best quality of tools you can afford, and be sure to put them safely away when you aren't using them.
- Select the right gloves for the protection you need for any given garden task.
- Choose a garden cart with a large enough cargo capacity for your needs.

Location Is Key

In This Chapter

- Determine the path of the sun on your property
- Calculate how much space you need to grow the plants you want
- Locate water sources
- Protect your neighbors (and your relationships) by anticipating unsightly or unpleasant aspects of your garden, and children from potential dangers
- Consider the effects on the garden of animals and children
- Learn about the environmental factors related to your garden's location, including USDA Zones

Think of the garden you are planning as a piece of real estate. Then remember everything you have ever heard about buying real estate. It's all about location, location, and location. You might have great ideas, lots of resources, and the skills to match. But if you put your garden in the wrong spot, don't expect good results. The better the location, the better the return. It's just like buying a house.

Finding the right location for a garden of edibles is even more critical than if you were growing an ornamental garden of flowers. If you are simply planting flowering plants and shrubs, you can adapt plant selections to the location—full shade, part shade, full sun, dry, soggy, hilly, and rocky. Find the plants that like the situation you have. But if you want to grow tomatoes and cucumbers, you have to have good drainage and full sun. In order to have an abundant harvest of fresh herbs, you need to plant them in a place where the dog does not go. There's no getting around it.

In this chapter we look at some of the important factors you should consider as you contemplate the location of your edible garden.

Put It Where the Sun Does Shine

Sunlight is essential for most plants to grow. Nearly all vegetables and fruits and most herbs require at least six hours of full sun every day in order to photosynthesize and thus produce the produce. This is pretty much nonnegotiable.

> ### Prof. Price's Pointers
>
> Most of the things we eat are part of a plant's reproductive or storage organs: leaves, fruits, seeds, tubers, and roots. All these represent a huge investment in carbohydrates (sugars and starch), which comes directly or indirectly from photosynthesis, and that requires light. Photosynthesis is the conversion of light energy into the energy that makes plants grow.

You have to know where the sun shines on your property so you can grow your plants in full sun. Sounds simple. But if you remember sixth-grade science, you'll know that the sun's path changes over the course of the year.

To figure out the best spot for maximum sun exposure, spend the day watching the sun move across your yard. If you do this in early spring, before the trees leaf out, be sure to allow for the shade produced by tree canopies. I can't tell you how many novice gardeners are shocked to find that the garden they spent so much time preparing is in full shade by 2 P.M. once the leaves have grown out.

Enough Room to Grow

How much space you need depends entirely on what you want to grow. If you've always wanted to experiment with several varieties of corn, you'll need land, lots of land. If, on the other hand, having a steady supply of fresh herbs is the full extent of your plans, you can get by with a few pots on the terrace.

Your garden style (see Chapter 3) determines the square footage, or acreage, you'll require to achieve your goals.

To help you estimate how much room you'll need, consider the space requirements of a few favorite plants.

Plant	Space Between Plants	Space Between Rows
Asparagus	2 feet	5 feet
Blackberries	5 feet	
Corn	10 inches	100 feet (between rows of different varieties)
Beans	6 inches	3 feet
Raspberries	2 to 3 feet	
Cabbage	1 foot	
Head lettuce	4 inches	1 foot
Summer squash	3 to 4 feet	3 feet
Jerusalem artichoke	15 to 18 feet	3 to 4 feet
Collards	1½ feet	3 to 4 feet

Access to Water (and the Bathroom)

In a perfect world, gardeners rely on rain to irrigate their gardens. But we all know that there's no such thing as a perfect world. Southeastern Pennsylvania, where I live, has experienced three years of serious drought conditions. And we are not alone. Much of the Northeast is in the same boat.

While ornamental gardeners can add plant varieties that require less water, those who grow vegetables have to resort to various methods of irrigation when Mother Nature is less than generous.

Unless you own stock in a company that makes garden hoses, you won't want to have to run miles of hose in order to get water to the garden beds. So it's important to locate the garden close enough to a reliable water source.

CAUTION

Compost Pile

If you will be spending long hours working in your garden, you might need to use a bathroom from time to time. Be sure to factor that into your location equation.

What Will the Neighbors Think (When I Spread the Cow Manure)?

For those who have acres of land with not a neighbor in sight, the location of a garden in relation to property lines is irrelevant. But most folks do have neighbors. It's important to consider the impact your garden will have on them.

First, if you plan to spend all your waking hours raising vegetables and you are heavily into power equipment, be sure not to put your garden a few feet from your neighbor's patio. Think about your garden as an attractive nuisance for neighborhood children, and protect your own interests by making it inaccessible to them.

CAUTION

Compost Pile

To keep the peace with neighbors, avoid using power equipment early in the morning, at dinnertime, and any time you see your neighbors entertaining outdoors. The noise can be really irritating. The same goes for smelly activities like fertilizing or adding manure to beds.

In a neighborhood where manicured lawns and well-tended beds are the norm, you might not want to locate your basic, utilitarian-style vegetable plot smack dab in the middle of the front yard.

It all boils down to using common sense and being considerate of others. If you play by those rules, you'll find the right location for your garden.

Out of Harm's Way

Plants don't do well in traffic, whether it's four-wheeled or four-legged. So when you select a location for your garden, you will need to assess a number of important traffic factors, including vehicles, animals, and kids.

Death by Vehicle

Most people don't intentionally drive cars through their gardens. Unfortunately sometimes cars will stray off the pavement. If you place your garden too near a driveway, it could be damaged by a not-quite-tight-enough turn or an overestimated back-up effort. Snowplows can overstep the pavement, too, resulting in compacted soil and crushed crowns on perennials. Bikes, trikes, and wagons also pose a threat to gardens.

To avoid death by vehicle in the garden, select a location well away from traffic patterns. This includes places where the kids have always thrown their bikes, the natural path you take from house to garage or shed, near a turn-around or back-up area of the driveway, or where the snowplows regularly push piles of snow.

Four-Legged Friends

Fido might be your best friend, but dogs and gardens aren't great together. It's not that dogs mean harm, but let's face it, if your dog pees or poops on the asparagus, it becomes less than appetizing. In fact, the acids in dog urine can eat right through tree bark, so just think what a regular visit will do to plants with thinner skins. Not a pretty picture.

If your dog has the run of the yard, you might have to fence the garden (see Chapter 6). Dog owners who use electronic invisible fences to contain their animals will want to put their gardens outside the electric perimeter if possible.

Cats are another animal all together. The location of the garden will have no impact on a cat's ability to use it for a litter box. See Chapter 21 for some hints on cat control.

Four-Legged Foes

While many warm-blooded pests can wreak havoc in your garden (and some of these are addressed in Chapter 21), deer are the worst. Many farmers and gardeners in our neck of the woods have long-running battles with these "rats with hooves." If you live in an area with a large deer population, just forget about having a successful garden without fencing. Some strategies for dealing with deer are discussed in Chapter 21.

You would be wise to not place your garden in a spot where you regularly see a large herd of deer grazing. But other than that, the garden location won't make much difference when it comes to these marauders.

Kids Rule

We love it when our children romp in the yard. It's wholesome and healthy and it deters them from whining or asking for stuff. But although we think of our gardens as wholesome, healthy places, a garden isn't always the safest place for a young child to be.

Prof. Price's Pointers

Animal excrement from meat-eaters like dogs and cats is not healthy stuff. All kinds of nasty microorganisms can live in it, so if, despite your precautions, your dog or the neighbor's cat has made deposits in the garden, remove it promptly to avoid the risk of contamination and illness.

Garden Guru Says

Here's an easy no-mess way to clean up after dogs or cats who have used your garden as a potty: Put your hand inside a plastic bag, pick up the poop with your plastic-covered hand, and then, using your other hand, turn the bag inside out, and tie the top of the bag closed before disposing.

Chemical herbicides, pesticides, and fertilizers can be especially toxic to small ones. Just touching leaves or fruits that have been treated can cause allergic reactions. And because really little kids often put their hands in their mouths, the possibility of them ingesting toxic products is high. Even organic products, like pyrethrins or iron phosphatecan make a child sick if it is swallowed. Garden tools, especially pruners and knives, can also be extremely dangerous in the hands of youngsters. To avoid accidents, never leave very young children unattended in the garden. Teach them to respect tools and instruct even the tiniest ones always to wash fresh produce before eating it.

If you have small children, it's a good idea to place the garden in a spot where you will have control over who comes and goes in it. In order to watch the kids and work in the garden simultaneously, locate the garden within sight of their play area.

> **Garden Guru Says**
>
> Once your children have graduated from swing sets and sand boxes, you might consider reclaiming the space this paraphernalia once occupied. The same goes for old dog pens and runs. You will have to do some extra soil preparation in these spots. See Chapters 8 and 9 for information on testing and preparing the soil.

> **Garden Guru Says**
>
> Watercress is an edible that likes to have what garden types call "wet feet"—that is, soggy soil that retains moisture and rarely dries out completely. (In the wild, watercress grows in streams.)

Environmental Factors

If your property is a small one, you might not have much choice in where to put the garden. It's either right here or nowhere. Larger lots, on the other hand, might have any number of sunny, childfree, dog-proof options.

The deciding factors might be environmental. Some issues could include the relative sogginess or dryness of the soil, previous uses of the land, wind patterns, proximity of tree roots, slopes, erosion, and lack of topsoil.

Wet Feet

Most of the plants we will look at in this book prefer to grow in well-drained soil.

So you will want to rule out setting your garden up in the swampy part of your yard at the end of the sump pump's drainpipe. Without elaborate modifications and drains, the wet yard will never support a successful edible garden.

Dry as a Bone

Some properties have sections that are dryer than others. Sandy soils that drain very quickly will dry out fast and might not retain enough moisture to satisfy the plants' need for water. Chalky soils also tend to be dry.

If the only land you have fits in this category, you'll need to do some heavy-duty amending of the soil. However, if there is another, less desert-like location, go for it.

Superfund Site

Superfund sites are no laughing matter. There are hundreds of sites around the country that have seriously contaminated soil caused by the dumping of toxic waste. Some of that land has been cleaned and reclaimed. Other sites are still contaminated.

Not all contaminated sites have been placed on the Superfund list. Some have yet to be identified. If you don't know who previously owned your property or what it was used for, find out before you start an edible garden. Be especially vigilant if your property fits any of the following descriptions:

- Located near a gas station or a former gas station
- Adjacent to an active or former military base
- Near any existing or former manufacturing plant
- Near an existing or former dump or landfill
- Close to a junk yard or automobile salvage facility
- On a former farm

Garden Guru Says

To find out whether your property is near a Superfund site, log on to www.epa.gov/superfund/sites. This website provides a state-by-state guide to hazardous waste sites, the names and addresses of the sites (including aliases), and what action has been taken to clean them up.

Compost Pile

Properties that border heavily traveled roads might have lead contamination in the soil. If your garden is near a highway or a congested traffic area, have the soil tested for lead before growing edibles.

Although the chances of your property being contaminated are small, you don't want to find out about it after you've consumed a few years' worth of harvests.

Toxic Trees

In addition to making shade, some trees add other obstacles to successful edible gardening. Trees whose roots grow close to the surface and reach out in a wide circle (known as the drip line) are not good companions for your vegetable garden. The roots will interfere with cultivation and will suck up moisture greedily. Most maple trees are in this category, with silver maples ranked as the worst culprits.

Black walnut trees are also bad neighbors for your garden. In fact, their roots produce a toxin that is deadly for a wide range of plants, including many edibles. (The toxin can also have an allergic affect on humans and horses.)

Both the Ohio State University and the West Virginia University Extension Service have published fact sheets about black walnut toxicity. They include a list of plants that will not grow within 50 feet (and in some cases up to 80 feet) radius of the trunk of a black walnut tree. Research shows that these plants will be injured or will die in a month or two of growth in proximity to this killer tree.

These plants include the following:

- Asparagus
- Cabbage
- Tomato
- Potato
- Blackberry
- Rhubarb
- Pepper
- Eggplant
- Blueberry

Plants that don't seem to mind the toxin include the following:

- Lima bean
- Beet
- Onion
- Black raspberry
- Snap bean
- Corn
- Parsnip

If you remove a black walnut tree in order to garden, pull out the roots and allow about two months for the toxins to break down. To learn more about black walnut toxins, visit ohioline.osu.edu or www.wvu.edu.

USDA Plant Hardiness Zones

If you have ever read a how-to gardening book or looked through a plant catalog you have probably seen a USDA Plant Hardiness Zone map. This map was created by the U.S. Department of Agriculture in 1960 (with revisions in 1965) to help gardeners and farmers determine what plants will grow where. The map is based on the average lowest winter temperatures throughout the country. Years ago, there were only 10 zones, but the USDA has expanded the number to 20 by adding "a" and "b" areas to Zones 2 through 10 and Zone 11.

To find which USDA Hardiness Zone your garden is in go to www.usna.usda.gov/ Hardzone/hrdzone.html.

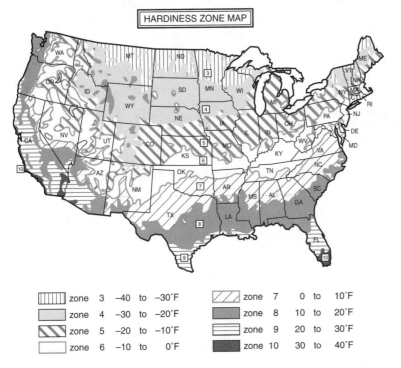

HARDINESS ZONE MAP

The U.S. Department of Agriculture Plant Hardiness Zone map will help you determine the zone where you garden.

zone 3 −40 to −30°F	zone 7 0 to 10°F
zone 4 −30 to −20°F	zone 8 10 to 20°F
zone 5 −20 to −10°F	zone 9 20 to 30°F
zone 6 −10 to 0°F	zone 10 30 to 40°F

Knowing the hardiness of perennial plants is particularly important when you buy them from websites or catalogs, as opposed from your local garden center. Many companies ship plants based on a formula of your order date and your hardiness zone. For example, the Burpee catalog says that if you live in Zones 6 to 10 and order by March 12, you will receive your plants during the week of May 10. It's a good system.

Prof. Price's Pointers

The U.S. Department of Agriculture bases the hardiness zone designations on more than 60 years of temperature data.

Food for Thought

USDA Zones give you an approximate idea of what you can grow where you live. Keep in mind that within these zones there are microclimates—sort of zones within zones—where the range of temperatures will be slightly higher or lower than indicated on the USDA map due to environmental and geographic factors. These factors can change from year to year.

For example, my home in southeastern Pennsylvania is in Zone 6b. But because my garden sits below street level, faces south, and is protected on all four sides with fences and white plaster walls that reflect the sun, the garden behaves more as if it were in Zone 7a. Other factors that might create a microclimate include prevailing winds and proximity to lakes, ponds, rivers, streams, mountains, hills, factories, and highways.

The Least You Need to Know

- ◆ Provide edible plants with at least six hours of sunlight a day.
- ◆ Calculate how much room each plant variety will require to grow.
- ◆ Put your garden conveniently near a water source.
- ◆ Don't allow young unattended children or pets access to your garden.
- ◆ Determine prior uses of your property to protect against contamination.
- ◆ Know your USDA Plant Hardiness Zone.

Chapter 6

Plotting and Planning

In This Chapter

- How to delineate the borders of your garden
- Learn how to use graph paper and a ruler to plot out your garden
- Take it to the next level with stakes and string
- Plan an irrigation system
- Explore fencing options
- The types of garden paths you might create

The plotting and planning stage of gardening is probably the least fun, especially for Type A personalities who like to get things done, fast. This work can be time-consuming and—well, let's face it—dull. But it's absolutely necessary. Skip this phase, and you'll most likely make mistakes that will result in a garden that could have been better. The good news is you really only have to do this stuff once.

In this section, you learn how to lay out the perimeter of your proposed garden *in situ* (right there on site). Then you can use graph paper to make a scale drawing of the garden and a plot plan that will serve as our planting guide. After that, you stake out the garden, giving yourself (or your hired hands) a blueprint for digging and for making paths. Then you can decide what kind of fences to use, the type of paths you want, and if and how to allow for an irrigation system. Finally, we look at growing seasons and how they affect your planning.

Lay It All Out

Now that you have a general idea of how much space you'll need for the kind of garden you intend to have, you'll want to lay it out. This step, though not essential, is helpful because it allows you to see exactly how your garden fits in your overall landscape, how convenient (or inconvenient) it will be and if, in fact, you have allowed enough space or if you have perhaps made it too big.

> **Garden Guru Says**
>
> Most vegetable gardens are rectangles or squares, though there is no rule that says you can't make it a parallelogram, a circle, or even a hexagon.

The easiest way to lay out the garden is with an old hose (or two or three depending on how big your garden ideas are). Take the hose and place it on the ground where you plan to situate the garden. You can create corners by sinking stakes, then shape the hose at a right angle around the stakes.

Once you have your garden shape delineated with the hose, you'll want to make a semi-permanent outline.

> **Garden Guru Says**
>
> If you find that your first attempt at laying out the guidelines is not going to work, mow the spray-painted grass and start over again.

The best way to mark your space is with landscaper's spray paint. This stuff is readily available at landscape supply stores or places like Home Depot or Lowe's. It's neon orange. Spray the paint right along your outline (be prepared: you will have permanently colored hose).

Remove the hose and there you have it—the layout for your future garden. Use the orange line to keep the digging you'll do within the framework you have planned, and as a guideline for setting up fencing.

Graph Paper and Ruler

Frankly, this next phase of the design is the part I don't particularly like. In the years that I ran a landscape design business, my partner did most of the drawings, and that made me very happy. But unless you are very good at visualizing the garden you want to create, it's not a good idea to skip this basic groundwork.

You have already decided where the garden will go and how big it will be (see Chapters 2 and 5). And you have created a basic layout using the old garden hose trick. Using this graph paper and ruler method is how you design the actual plot plan that describes where the entry will go, where paths and walkways will be placed, the location of any irrigation elements, and the placement for each plant variety.

To draw your garden plan, you will need graph paper (use any scale that you like); a sharp pencil; sharp colored pencils or colored markers; a ruler or straight edge; and a flat surface like a desk, table, or kitchen counter.

Next, follow these steps to make a scale drawing of your proposed garden:

1. Determine your scale. The simplest way is to have one square on the graph paper represent a certain number of square feet in the garden.

2. Plot out the square footage by counting off the squares on the graph paper. For example, if you are planning a 1,000 square foot garden, and your scale is one graph paper square per square foot of garden, count off 20 squares across and 50 down. Mark the beginning and the ending points.

3. Use the pencil and the straight edge to draw lines connecting the marks.

4. Count off squares within your framework to determine the placement of fence posts, gates, arbors, paths, and any other *hardscape* elements.

5. Count off more squares to measure specific planting areas. Use square footage needs based on seed packet information or estimates you will find in Part 4 of this book.

6. Use the colored pencils or markers to indicate different planting areas. Make a key for yourself on the plot plan so you know what plant or group of plants each color represents.

7. Indicate where irrigation system elements will be positioned. (You might want to share your plot plan with the irrigation specialist if you hire one to install a system.)

8. Indicate the source of electricity for the electric fence should you elect to install one.

Once you have completed your scale drawing, you are ready to move on to the next step, staking out the garden.

Prof. Price's Pointers

If you are comfortable using a computer, you might want to explore some of the gardening software that is now on the market. Though most programs are focused on landscape design, a few will work for edible gardens. Use these software programs to help you design your garden spaces and skip the traditional graph paper step.

Prof. Price's Pointers

The **hardscape** is the collection of structural elements in the landscape. Walls, fences, walkways and paths, gates, arbors, and buildings are all part of the hardscape.

Stakes and String

With a plot plan in hand, you can stake out the garden more precisely. You might or might not have spray-painted the outline of the garden. If you have, you can go right to step 2: placing stakes at the corners and running string between the stakes. (If you have a garden with a curved outline, spray paint is your best option.) If you have skipped the hose and spray paint option, you'll need to do some measuring before you put in your stakes. And if you are a complete fly-by-the-seat-of-your-pants type, just stick the stakes in any old place, or just start digging.

Once your corner stakes are in and the perimeter outline is marked with string, you can stake and string the entry and any paths you plan to create. If you plan to have grass areas between growing rows, stake them out, too. Also use stakes to mark where irrigation system elements will be placed and where the electric current will enter the space in the case of an electric fence. Be sure to refer to your plot plan as you stake, but be prepared to make alterations as you go along. Even the best garden designs can be changed for the better at this stage. You'll want to make the changes on your plan as well as on the ground for future reference.

Note: At this stage of the game, you might want to do your heavy digging. This is the critical part of the job where you remove sod, turn the soil, and improve it. We will look at this step in depth in Chapter 9. From this point on in this chapter, we will assume that you have dug the garden.

Advance Planning for Irrigation

It would be wonderful if we could grow edibles without worrying about watering. Somehow, it never works out that way. And because some vegetables and fruits require great quantities of water in order to produce, some form of irrigation might be the only option.

If you are going to install an underground irrigation system, this is the stage at which you lay the underground piping. Although it can be done later in the game, it's best to do it now, after the garden is dug, but before anything is planted.

Note: You might want to check out Chapter 19 to review the various irrigation options.

Fence Me In

There are a couple of good reasons to put fences around edible gardens. The number one reason is to keep marauding animals out. A fence around the garden plot is also a safety measure to protect children and pets, whether they are yours or the neighbors'. An attractive fence is the best way to keep the sometimes-untidy appearance of a productive edible garden out of sight, especially in a formal or otherwise well-manicured landscape.

In order to select the right kind of fence for your garden, you should determine what you want the fence to do. If deer are a big problem, the height of the fence is an important factor. Digging animals will need another solution. To make the vegetable plot an integral part of the backyard, a well-designed decorative fence might be the right choice. The following sections will give you an idea of what you might want to do.

 **Garden Guru Says**

Many municipalities and homeowners' associations have strict regulations about fencing, including height restrictions and materials allowed. Be sure to check with the appropriate governing bodies before installing fences on your property.

Simple Solutions

The most basic garden barrier is nothing more than a roll of wide wire fence material or plastic mesh strung between wooden or metal stakes. The stakes are set into the ground at intervals around the perimeter of the garden. You will need to secure the fencing to the stakes somehow. This can be done with twist ties or wire. Or if you are using wooden stakes, fasten the wire with heavy-duty staples.

Plastic mesh fencing is becoming increasingly popular because it is relatively inexpensive and durable, easy to install and it sort of blends into the background. Another plus is that it is available in widths up to eight feet or more, making it a great option for keeping deer out.

These kinds of fencing are not pretty. But if the look of the garden isn't an issue, go for it. Just be sure to devise an entry to the garden.

Food for Thought

To keep digging animals like rabbits, moles, voles, and dogs out of your garden, you will need to place wire fencing or plastic mesh below ground level. The easiest way to do this is to dig a trench along the perimeter of the garden. You might have to go down as much as a foot. Then attach your metal fence material securely in the soil every couple of inches with steel pins or use metal rods, flat metal bars, or strips of wood to hold the fencing in place. Curve the fencing outward just slightly to make it even more difficult for the pesky critters to tunnel under. Be sure to factor in the underground portion when you measure how much fence material you'll need to buy. You can add this underground insurance to any style of fence you choose to install.

Another simple option is a chain link fence. Also not pretty, and certainly not as inexpensive as wire or plastic mesh, chain link is usually less expensive than wood, PVC, or decorative metal fences. And it's very sturdy and durable.

Attractive Options

If the look of the garden is important to you, you might want to opt for a more decorative fence. You can choose from a broad range of styles and materials. There are do-it-yourself fences with elements available at home and garden centers; component fences with mix and match elements; custom-made fences; and some that have to be ordered online or by mail from companies in New Zealand (thatch) or England (waddle).

The style of decorative fence you choose is all a matter of taste. If you only want the fence for decorative purposes, you won't need any modifications. If, however, you want an attractive fence that also serves as a barrier, you might have to modify it with wire fencing or plastic fence tacked on to the inside perimeter.

The following decorative fence styles are just a few you might want to consider:

- ◆ **Hurdle.** Developed in England, and originally a movable wood fence, it features upright end posts, four or five thin rails, an upright center post, and two diagonal posts forming a triangle at the center.

- ◆ **Post and rail.** Generally made of wood, but also available in PVC, each section consists of two upright posts with two, three, or four cross rails. Cross rails are usually round or squared. The crossbuck variation is similar to the hurdle fence but has two rails forming an X between the top and bottom rails. The rails either fit into notches in the posts or are attached with nails or screws.

- ◆ **Split rail.** Slightly more rustic than the post and rail style, the split rails are more roughly hewn. Generally there are two, three, or four rails, which are chamfered at the ends and fit into slots on the posts.

- ◆ **Stacked split rail.** Many variations include worm, snake, Virginia, Vermont, crooked rail, rick rack, and zigzag. All are made of rails stacked on top of each other. Some are supported by sunken posts, others by posts that form Xs. Still others have no posts at all.

- ◆ **Picket.** This is the old-fashioned cottage fence. It comes in hundreds, if not thousands, of forms ranging from standard stock pointed pickets to hand-crafted styles. Usually made of treated, stained, or painted wood. Also available in PVC.

- ◆ **Stockade.** Narrow, picketlike, and usually roughly hewn boards are set flush one next to the other. Secured across the back by horizontal boards attached to posts set in the ground. Usually available in four, five, six, or eight feet heights. Tall stockade fences cast shade so these are best for large gardens where some shade won't matter.

◆ **Thatch.** From the days of thatched cottages in England, a thatch fence is made of bundles of twigs and small branches tied together with wire, rope, or vines and formed into panels. The panels are attached to twiggy posts and set in the ground. Very decorative.

◆ **Waddle.** Originating in England, and also used by early American farmers including George Washington, the waddle fence was made of willow branches woven in a basket weave pattern between upright sticks. Also made in Asia of bamboo.

◆ **PVC.** Long-lasting, durable new fence material. Is made to look like picket, post, and rail fences.

◆ **Powder-coated wire.** An inexpensive barrier fence that is better looking than plain wire or plastic mesh. Easy to install.

> **Garden Guru Says**
>
> When you install your fence, you'll need to allow for an entry point. This should be at least three feet wide. But you might want more room than that depending on how you will use and maintain the garden. Is your entry large enough for your garden tractor, cart or wheelbarrow, mower, and so on?

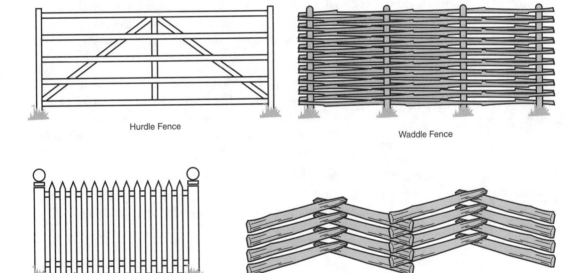

Hurdle Fence

Waddle Fence

Picket Fence

Split Rail Fence in Worm Pattern

There are a variety of fences you can use to fence in your garden.

Wooden fences can last up to 20 years if they are made of treated wood. Cedar and redwood are the most durable, followed by Douglas fir, spruce, and pine.

An Electrifying Situation

When my parents had their large wooded property, an electric fence around the perimeter of the planted areas was essential. Until the fence was installed, the deer ate themselves silly. If deer are a problem in your area (that would be just about the entire Northeast, as well as other large areas of the country), you might want to consider an electric fence.

Be prepared. Electric fences are not pretty and they don't come cheap. But if you have devoted a lot of time and energy into growing edibles for your table, you don't want to be providing fancy feasts for Bambi and his friends.

Most homeowners will call on specialists to install an electric fence on their properties. If you elect to do it yourself, be sure you know what you are doing.

Down the Garden Path

Unless your garden space is really tiny, you will probably need to have some kind of paths or walkways, even if they are nothing more than the spaces between rows or planting beds. A path inside a garden should be at least two feet wide. Three feet is even better.

Whole books have been written about garden paths and walkways (I actually wrote one— *Paths and Walkways* [Friedman/Fairfax] a few years ago!), so if you are really interested in this topic, check out a couple of them. In the meantime, consider the options discussed in the following sections.

Packed Earth

The packed earth path is the path of least resistance, if you will. After you have stripped the sod from your garden space (see Chapter 19 for more on this), simply leave the spaces you have designated for paths as is. Over time, the soil will become compacted from being walked on, which will help keep weeds from sprouting.

Grass

Very large gardens will often have grass paths and walkways, just because it's a lot less work to leave some of the sod in place than to strip it all. Grass paths are an attractive foil to planting beds. But they do have to be mowed. Be sure the path is wide enough to accommodate your mower. You don't want to wind up mowing vegetables by accident.

Mulch

A thick layer of some form of mulch on top of a bare, packed earth path is easy to maintain and has a neat, clean appearance. Use wood chips, pine bark, salt hay, seaweed, or even grass clippings. You will have to add to the mulch as it gets worn down over time.

Fancier Solutions

If you are hoping to create a more formal garden space, you will most likely want to design paths with a decorative touch. While grass paths will work in a formal situation, there are other materials you might want to consider:

- Gravel
- Stone
- Wood rounds
- Cement rounds
- Brick
- Wood planks
- Cement pavers

In the next chapter, we look more closely at how the garden path works in the overall design of a garden.

The Least You Need to Know

- Use spray paint and a garden hose to delineate the borders of your garden.
- Draw a plot plan on graph paper before you start digging.
- Use stakes and string to determine planting areas, entry points, and paths.
- Plan an irrigation system before planting.
- Select a fence style that meets the needs of your garden.
- Make paths with materials that suit your style of gardening.

Chapter

7

Design Dilemma

In This Chapter

- Explore some popular garden styles
- Design a basic, productive garden with minimalist sensibilities
- Try on different or unusual gardening styles
- Incorporate decorative elements into your garden space
- Deal with compost piles, utility areas, and other unsightly garden details

At this point, you probably have a pretty good idea of how big your garden will be, what kinds of things you are going to grow, where you'll put the garden, and how to put some of your ideas into action.

This chapter is a little different because it's not about essential stuff. Instead, we go over some of the aesthetics of your garden. Not the nuts and bolts things, but how the garden will look. Do you want a basic vegetable garden, or do you want to re-create a mini version of a royal French *potager?* Do you want to add a little sitting area, a small terrace, a fountain, a potting shed, or other decorative feature to enhance the looks of your garden? Do you want to follow feng shui principles? Read on and then decide.

Prof. Price's Pointers

Potager is the French word for kitchen garden. These highly structured gardens were usually laid in perfectly manicured geometric beds intersected by axial paths. Several or even many paths might intersect forming a series of geometric planting beds. This patterned approach is called a parterre. A pergola is a structure like an arbor with upright supports and cross pieces overhead that create a room-like space underneath.

A Sense of Style

We all have our own sense of style. Usually we express our style in the way that we dress and the way we furnish our homes. Sleek modernists often wear basic black and favor smooth granite countertops and unadorned floors. Traditionalists, in tailored sportswear, frequently have homes with lots of chintz and tabletops cluttered with frames and decorative mementos.

Our sense of style can also be reflected in our gardens. Do you like cute vegetable-shaped plant markers and lots or ornaments? Or do you prefer to take an unadorned approach? Whatever appeals to you most is what you ought to do. Some garden styles are more, well, stylized. In this chapter, we'll look at a few different approaches.

The Island Bed

Think of your lawn as a body of water. Now create an island in that body of water. The island is the garden bed floating in the sea of lawn. Okay, I know that sounds kind of corny, but that's the best way to describe an island bed.

It should be free form, with gently curving lines. Right away, because of the form, you know it is an informal space. And because it is free form with a curved outline, a wooden fence isn't going to work. If possible, leave an island bed unfenced. A large island bed will need a path through it in order for you to tend all the plants. Make your path twist and turn gently from one end to the other. And because the island bed is meant to be seen from all sides, plant taller things toward the center, then medium-size plants all the way around with the lower plants along the outer perimeter.

Here are some suggestions for various-size plants:

Tall plants for center of island bed:

- Corn
- Peas or beans on teepees or trellises
- Large variety tomato plants
- Broccoli
- Brussels sprouts
- Dill
- Sunflowers (not really a vegetable, but has edible seeds)

Medium height plants:

- Spinach
- Leeks
- Eggplant
- Onion
- Basil
- Chard
- Cabbage
- Pepper
- Sage

Lower plants for perimeter of island beds:

- Parsley
- Oregano
- Radish
- Thyme
- Scallions
- Carrot

The Country Cottage

The English cottage garden was all the rage a few years ago. And it's not hard to understand why. This is a very appealing garden style.

The cottage vegetable garden is equally appealing. It's easy on the eye, not too fussy, but not too bare. Each might have its own personality, but the best country cottage gardens have a few common elements, including a nice picket or split rail fence; an arbor over the gate; a little shed at one side; a bench; plenty of neat, straight paths in gravel, grass, or mulch; and a wide variety of well-tended plants.

Crisp edges aren't a priority in a country cottage garden. In fact, plants should appear to tumble out along the path. One of the lessons I learned from English gardeners is to design axial paths (straight intersecting perpendicular paths) bordered by thickly planted beds with plants that overstep the bounds of the beds on to the paths. It produces a controlled chaos that is enormously appealing.

Feng Shui

You have probably heard about the Chinese belief and practice called feng shui. Feng shui literally means "wind-water," and it refers to the flow of *chi*, or energy, in a space. The belief is that energy affects wealth, health, and relationships. In a house, feng shui dictates the placement of doors, windows, furniture, and other elements. The same principles can be applied to the garden.

In a feng shui garden, the placement and shapes of beds is important. So is the use and location of certain materials and elements including metal, wood, water, and color. There are feng shui experts who will advise clients on the best way to achieve proper feng shui in the home and in the garden.

To get you started without a professional, here are a few suggestions:

◆ Avoid having corners in the garden.

◆ Avoid straight lines or sharp angles.

◆ Use curving lines to encourage the flow of energy.

◆ Balance dark (yin) and light (yang) elements.

◆ Place water features and tool sheds to the north, never in the south.

◆ Use stone or earthen elements (brick, for example) in the northeast section of the garden.

◆ Use triangle shapes in the south.

◆ Use circular or arched shapes in the west.

◆ Avoid the use of metal to the east.

◆ Grow fruits and herbs and incorporate columns in the eastern part of the garden.

Feng shui is much too complicated to cover completely here. Look in the reference section for a few books on the subject, or consult an expert.

Children's Gardens

Many years ago, I attended a symposium on gardening for children hosted by a national gardening organization. In addition to all the speakers, forums, and booths, the event featured a dozen real gardens designed for children. They were really fantastic with little places to sit or hide; wonderful colors, textures, and fragrances; amusing decorative details; and lots of opportunities for learning and pretending.

In Chapter 3, we looked at some of the things children enjoy growing and explored some ways to introduce kids to gardening. Here are a few design ideas that will make a children's vegetable garden an inviting and fun place to explore.

◆ Laminate seed packets and attach to Popsicle sticks to use as row markers.

◆ Make and install a scarecrow.

◆ Add a child-size bench or table and chairs so the garden becomes a living space.

◆ Construct a teepee for vines (see Chapter 3).

◆ Add fun decorative elements like a toad house, fountain, birdbath, bird feeder, or wind chimes.

◆ Install a child-size arbor.

◆ Plant flowers with the vegetables.

Formal Vegetable Gardens

Although all parterre gardens are more or less formal, not all formal gardens are constructed with parterre patterns. The formal feel of a garden is reinforced by the use of straight lines as opposed to curves, but they don't necessarily form patterns.

A simple formal garden might be a rectangle divided by two intersecting perpendicular paths. It might have a small, paved seating area covered by a pergola at one end and an open view at the far side.

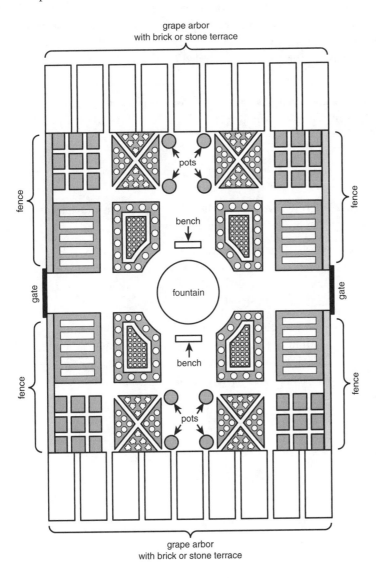

This is a variation of the formal vegetable garden I designed several years ago. The original design had brick paths.

Neatness counts in a formal garden. Everything should be in its place. Planting beds are well defined with well-trimmed, edged borders.

Some of the most beautiful formal vegetable gardens are reproductions of historic gardens like Thomas Jefferson's kitchen garden at Monticello, George Washington's kitchen garden at Mount Vernon, and the great *potagers* in France.

Parterre

Parterre is just a fancy word for describing the layout of paths and beds in a garden bed. The kitchen gardens at Monticello and Mount Vernon were done in a simple parterre style while the seventeenth century kitchen gardens at Versailles and Villandry in France were elaborate affairs that went on for acres and included great fountains and fancy trellising.

Though these gardens require an enormous amount of work to plant and maintain, it is possible to re-create your own, though I would recommend a smaller scale than Versailles.

Formal Herb Garden

Because herbs tend to be easy to grow and because they don't take up as much space as many vegetables do, they make the perfect plants for creating a small formal garden.

Some of the most beautiful formal herb gardens are designed as knot gardens. Dating to medieval times, the knot garden features tiny hedges of evergreen herbs forming intersecting lines in simple patterns. Most often, herbs with contrasting colors are used so that the intersecting little hedges stand out and the pattern is more vivid.

A typical eighteenth-century-style American herb garden is easily reproduced today. Typically a square space, the garden might have had a central space shaped as a diamond or as a square turned on its axis. Straight paths of brick or gravel might form an X at the center square and divide the other spaces into triangular planting beds. Most formal herb gardens are symmetrical.

Parterre garden

The parterre garden pictured here might not be as overwhelming a project for the home gardener as the Versailles gardens.

1) tepee for peas or beans

2) cabbage

3) lettuces

4) tomato in cage

5) onions

6) kale or spinach or chard

× various herbs

boxwood hedge

dwarf boxwood hedge

Architectural Elements

Any kind of a wall or building in a landscaped area is known as an architectural element, and landscape designers love them. An architectural element creates a framework and a foil for plants.

If you already have an architectural element on your property and it's in an appropriate spot for the garden, give some serious thought to putting your garden nearby or even bordering it.

Consider some of these structures if you want to add architectural elements to your design. Any one of these would add architectural interest to your edible garden space:

- Garden shed
- Tool shed
- Chicken coop
- Carriage house
- Smoke house
- Spring house
- Oversize cold frame
- Potting shed
- Old outhouse
- Garage
- Lean-to
- Pool house
- Greenhouse

So let's imagine that you are fortunate enough to have one of these architectural elements in close proximity to your garden. How do you use it?

If you have a small building, use one wall, preferably not facing north, as one side of your garden. Enclose the other three sides with fence and your garden becomes a more important feature in the landscape. Add espaliered fruit, vining vegetables, hanging baskets, or window boxes along the wall, and it becomes even lovelier.

Out of Sight

If you are doing a down and dirty garden, you might as well skip this part. In this section, we're going to look at ways to hide or disguise the less attractive, but necessary, elements of the garden like compost piles, equipment, supplies, and other not so pretty but essential things.

Take Out the Garbage

Compost piles can be unsightly. I mean, let's face it. A compost pile is basically a pile of garbage! But that garbage eventually becomes compost and there's nothing like it to make your soil rich. So in a garden where aesthetics are important, the compost pile is a liability.

There are a number of ways to hide or disguise the compost. You can put it on the other side of the garage or garden shed, if your yard is blessed with these structures. You can create a screen with panels of fence or trellis. Or you can grow a screen with bamboo, forsythia, evergreens, or another thick hedge.

Food for Thought

A clever and fruitful method of disguising your compost pile is to grow a vining vegetable or fruit like pumpkin, squash, or melons right on top of the pile. The vines grow rapidly, produce large leaves, and sprawl all over the pile. You can still add more scraps, clippings, and stuff to the pile just by moving the vines around a little bit. Although this won't completely hide the pile of compost, it will cover it up a little. And once the pumpkins, squash, or melons start to grow and ripen, they will take center stage.

Another way to hide or disguise the compost pile is to keep it in nice tidy containers. You can either build your own or buy one of the many different styles available commercially. A large wooden compost bin can actually become an architectural element in your garden.

Storage

Large gardens might require large quantities of mulch and fertilizer, a mower or tractor, lots of tools and hoses, and other equipment and products. Most of these things aren't all that decorative, so you might want to think about having some sort of structure for storage.

Custom-made or prefab tool and storage sheds are the ideal answer to garden storage problems. Some are more attractive than others, but even the ugliest prefab metal shed will look better than a big pile of peat moss and fertilizer bags, mower parts, mulch cloth, and any of the other stuff that seems to accumulate around the garden.

Garden Guru Says

An out-of-use outhouse can make a very attractive little tool shed. Though not easy to find, they are sometimes available when a developer takes over a country property. Old chicken coops also make great garden sheds.

Prof. Price's Pointers

Cloche is French for bell jar. A bell jar is a bell-shape glass jar often placed over a delicate seedling to protect it from cold.

To improve the look of a garden shed that is more practical than pretty, you can always attach a few sections of lattice along the walls and encourage vines to grow. The disguised wall then becomes a nice backdrop for other plantings, and voilà, the ugly old garden shed becomes an architectural element.

The Minimalist

The minimalist design is a garden style that will appeal to people who don't like a lot of clutter. People who like these rarely have more than one thing on their coffee table and the kitchen counters are often bare. Clean lines. No fussy tchotchkes littering the scene.

A minimalist garden isn't necessarily simple. It just uses clean lines without excess ornament. Long, straight, well-manicured rows with neatly placed plantings is what's needed.

A Decorative Touch

If you like lots of stuff around your house, you might feel comfortable with decorative items in your garden as well.

Here are some things you might add to your garden to give it that homey feel:

- Benches
- Ornaments
- Paths
- Pergolas
- Trellises
- Fountains
- Scarecrows
- Teepees
- Fences
- Arbors
- Pots
- Sundials
- *Cloches*
- Edging

The Least You Need to Know

- Look for an architectural element to enhance your garden's design.
- Let your personality help define your garden style.
- Try to disguise unsightly elements in your garden like compost piles or storage areas.
- Call on an expert if you want to utilize feng shui in your garden.

Part

Get Ready to Plant

Now we can get our hands dirty. This part of the book is all about soil and digging. First, in Chapter 8, we actually look at what soil is, how it functions, and how to make it as good as it can be. We also explore the mysteries of pH. And there's a section on making compost, which some gardeners get nearly spiritual about. Later in this section are rules to follow for preparing garden beds, including the arduous double digging that the English are so fond of. You'll find out why in Chapter 9, where we also go into quite a bit of detail on how to create raised beds and how to amend the soil. There's a little bit in there about machine tilling too for gardeners who like that kind of thing. Even if you are science phobic, I think you won't have any trouble understanding the plant biology lesson in Chapter 10.

Chapter 8

Essential Soils

In This Chapter

 ◆ Get the dirt on soil
 ◆ Figure out the pH of your soil
 ◆ Find out how to test your soil, and why you will want to
 ◆ Get a feel for the soil texture plants like
 ◆ Find out what goes into compost, and what does not

For farmers, gardeners, and plant scientists, soil is a really big deal. People get a Ph.D. in soil science. There are entire departments at state universities devoted to the subject. In this chapter, we will look at the many properties and variables of soil, find out what pH is and why it is so important to gardeners (and plants!), and learn about the various nutrients that enhance the quality of soil. This is also where to find out everything you've ever wanted to know about compost.

Dirt Is a Dirty Word

If you want to call yourself a gardener, you must swear never again to use the word *dirt* when you mean soil. Just remove *dirt* from your vocabulary.

Now that we have that out of the way, here's the dirt on *soil*. In order to provide plants with an environment in which they can thrive, gardeners need to know at least a little bit about the chemical and physical makeup of soil.

Soil is made up of several layers of different materials. The top layer consists of leaves and organic debris. Just below that is what we think of as topsoil. It's also called surface soil and it usually includes a fair amount of organic matter. Next comes the subsurface layer with decomposed organic matter and mineral compounds. Below that is the subsoil that can be a combination of enriched clay, minerals, organic compounds, and loose rocks. All these layers lie on top of bedrock. Different parts of the country have different thicknesses and even concentrations of materials at each layer, but the basic set of layers is more or less the same.

This drawing shows the profile of all the layers of typical soil from the surface organic debris all the way down to bedrock.

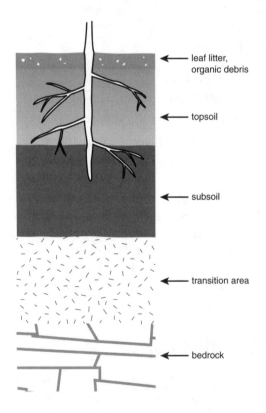

← leaf litter, organic debris

← topsoil

← subsoil

← transition area

← bedrock

Soil is also made up of mineral materials including particles of gravel, sand, clay, silt, and organic matter, including broken-down plant and animal remains. There is also air and water in soil.

Most of the components of soil—such as clay particles, sand, and organic matter are important for the physical structure of the soil. They determine how well water and nutrients become available to plants. Soil also contains tiny amounts of minerals that actually are the nutrients. We'll learn more about these nutrients and how they work in Chapter 19.

The Feel of the Soil

Soil texture is another important factor, which affects how water passes through soil and how quickly it warms up and retains heat. Soil texture ranges from the finest silt loam to the densest clay. In between are loam, silty clay loam, sandy loam, clay loam, sand, loamy sand, and sandy clay loam. Most vegetable plants like to grow in loamy soils.

You can improve the texture of your soil by adding peat moss, leaf mold, decomposed grass clippings, manure, and compost. Be cautious with peat moss because it can become compacted and will act like a moisture barrier preventing moisture from descending to the plants' root zones.

Tip-Top Soil

Surface soil or topsoil is the best for growing plants. It is usually made up of 50 percent solid materials that are a combination of minerals and organic matter. The other 50 percent is open or pore space that is filled with either air or water. Ideally the pore space is half air and half water. After a rain or a period of irrigation, there will be more water than air. When it's been dry for any length of time, there is more air than water.

Organic Matter

Organic matter in soil refers to the remains of plant material. It can take the form of sawdust, wood chips, pine needles, kitchen scraps, dried leaves, straw, grass clippings, and manure. Over time and given the right conditions, organic matter decomposes.

 Food for Thought _____

The process of decomposition converts large chunks of organic material into much smaller particles, some even too small to see under a microscope. These particles act like miniscule sponges that soak up water. Then they attach themselves loosely to the minerals and nutrients in the soil. The result is a soil that is much more friable (that's the optimum soil texture), more moist, and more fertile.

In healthy soil, worms, insects, bacteria, and other microorganisms eat the organic matter and produce _humus_ and soil nutrients.

Soil Structure

People who really know their soil usually classify the soil's structure as either weak or strong, with varying degrees of strength or weakness. This is a description of the shape of soil particles and how they group together. It's important to understand this because it will determine how air and water move through the soil.

Soil particles cluster together in little groups called aggregates. The shape of these aggregates will determine the structure of the soil. The aggregates range from microscopic grains of sand to what is called "massive" chunks. Some look like tiny pebbles, others like slivers of mica. Some are porous, others solid.

Granular soils—with a texture like miniscule pebbles—allow water and air to pass through easily. This kind of soil has a strong structure. A weak soil has massive kinds of aggregates making it more difficult for water and air to pass through and for roots to take hold.

You can improve the structure of the soil in your garden by adding things like course sand, vermiculate, perlite, peat moss, compost, manure, leaf mold, sawdust, seaweed, and straw.

Be cautious with peat moss as it can easily become compacted, thus preventing water from penetrating.

The pH Story

When we talk about *pH*, we are referring to how acid or alkaline the soil is. Sometimes this is expressed as how "sweet" (alkaline) or "sour" (acid) the soil is. It is a logarithmic scale (which is way over my head—my high school math only went as far as a poor showing in algebra). But put simply for idiots like me, it means that a pH level of 6.5 is 10 times more alkaline than a reading of 5.5.

But why is pH so important? If the pH of the soil in your garden is out of whack with the requirements of the plants you are trying to grow, the plants will struggle to absorb the nutrients they need. For example, most vegetables like to grow in soil with a pH of about 6.5, which is just slightly acid. If your soil measures 5.5, your tomatoes and peppers will grow slowly, won't produce as much fruit, and will be more prone to disease. On the other hand, blueberry bushes will be much happier in 5.5 soil than 6.5 because they like a much more acid soil. Get it?

> **Garden Guru Says**
>
> Microorganisms need to eat to multiply, but it can take them a long time to digest intact plant material. Give these bugs an energy boost with a big dose of sugar simply by emptying the dregs of soft-drink or beer bottles onto the pile after your next backyard picnic.

Soil That's Too Acid

If your soil proves to be too acid for the plants you plan to grow, you can raise the pH by adding ground limestone. Because relatively little lime is needed to raise the pH to the desired levels, you might want to consult with your local County Extension Office or Farm Bureau to help you determine the proper amounts for the soil in your area.

In regions like the Northwest and the Northeast which tend to have acid soils, an application of lime every four or five years using a formula of about 4 pounds for every 100 square feet of garden is usually enough for most vegetable gardens. It might take several months for the lime to affect the pH level throughout the beds. The best time to apply lime is at the end of the growing season so it will have plenty of time to produce its affect.

Soil That's Too Alkaline

If the pH is too high or alkaline, you'll want to add sulfur, gypsum, or aluminum sulfate. Aluminum sulfate is water-soluble so it will do the trick quite quickly. The other products take a bit more time. A good formula to follow is about 3 pounds of sulfur or 5 pounds of aluminum sulfate for every 100 square feet of garden.

The Drain Game

The way water passes through soil is called drainage. Good drainage qualities help to maintain a deep root zone, eliminate frost heave, bring warmth to soils earlier in the spring, improve soil aeration, and lower disease problems.

> **Garden Guru Says**
>
> Moss growing on the soil is a pretty good indication that soil drainage is poor.

Soil with serious drainage issues will be easy to spot. It will be wet and squishy, puddles will form easily in depressions and low spots when it rains, and the water will stay there for a while.

The more organic matter there is in the soil, the better able the soil is to retain water. Thus, if you have drainage problems, you should consider adding organic material to the soil, though if your drainage problems are really serious, this won't be enough. You might have to consider cutting swails (ditches to divert water), installing drains, or bringing in a dump truck load of additional soil.

Soil Tests

Soil tests help gardeners determine the pH of the soil and the level of available nitrogen, phosphorous, and potassium. You'll also receive other information on the texture of the soil, the lime and salt content, and sometimes levels of toxic materials. This information will help you understand what adjustments you'll need to bring the soil to the fertility, texture, and pH you'll need to grow specific crops. Unless you are growing particularly demanding crops or your land is flooded, you'll only need to test the soil every three or four years. It's best to test in the fall so that you can add amendments and allow them to "percolate" through the soil over the winter.

Follow the directions on the soil test kit. Usually they will suggest 8 to 10 samples from various parts of the garden. If you have a tiny patch, five or six samples will do. However, if your gardens consists of a number of remote areas—the raspberry patch here, veggies over there, and a half acre in corn—you'll need to perform several different tests.

CAUTION

Compost Pile

If your garden is near a heavily traveled road or in the vicinity of an older home that might have had lead-based paint scraped off, or if there was any kind of industrial activity near where your garden is now, the soil might be contaminated with lead. You don't want to grow edibles in lead-contaminated soil. Be sure to have it tested.

Compost

Compost is what we call the decomposed plant material that we collect from the kitchen, yard, garden, and barnyard for reuse as a soil enhancer. Just about any material that started out as part of a plant can be composted, including the manure of plant-eating animals.

Compost piles need air circulation, moisture, and heat in order to do their magic, so you will want to place your pile accordingly. Do avoid putting the pile in a spot that gets full sun all day unless you are prepared to water it regularly. A part-shade location is ideal.

Prof. Price's Pointers

Compost is plant material that has been decomposed by microorganisms.

Take the following steps to create a compost pile for your garden:

1. Establish a location for the pile. It should be close to the garden, but also convenient to your kitchen.

2. Dig a pit about 4 × 4 or 4 × 5 foot and about 1 or 2 foot deep. (This step is optional; but having the pile start out in a pit helps to keep moisture in.) A pit is not a good idea if drainage is poor.

> **Prof. Price's Pointers**
>
> **Compost microorganisms** are those bacteria and fungi that can digest plant material. They occur naturally in soils.

3. Add an 8- to 10-inch layer of organic material like kitchen scraps, leaves, grass clippings, or seed-free weeds.

4. Cover the first layer with a thin layer of soil.

5. Water thoroughly, but not to the point of making it soggy.

6. Add more layers of organic material, alternating with thin layers of soil and watering between layers, until the pile is about four or five feet high.

7. Let it sit for a while—a month or two.

8. Keep the soil moist, if it's very hot or if there is no rain. Water the pile occasionally but make sure it never becomes soggy.

9. Cover the pile with a tarp if there are heavy rains for more than a day or two in a row.

10. After two months, and then once a month for three to five months, turn the pile over with a pitchfork or a special "compost screw."

11. With each turn, check to see that the pile is "cooking." It should feel warm to the touch.

12. When the material in the pile looks like soil, it's ready to use in the garden.

It's always a good idea to have a relatively even mix of green and brown materials, like grass clippings and dried leaves, for example, for good quality and rapid compost. To accommodate all the organic material you might accumulate, you might want to have more than one pile going at a time. And you could consider one of the commercial compost bins or tumblers that work faster than a traditional pile.

Good composting material includes:

◆ Weeds (without seeds)

◆ Green plants (disease-free)

Compost Pile _____

Never, ever add grease, meat or fish scraps, dairy products, or bones to your compost heap. It will attract vermin, and even worse, the bacteria that works on breaking down animal products can cause disease. Another big no-no is pet poop. And to prevent the spread of disease or invasive plants, avoid diseased plants and weeds with seeds.

- Leaves
- Grass clippings
- Dryer lint
- Kitchen waste (except animal products and grease)
- Newspaper
- Thin cardboard
- Pine needles
- Straw
- Woodchips
- Cornstalks
- Manure from horses, cows, sheep, goats, rabbits, and chickens

The Least You Need to Know

- Never say _dirt_ when you mean _soil_.
- Have your soil tested to determine the pH, texture, and mineral content. Test for lead if you have even the slightest idea that it might be present.
- Adjust and amend your soil based on the results of a soil test. Use organic matter as an all-purpose amendment.
- Make sure your soil has adequate drainage.
- Compost organic matter to make a rich amendment for your soil.
- Compost piles need air circulation, moisture, and heat in order to function properly.

Tilling and Toiling

In This Chapter

- Learn how to prepare the soil for your garden
- Find out how to turn newspapers into a grass-killing tool
- Discover the benefits of double digging
- Pursue the pleasures of plastic mulch
- Read about raised beds
- Introduce yourself to Rototillers

Up until this point, getting the garden ready has been a lot more thinking than doing. But now you'll have the opportunity to really get your hands dirty. Preparing the soil and getting it ready is pretty important, some might even say more important than all the learning and planning you have done so far. The quality (and quantity) of the work you do at this point will help determine the quality of your garden and the quantity of the produce you will grow.

In this chapter, we go over the steps to take for killing and removing sod. We look at various methods of preparing the soil for maximum friability and fertility. And we explore some of the options to consider when it comes to creating planting beds.

Preparation Is Everything

It's impossible to over emphasize the importance of well-prepared garden beds. The health and fitness of the soil is as important to the future of the plants you grow as is the health and fitness of your body to the way you live. After all, the soil provides the support and the nutrients without which plants will not survive. So do give it your best shot. You will have plenty of time to make improvements over time, but why not start out with the best you can create.

If you do it right, right from the start, you won't have to make up for mistakes later on. And the beauty of it is, if you do prepare quality beds from the get-go, you won't have to do all that really difficult work again. Any necessary improvements or adjustments will be comparatively easy.

Unsod It All

If your future garden space is nothing but bare soil, skip to the next section. But if you are like most home gardeners, you will be creating new garden spaces in areas that are currently lawn. Lawn, or sod, covers vast parts of America, and most homes, especially new ones, are surrounded by acres of green grass. Let's get rid of it. Lawns, after all, are responsible for all kinds of pollution: noise and air pollution from lawnmowers, and water pollution from fertilizer runoff.

So here's how to kill your lawn.

The Old Paper Trick

This is the low energy, low impact approach to lawn killing, and it's a favorite of the organic gardeners among us. After you've finished all the plotting and planning tasks, and you've staked out your garden, you can begin.

> **CAUTION**
>
> **Compost Pile**
>
> Remove the comics and advertising pages from your collection of newspapers. The colored ink could leach out into the soil and might not be the healthiest additive. The occasional color photo in the paper shouldn't make much difference.

You'll need lots of old newspapers and some big stones or several wood boards. The amount of newspapers and rocks and the length of board will depend on how big your garden will be.

Take sections of the paper (the thickness of the first section of *The New York Times* on a nonholiday Sunday is about right) opened at their midpoint, and place them on the grass, weighting the paper with stones or boards. Cover every inch of the space with papers and secure the paper thoroughly. Then walk away. For a long time. Eventually the grass will die. It can take many months, but if you're not in a hurry, nature will do most of the work for you.

Garden Guru Says

Alternatively, you can hold the newspapers in place with a thick layer of manure, rinsed seaweed, salt hay, grass clippings, compost, leaves, or soil. The advantage is that when the lawn is dead, you won't need to remove anything from the area and can simply move on to the next step, which is tilling. The newspapers and the organic material on top will be well on their way to decomposing.

This technique is best for small to medium-size gardens. If you are planning a very large garden, use another method.

The kill-your-lawn-with-paper trick is a good one to try in late summer or early fall. Leave the papers in place through the winter and by spring, the grass should be nice and dead.

Heavy Lifting

As low energy as our first grass-killing option is, the next method is hard on the body. I've seen many a burly landscaper get weak in the knees at the thought of some heavy sod busting. Digging up the lawn is tough, physical labor, but if you are in decent shape, and your garden space isn't overwhelmingly large, it's an inexpensive method, and one that will get the job done in a matter of hours, or at the most, days. And, speaking of burly landscapers, this is one of those times when a hired hand might make a lot of sense.

Here's how to dig up the lawn. Use a spade with a sharp blade to cut through the grass, making sure that you get down deep, to where the roots are. Work across the space with an overlapping pattern so that you don't miss any bits of sod. After cutting through the sod, remove the clump and place it to one side. Dig down one more spade depth and place that soil back in the hole. Return the clump of sod to the hole, roots side up, exposing the roots to the sun and air. You want the soil that clings to the roots to dry out a bit before the next step.

Food for Thought

The last time I dug a garden bed myself, I wound up with terrible blisters on the bottom of my right foot—the foot I used to push the spade into the sod. If I were to do that again—well, I actually will never do that again!—but, if I were to, I would use a spade with a small lip at the top of the blade which spreads out the point of impact on the foot. And I would wear sturdy boots. Deck shoes just don't cut it.

When you have finished digging the entire space, you should have an evenly distributed surface.

Hand-digging a garden takes a lot of time. I spent the better part of an entire weekend (and I'm talking eight hours or more each day) to dig a 6 foot by 30 foot bed in rich, loamy soil. And I was in pretty good shape back then. Plan on needing much more time if your soil is hard and rocky, and if your lawn is thick and healthy.

Sod Cutters

There is yet another method for removing unwanted sod—with a contraption called the sod cutter. There are two types of sod cutters: the gasoline-powered machine and the distinctly low-tech kick-type.

The heavy-duty machine looks a little like a power tiller but instead of having tines on rotary blades, it is fitted with sharp, flat blades. The machines are usually self-propelled. As they move across the sod, the blades penetrate the sod and cut through just below the roots. The grass is cut in long strips which can be rolled up and used to make new lawn somewhere else.

The kick-type sod cutter looks a lot like an old-fashioned plow without a plow blade. This method of sod busting requires heavy physical labor.

(Illustration courtesy of Quail Manufacturing)

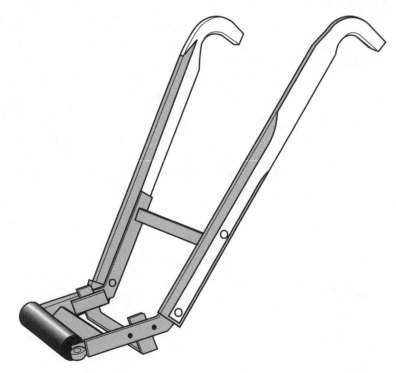

A kick-type sod cutter looks like an old-fashioned plow handle with a flat metal blade attached where the plow blade would go. Just above the blade is a metal bar that the user steps on as he pushes the cutter forward. The weight of the user pushes the blade below the grass in a forward-cutting motion.

Once the sod is cut, the soil must still be turned, either by plain old hand digging or with a tiller.

Few home gardeners will need to actually buy a sod cutter unless they plan on creating lots of new beds over a long period of time. These tools are usually available from equipment rental businesses.

Tillers

There are times when machines make so much sense. The preparation of a large garden is one of those times. *Rotary tillers*, commonly known as Rototillers, are a wonderful invention and you should take advantage of one if your garden plans run to many hundreds of square feet or more. If your garden space is a small one, a Rototiller will cut your preparation time substantially.

Tillers are machines with a couple of sets of rotary tines or blades attached. The engine turns the blades that dig through sod and deep into the soil, turning it over and breaking it up. Some of the large, gasoline-powered tillers are self-propelled and can be used for cutting through sod and tilling expansive areas of ground.

Some smaller tillers have electric engines and are much easier to handle than their larger counterparts. The Mantis Tiller, for example, advertises its ease of use with photos of a diminutive woman guiding the machine with one hand. These small versions of the rotary tiller are not meant for really heavy soil preparation. Use them instead to turn cleared ground or to cultivate an already prepared bed, between rows, for example.

Prof. Price's Pointers

The first **rotary tillers** were horse-drawn steam engines used by German, French, and Swiss farmers in the late 1850s. In 1910, Konrad von Meyenberg, a Swiss inventor, was granted the first patent for the kind of tiller we still use today. In 1932, C. W. Kelsey, an American distributor of Swiss-made tillers, trademarked the name Rototiller.

Compost Pile

When using a large tiller, exercise caution. It can kick up and back when the blades hit a buried rock, root, or stump. And the blades are very sharp. My husband still has a scar on his leg from a run-in with a tiller more than 15 years ago.

Prepare the Soil

Now that all the sod has been cut, it's time for the next step: removing debris, rocks, roots, and clods of leftover grass. An efficient way to do this is to rake through the dug bed with a sturdy garden rake, pulling all the undesirable material to one spot. At that point you can go through the pile by hand tossing out rocks and roots, and shaking loose any soil that is clinging to the clumps of sod.

Food for Thought

Back in my obsessive bed-making days, I would sift the soil through a homemade screen made of rat wire attached to a frame of 2x4s. The rat wire was just the right size mesh to allow the soil to pass through without releasing the stones, roots, and so on that I hate to have in garden beds. Although a very time consuming task, I think it was worth every minute. To this day, the texture and consistency of my soil is nearly perfect.

Double Digging

This classic soil preparation technique all but guarantees great soil. But be prepared, it's time consuming and really hard on the old back. You will need a sturdy, sharp spade; a spading fork; and a wheelbarrow or garden cart. In addition, depending on the quality of your soil, you might need quantities of compost, well-rotted manure, or peat moss. Here is how to double-dig a garden:

1. Divide your garden space into sections about the width of your spade blade. Your work will be a bit easier if you make your sections across the shorter length of the garden.

2. Use the spade to dig a six to eight inch deep (or as deep as the layer of topsoil) trench the length of the first section.

3. Place the soil from the first section in the wheelbarrow.

4. Break up the subsoil with your spading fork, going down as far as you can. About a foot deep is ideal, but if your subsoil is very hard, just do the best you can. Remove any loose rock.

5. Add a two to four inch layer of compost, rotted manure, or peat moss to the bottom of the trench.

6. Repeat the process in the second section. But instead of placing the topsoil in the wheelbarrow, put it in the first trench on top of the peat or compost.

7. Repeat this process in each section, each time placing the topsoil from the current trench in the previous trench. In the last trench, use the topsoil from the wheelbarrow.

8. Finally, dress the top of the entire bed with a couple of inches of compost or well-rotted manure.

9. Mix the top dressing with the top few inches of soil and rake smooth.

Double digging is really hard work, but the payoff is a high quality garden bed—one that will help plants thrive.

Garden Guru Says

Once you have completed your double digging and your garden bed is ready for planting, try to avoid stepping on the soil. You want the soil to remain light and fluffy and walking on it will compact it, undoing all that hard work you have done. When planting seeds or seedlings, lay a wide board along the row you are working on and stand or kneel on the board. This will spread your weight out over a wider area, keeping compaction to a minimum.

Plastic in the Garden

If weeding the garden makes you crazy, you might want to consider installing plastic mulch or mulch cloth after you have prepared your beds. Though not particularly pretty, this material will greatly reduce the need for weeding. This is one of Prof. Price's favorite planting techniques.

Shiny black plastic sheeting was the standard many years ago. And while it works well enough, there are disadvantages. It rips easily, water and air don't penetrate so the soil underneath is compromised, and it's really ugly.

Mulch cloth is the next-generation material and it's a big improvement. It's a finely woven mesh fabric, usually black, and is sold in large rolls. Because it is mesh, air and water can pass through to the soil beneath, but it is still dense enough to prevent sprouting weeds from penetrating, and they are also robbed of light so they will not grow.

To install mulch cloth simply lay it out over your prepared beds. Overlap edges by several inches to ensure that no soil is exposed. Secure the edges with rocks, boards, or metal U-shaped pins. Or bury the edges in a shallow trench around the perimeter of the garden. (How to plant in mulch cloth is discussed in Chapter 12.)

Raised Beds Are Not for Sleeping

Raised bed gardening is a time-honored technique ideally suited for gardeners with serious soil problems, drainage issues, space limitations, time constraints, and physical disabilities.

Plants grown in raised beds live in soil that is above the natural level of soil in the garden. Some raised beds are actually large containers and others are simply beds of soil.

Railroad or landscape ties will hold a raised bed together and give it a neat, tidy appearance.

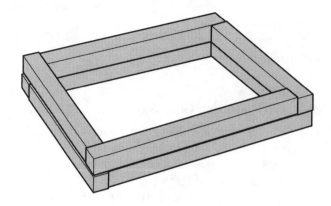

Sick Soil Solution

There are any number of reasons why your soil might be unacceptable for gardening: contamination from pollutants, poor drainage, too much rock, too much sand, too compacted, or not enough soil. Instead of doing a complete overhaul of the soil, which in the case of contamination might not actually be possible, you could consider installing a raised bed, or even a collection of raised beds.

Space and Time-Saver

If your garden space or the time you have to work in the garden is severely limited, growing edibles in a raised bed could work for you. That's because you can grow plants intensively (planted very close together) in the high-quality soil you will be using. Weed control is easier in the confined space and watering takes less time than in large gardens.

Raised Beds for Disabled Gardeners

Raised garden beds built up to wheelchair or waist height make it possible for the disabled or those with knee or back problems to enjoy the pleasures of gardening. These raised beds are generally constructed of wood like a table with sides. It should be high enough for a wheelchair to fit underneath and should be a bit narrower so that reaching the center of the bed is not too much of a reach. For wheelchair access, you'll want to make sure the surfaces surrounding the beds are smooth enough for the wheelchair to glide across.

Make Your Bed

To build your raised bed, follow the steps we have already outlined for staking out the garden. The bed or beds should be narrow enough for you to reach all the way to the center from one side. Four or five feet is about right. This way the bed can be worked from the perimeter. The length is up to you.

Kill any grass in the space. Loosen about 6 to 12 inches of the soil using a spade or spading fork. Then bring in enough soil to create a planting depth of 12 to 14 inches. You can buy good quality topsoil by the truckload or in bags. Rake the soil out until it is a smooth, flat mound.

If you have determined that your soil is contaminated, dig out about 12 inches of soil and remove it. Replace that 12 inches of soil with new, clean soil and then add another 12 to 14 inches worth to create the raised bed.

Enclosing a raised-bed garden with walls will help hold the soil in place and can give it a neat, even architectural appearance. Railroad ties or landscape ties, treated wood boards, or even cinder blocks are frequent choices for raised bed enclosures.

Garden Guru Says

The soil in a raised bed will usually warm faster than ground level soil and it will tend to dry out faster. In the hottest part of the summer, you should plan to water raised gardens more frequently than standard garden beds.

Prof. Price's Pointers

Rotating the kinds of plants you grow each year in your raised beds will help avoid depletion of and deterioration of the soil. That's because different plants will use more of certain nutrients than others. If the same kind of plants are planted year after year in the same spot, the nutrients are depleted.

Amen to Amending the Soil

There is such a thing as perfect soil and you have the opportunity to create it now. You've tested the soil, examined its texture, and determined the drainage situation. If there are problems, you can fix them. Do it at this stage of the game, after the soil has been tilled but before you've planted one seed, and you'll save yourself a world of trouble.

This is when you add the ingredients you need to raise or lower the pH, to make the soil lighter, or to improve drainage. Now is also the point at which you can add compost, rotted manure, or fertilizer to boost the richness of the soil. Just dump it on top and mix it in thoroughly. If we are talking huge quantities, you'll probably want to give it a quick once over with the tiller again to make sure everything is thoroughly combined. But if the amounts are small, spreading it all around evenly with a rake will be fine.

The Least You Need to Know

♦ When hand-digging the lawn, be sure to get down to the roots of the grass. And be sure to remove all the clumps of sod from the soil.

♦ Build raised beds to accommodate disabled gardeners.

♦ Use a mechanical tiller for large spaces; and always exercise caution when operating a tiller.

♦ Take the time to double-dig a garden bed to create the optimum growing environment.

♦ Use mulch cloth over prepared soil to reduce weeds.

♦ Enrich your soil with compost or well-rotted manure.

10

Plant Biology 101

In This Chapter

- ◆ Learn to identify different plant parts
- ◆ Peek inside a plant's organs
- ◆ Find out when a vegetable is a fruit
- ◆ Study up on the sex life of plants
- ◆ Learn about the drinking habits of plants
- ◆ Discover the difference between annual and perennial plants

Before you can begin the tasks of actually sowing seeds and tending plants, you probably should know a little about how plants grow. If you remember everything you learned in freshman biology, you can probably skip this chapter. If not, read on. And be prepared, this stuff is pretty technical.

Plant Parts

To understand how plants grow and reproduce, you need to become familiar with their various parts. It's pretty easy to understand actually. To make it even easier, we look at this in terms of edible plants.

A Little About Leaves

Leaves are lateral outgrowths of a plant's stem. Most leaves are green (at least at some stage of their lives). Edible leaves include lettuce, cabbage, kale, mustard greens, bok choy, spinach, and parsley, among many others. The role of the leaf is to soak up the sun's energy.

Most leaves are green because they contain chlorophyll, the plant's green pigment (*chloro* means "green" in Greek). The chlorophyll traps the energy from the sun. This is part of a process called *photosynthesis*, which we look at a little later in this chapter.

The Story of Stems

The stem is (usually) a slender growth of plant material that supports or connects one plant part to another. Stems function like arteries and veins distributing water and nutrients throughout the plant. For example, a stem connects leaves to each other and supports a flower or fruit. Some of the stems we eat include celery, asparagus, and rhubarb.

The story of stems can get a little more complicated. Stems can also grow underground as stolons. The runners of strawberries are a good example of stolons. Some other underground stems are called tubers. Potatoes, yams, jicama, and Jerusalem artichokes fall into this category.

Get Back to Your Roots

The root is the part of the plant that usually lives below the soil. It serves as a sort of anchor for the plant and is the machinery the plant uses to absorb water and nutrients.

> **Garden Guru Says**
>
> Bulbs like onions and garlic are a collection of modified leaves that live underground in the form of bulbs. If you've ever peeled an onion, you can see how it is made up of tightly wrapped leaves. These modified leaves don't have the same role as green leaves that are exposed to sunlight. Instead, they store energy.

Roots also can enlarge and become a kind of storage tank of nutrients the plant will call on later in its life cycle. Usually, people eat these little warehouses before the plants get to use them. Among the edible roots we humans enjoy are carrots, radishes, beets, turnips, and parsnips.

Most plants have a primary root that goes more or less straight down into the soil with smaller lateral roots that reach out from the main root. At the ends of lateral roots are tiny root hairs that are responsible for absorbing nutrients and water from the soil. Finally, there is a root cap at the very end of the root.

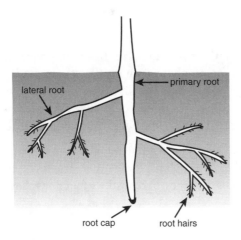

A plant's root system helps to keep it stable in the soil and helps it to soak up water and nutrients.

Some plants develop large main roots with some lateral roots. This main root is called a tap root. Carrots, parsnips, and radishes are good examples. Other plants have fibrous roots which are what you see with tomatoes, peppers, beans, and most other vegetable plants. The fibrous roots have a much smaller main root and lots of lateral roots.

Beautiful Buds

The bud is either a stem or a flower in the very earliest stages of its development. Some buds are vegetative and can become new stems and leaves. Others will develop into flowers. Some flowers eventually become fruit.

Food for Thought

Vegetables like peppers, tomatoes, eggplant, squash, and cobs of corn are actually, botanically speaking, fruits, which, as we have just learned, are fully developed buds. Some other vegetables are actually flowers. Artichokes are flower buds. We eat the unopened petals one by one. The parts of broccoli and cauliflower that we eat are clusters of flower buds. Fruits including berries and watermelons are, well, fruits.

Inside Plants

The really interesting parts of plants are buried—but not hidden—inside of the cells that make up plant organs. Most of these parts are very much like those in humans and other animals, such as the nucleus, which contain the cell's DNA. But some of the tiny structures inside plants are very different from anything found in animals.

Chloroplasts

The one, big exception where plants differ from animals is that plants have chloroplasts. These are little green engines that carry out photosynthesis (be patient, we'll get to it). Chloroplasts are green because they contain chlorophyll. (Remember, *chloro* means "green" in Greek.) Chloroplasts typically appear in leaves (which is why leaves are green), but they can also be found in other green organs like buds (broccoli), stems (celery), and fruits (bell peppers).

Several structures are closely related to chloroplasts; these other structures are not green and they don't carry out photosynthesis, but they have distinct functions that are critical to the life of plants.

Amyloplasts

One relative of chloroplasts is the amyloplast, which contains starch (*amylo* is Greek for "starch"). Amyloplasts are found in very large quantities in seeds and tubers. The starch they hold is where much of the energy we get from food originates. But the reason plants have amyloplasts is actually to fuel their own reproduction. Developing seedlings harvest the energy from the starch stored in the amyloplasts as they grow until they are mature enough to soak up sunlight.

Chromoplasts

Chromoplasts are another relative of chloroplasts (*chromo* means "color" in Greek). They accumulate large amounts of yellow, orange, and red pigments (called carotenoids), which are found in foods like carrots and tomatoes, in nasturtium flowers, and in squash blossoms.

How Seeds Grow

Seeds, which are made by plants so they can reproduce themselves, are basically tiny undeveloped new plants with some extra things added on. Each seed contains an embryo (the undeveloped new plant) and some tissue that is packed with food that will feed the developing seedling until it is able to survive on its own.

The seed is enclosed in a tough jacket that protects it from the elements until the conditions for *germination* are just right. Usually this is when there is enough moisture and warmth in the seed's environment. When the seed senses that it's warm enough and that there is enough moisture, it breaks out of *dormancy* and begins to grow.

Prof. Price's Pointers

Dormancy is a rest period in a plant's life cycle. **Germination** is when a seed's dormancy is ended and it begins to develop as a new plant. Plants also have an internal clock that is set by the length of the night. So when nights become shorter in the spring, the seeds of some plants, such as lettuce, say "Wake up! It's time to germinate." Our plants use this clock to decide when it's time to flower.

As the seed grows into a seedling, it uses its little storehouse of food. The stem of the seedling will push up through the soil toward sunlight. When it finally "sees" the sun, it puts its energy into expanding the tiny leaves. At this point, the colorless leaves begin to turn green.

Photosynthesis

One of the great triumphs of plant science in the middle twentieth century was unraveling the mystery of *photosynthesis.*

Photosynthesis takes place inside the plant's chloroplasts in two separate processes called "the dark reaction" and "the light reaction."

The dark reaction occurs when carbon dioxide is converted to sugar. This process can happen in the dark, but only for a few seconds. To keep on going, it needs a huge input of light energy. That's when the light reaction kicks in. This process starts when the chlorophyll in leaves soaks up the sun's energy, which is then converted through chemical processes to electrical energy. For all you chemistry buffs, this is when an electron is separated from a hydrogen atom, a lot like when you charge a battery.

The electrical charge is then converted to a complex chain of reactions that eventually fuels the dark reaction, which makes the sugar. Finally, the waste product of this process—oxygen—is released. Simple, right?

Photosynthesis, in a nutshell …

  ◆ Produces food for plants.

  ◆ Occurs in cells that contain chloroplasts.

  ◆ Uses water and carbon dioxide.

  ◆ Requires the energy of the sun.

Prof. Price's Pointers

Photosynthesis is the conversion of carbon dioxide and water into glucose and other sugars and starch using the energy of sunlight, and producing oxygen as a waste product. It is how plants manufacture their own food.

How Plants Drink

Do you remember the science "experiment" you did in third grade when you took a stalk of celery and put it in a glass of water mixed with red food coloring? After a few hours the celery had magically turned red! That was a lesson on how plants drink. You might even remember that the process was called osmosis. That elementary school lesson gave you part of the story about how plants drink, but it's a little more complicated.

Why Plants Wilt or Don't Wilt

Plant cells are filled with solutes—these are salts, sugars, organic acids, and so on. The solutes create what is called an osmotic potential, which decreases the energy of the water. As a consequence, plants absorb water until the pressure inside the plant cells matches the osmotic pressure. The balance of osmotic pressure and internal water pressure is what makes plant stems get stiff when they have enough water and to wilt when there's not enough. The firmness of the plant's tissues is called turgor.

More Drinking Stories

Osmotic potential pulls water into a plant only so far. So plants have another trick: evaporation. The leaves of plants have thousands of tiny openings called stomata that allow water vapor to diffuse out. (They also permit carbon dioxide, needed for photosynthesis, to diffuse into the leaves.) The loss of water by evaporation through the stomata creates a negative pressure that literally sucks water up through the stems. This process is called transpiration.

Food for Thought _____

Because leaves don't photosynthesize at night, the stomata in the leaves close down and save water. When the sun comes out, they open again for business. If the water pressure in the plant drops too low, the stomata will close up again to save water. So if you forget to water the tomatoes, the plants themselves will bail you out. But don't do it again, there's only so much a plant can do on its own.

How Plants Reproduce

When it comes to reproduction, plants are a bit more flexible than animals (and no, I'm not talking about acrobatics!). Plants can reproduce using sexual reproduction or asexual, or vegetative, reproduction.

It's All About Sex

Sexual reproduction in plants happens when the ovules (egg) and pollen (sperm) from flowers are combined and form an embryo. While most plants produce "perfect" flowers that contain both pollen and ovules, in some plants the sexes are separated. In members of the squash family, for example, the first flowers to appear on the stem are strictly male, producing only pollen. Later flowers are strictly female, with the baby fruit looking like a slight swelling behind the petals.

Birds, bees, other insects, the wind, and sometimes even humans all help plants with sexual reproduction, which occurs when the pollen, which is usually carried on the stamen (the little yellow bundle inside the flower), is mixed with the ovule, which is usually at the center of the bloom inside the ovary. Bees and other insects and some birds visit flowers to drink the nectar in the petals. As they pass by the stamen, a little of the pollen rubs off on their wings or feet and then lands at the stigma where it can enter the ovule.

When bees are scarce, pollination might not happen as often as it should, and plants will produce less fruit. Sometimes gardeners will help with the process by hand-pollinating their plants.

A Vegetative State

Some plants are sterile (they can not reproduce on their own) so the only way to make new plants is by vegetative reproduction. This is usually done with stem or root cuttings. Most vegetative reproduction is done with woody plants or houseplants and rarely with vegetables. Fruit shrubs and grape vines can be reproduced with root or stem cuttings, as can some herbs. Vegetative reproduction is considered asexual reproduction.

Growing Seasons

So far in this chapter we've looked at the parts of plants and what makes them tick. Now it's time to talk about how they actually grow. Instead of thinking of growing seasons in terms of simply summer, spring, fall, and winter, gardeners look at seasons of development, growth, fruit production, and death or dormancy.

Plants have a growth cycle that basically goes like this:

1. The seed germinates.
2. It becomes a seedling.
3. Then it becomes a full-grown plant.
4. The plant grows.
5. It produces food (photosynthesis).

6. It reproduces itself by growing a fruit that produces a seed.

7. The plant dies.

8. The seed grows into a new plant.

Some plants, notably woody plants like trees and shrubs, go as far as producing the seed and then go into a dormancy period that is usually related to temperature and daylight. At the end of the dormant stage, they wake up and start over again. And of course trees, such as maples or redwoods will go on for years, even centuries, with this cycle.

But herbaceous plants, that is plants with a soft, non-woody stem, like tomatoes or oregano, have a different life cycle. They are usually classified as either annual or perennial plants.

Annual

Just about all the common garden fruits and vegetables that we grow from seeds or seedlings (tomatoes, peppers, squash, watermelons, and so on) are annual plants. This means that their entire life cycle is spent in one growing season. They sprout, grow into a plant, produce fruit, make seeds, and then they die.

Perennial

Perennial herbaceous plants, on the other hand, have a longer life cycle. They sprout, grow into a plant, produce fruit, make seeds, and then they die back to the ground. Their roots or stems, especially underground stems, remain in a dormant state. At the start of the next growing season, new growth forms and they start over again. Perennial edible plants include asparagus, artichokes, rhubarb, and many herbs.

The Least You Need to Know

◆ Plant parts include leaves, stems, roots, buds, and flowers.

◆ Plants use photosynthesis to harness sunlight in the manufacture of food.

◆ Plants reproduce sexually and asexually.

◆ Plants pull water into themselves using osmosis.

◆ Bees, other insects, birds, the wind, and humans help plants reproduce by distributing pollen to the stigma where it might eventually reach the ovule of a plant.

◆ Most vegetable plants are either perennial (they live through several life cycles) or annual (one life cycle).

Chapter 11

Seeds and Seedlings

In This Chapter

- ◆ Learn how to get a jumpstart on the growing season by starting seeds indoors
- ◆ Mix up some homemade potting soil
- ◆ Look at cold frames
- ◆ Find out what to look for when selecting seedlings
- ◆ Establish time frames for starting seeds and setting out plants

In this chapter, we finally arrive at what many consider to be the best part of gardening—planting seeds. Here we focus on starting seeds indoors and the steps to take to take them from seed to healthy young plants. We learn about starting plants from sets, crowns, and plant divisions, and we also talk about what you should look for when you buy young vegetable seedlings.

Later in the chapter, we look at cold frames and old-fashioned bell jars that help extend the growing season. This chapter finishes with information on when to plant and how to create support systems for growing plants.

Sowing Seeds Indoors

Gardeners who live in Florida, Southern California, and other warm spots won't need to spend much time with this section. But if you live where it gets cold, pay attention. One of the reasons gardeners start seeds indoors is to get a jump on the growing season.

Some seeds take many weeks to germinate and then many more weeks to produce ripe fruit. If, for example, the growing season (that is when it's warm enough to plant tender plants without risk of frost) doesn't start until May 15 and if seeds require 10 days to germinate and about 80 growing days until the fruit is ready to harvest, you'll be waiting until the middle of August before you get those juicy Beefsteak tomatoes. But if you start the seeds indoors and have nice hearty seedlings ready for that set out date of May 15, you might have tomatoes for your salad by the end of July.

There are other good reasons to start seeds indoors, including …

♦ You can ensure the quality of the plants you will grow.

♦ You know exactly what your plants have been exposed to (this is especially important for those concerned about an organic, chemical-free approach).

♦ There is far more variety to choose from in seed catalogs and specialty vendors than with seedlings from garden centers and nurseries.

♦ There is less chance of introducing disease to your garden than when you bring in seedlings or plants from other places.

♦ Starting seeds indoors has a very low cost.

Containers for Seeds

Finding containers for seeds is an area where ingenuity counts. You can start seeds indoors in all kinds of containers. I've seen it done in cardboard milk cartons, wooden fruit crates, aluminum pie plates, and olive oil cans. More traditional methods are plastic cell packs and trays, peat pots, fiber packs, and flowerpots. And in more than one catalog I've seen a clever device that forms cute little pots from old newspapers.

The key things that a container must do are hold soil and allow for drainage. Unconventional containers like pie plates and milk cartons must have holes punched in the bottom so water will drain out. The peat pots, fiber packs, and little newspaper pots are all biodegradable so you can plant the container and the seedling together directly in the soil, without the risk of disturbing tender new roots.

If you reuse old containers, be sure they are scrupulously clean. Wash them with disinfectant or a diluted bleach solution.

When you are ready to start seeds indoors, fill the eggshells with potting soil or seed starting mix, plant a seed in each shell, and water. Keep the egg carton on a tray because it will drip. Then proceed with the other steps for starting seeds indoors. When it's time to transplant the seedlings outdoors, plant them shell and all. The little roots won't be disturbed, and eventually the shell will break down.

Mixed Media

The quality of the planting mixture you use to start your seeds indoors is a crucial element to the ultimate success of your plants. After all, it's the first home to the tiny, emerging plant so it has to be a safe and nutritious environment.

There are any number of potting media that will work well for starting seeds. These include the following:

- Commercial potting mixes

- Commercial seed starting mixes

- Horticultural vermiculite

- Half perlite and half horticultural vermiculite

- One part each of vermiculite, perlite, and peat moss

- One part each of peat moss, sterilized commercial compost, coarse sand, and vermiculite

- One part each of commercial potting soil, sterilized commercial compost, and vermiculite

Prof. Price's Pointers

Vermiculite is a mica-like mineral that is added to soils, especially in container gardening, to increase the water-holding capacity of the soil. Perlite is a volcanic lava that has been crushed and heated at very high temperatures to create a lightweight material used in potting mixes.

Garden Guru Says

To sterilize your potting mix, you can heat it on a baking sheet in a 250 degrees Fahrenheit oven for about a half hour. Don't overheat or overcook it. Although it won't smell very good, the process will kill off bacteria and fungus that could damage or kill young plants.

The key to a good quality planting medium is that it be light and fluffy so the tiny roots and shoots will have an easy time pushing their way through the mix. It should drain easily. And it's really important that it be disease and pest free.

The perlite and vermiculite in the previous list are natural mineral products available at home, farm, and garden centers. The easiest way to measure these products and the peat and compost is with a coffee can, children's sand pail, or large measuring cup. Mix up your potting soil in a large bucket or trashcan for handy access.

How to Plant

When you plant your seeds indoors will depend on when you want to set out your seedlings. And that date will depend on the weather. You'll learn a little more about that a little later in this chapter.

Once you have established your set-out date, you simply consult the information on the seed packet that will tell you how many days before the set-out date to plant the seeds. This will range from a couple weeks to as many as 12 weeks.

To plant the seeds, follow these steps:

1. Fill your containers to about a half-inch or so from the top with the planting medium you have chosen.

2. Sprinkle the mix gently with water. You might find a mister helpful for this task.

Food for Thought

One of the easiest, least expensive, and most earth-friendly ways to plant seeds is to use eggshells. After you've had eggs for your breakfast, rinse the shells and store them in egg cartons. Try to keep them as intact as possible. You can even snip off ragged edges.

3. Press the planting mix gently with your palm or with a flat surface. You don't want to create any dips or impressions.

4. Sow the seeds according to the directions on the seed packet. We'll talk more about this in later chapters.

5. Mist with a fine spray of water.

6. Place the container in a warm spot, preferably about 70 degrees Fahrenheit.

Off to a Good Start

You will need to keep your germinating seeds warm and moist until they pop through the surface of the soil. After they pop through the surface of the soil, the tiny seedlings will need a little less warmth but a lot more sun.

The ideal temperature for most seedlings will be about 65 degrees Fahrenheit during the day and 5 or 10 degrees cooler at night. Some plants might have different requirements so you will want to consult the seed packet.

Ideally, you should place the seedlings in a southern window where they will get as much sunlight as possible. Turn the pots or trays every day so that all the seedlings get an equal exposure to the sun.

If you don't have adequate window space, install a special grow light for the plants. You can even rig one up in the basement. When the seedlings are very small, put the plants about six or eight inches from the light. As they grow, move the lighting fixture up so that it doesn't burn them. Keep the light on at least 12 hours a day and up to 16 hours. Install a timer for convenience.

The Next Step

Once the plants have grown their first set of true leaves, you can begin transplanting them to larger containers. Don't do this if you have planted individual seeds in peat pots, eggshells, or cell packs. You can allow the seedlings to mature if they are in their own containers.

At this stage you should also start a feeding regimen. Use a liquid fertilizer about every two weeks according to the directions on the package. If in doubt, err on the side of a weaker solution.

Keep the seedlings moist but not wet. A fine mist is better than direct watering. Over-fertilizing and overwatering young seedlings are the most frequently made mistakes people make when starting seeds indoors.

> **Prof. Price's Pointers**
>
> Many seedlings succumb to a condition known as **damping off**. The seedlings die from excessive moisture. But it is a fungus that comes with the overwatering that actually causes the plants to die.

Hardening Off

About two weeks before your set-out date, you will need to get the seedlings ready for transplantation. They will need to be *hardened off*.

To do this, you can start by lowering the temperature in the room where the seedlings are growing and reduce the amount of light. After a couple days, you can move the plants outside to a protected, shady spot during the day. Don't do this if it's windy, raining, or below 45 degrees Fahrenheit outside. Try the garage or an unheated sunroom instead. Bring the plants back inside at night. During this process, water regularly, but sparingly. In about two weeks, your seedlings should be acclimated enough to make the big move to full-time life in the great outdoors. But don't push it. Keep a close eye on weather forecasts and be prepared to rush outside with protective coverings for your newly planted babies should a cold front come through.

> **Prof. Price's Pointers**
>
> **Hardening off** is the process of slowly acclimating plants to a new environment, usually from indoors to outdoors.

Cold Frames

A cold frame is essentially a greenhouse device, usually placed directly on the ground and made of glass or transparent plastic. Using one gives gardeners the opportunity to start the spring planting season early and to extend fall growing time past frost dates.

Use a cold frame for hardening off young seedlings without the nuisance of moving pots in and out of the house. Or plant seeds of cool tolerant plants (like peas, lettuce, or spinach) directly in a cold frame laid on prepared soil. The sun will warm the soil inside the cold frame well before it does the exposed garden soil.

> **Food for Thought**
>
> Make your own cold frame using old storm windows and some scrap lumber or scrap metal, cinder blocks, or bricks. You can find precise instructions from a number of sites on the Internet. Just type "make a cold frame" into Google or another search engine.

Cold frames should have the slanted, glazed top facing south for maximum sun exposure. It helps to place them up against the southern wall of the house, garage, barn, or garden shed because the wall will help capture warmth. Painting the interior white and sinking the foundation a few inches will also make it warmer.

Cold frames can become too warm inside, which can encourage disease and fungus. Keep a thermometer inside the frame; if the temperature goes above 70 degrees Fahrenheit, you'll want to open the frame to vent it. Most commercial cold frames have optional automatic vents like a greenhouse.

Planting Seeds Outdoors

Planting seeds outdoors is a far less complicated undertaking than doing it indoors. Prepare the soil properly and plant the seeds according to the directions found on the seed packet.

Although just about all plants can be grown from seeds (there are a few exceptions, but we'll get into that later), it's not always the most practical approach. The seeds of some plants can be difficult to germinate or might take an inconveniently long time to sprout. Home gardeners typically grow some plants from sets, tubers, crowns, divisions, and offshoots.

Set Out the Onions

Onions, garlic, and shallots are all members of the same plant family. And as we learned in Chapter 9, the bulb part that we eat is actually a collection of leaves that grow underground. Almost no one, except commercial growers, attempts to grow these plants from seed. Instead, we use sets. Usually the sets are sold in bunches of 50 or 100. They look like tiny flower bulbs. Some might have sprouted a little stem by the time you buy them in the spring. Each individual set will grow into one large plant.

One Potato, Two Potato

Potato (*Solanum tuberosum*) and sweet potatoes (*Ipomoea batatas*) are usually grown in the home garden from little tubers. These are basically tiny potatoes that are grown commercially as seed stock.

Other plants that aren't generally grown from seed by home gardeners are asparagus that are usually started with dormant *crowns*, and rhubarb, which are grown from rooted offshoots or divisions of existing plants. These are available from garden centers, nurseries, and specialty mail order houses.

> **Garden Guru Says**
>
> While most onions are grown from sets, there is one exception. Scallions, the small green onions with edible stems, are typically grown from seed.

> **Prof. Price's Pointers**
>
> A **crown** is the part of the plant where the roots and the stem meet.

Seedlings

Many gardeners who want more immediate gratification will start their gardens using seedlings. It's really a much easier way to go and is also helpful if you get a late start in the spring or early summer.

Vegetable seedlings are readily available at garden centers, nurseries, farm markets, and even grocery stores and places like K-Mart and Home Depot.

When you pick out seedlings, look for plants with strong, thick stems and plenty of healthy looking leaves. Avoid any wilted plants. Stay away from yellowed leaves, those with brown or curling edges, and any with signs of insect damage. Look under the leaves to make sure there aren't any nasty bugs lurking there either. Plants with some tiny flowers might set fruit earlier, but that's not guaranteed.

> **Compost Pile**
>
> The containers of some commercially grown seedlings are treated with a growth-inhibiting agent that will affect how quickly the plant grows in the garden. Growers use this technique to keep young plants from outgrowing their containers before they are sold at retail markets. There really isn't any way to know in advance whether the plants you have bought are in treated containers, but if your plants take a very long time to grow, this could be the reason.

When you take your new plants home, water them thoroughly, and put them in the shade until you have time to plant. They have probably had a rough life up till this point, so you'll want to pamper them a bit.

Time Frames

Most plants have a preference as to what time of year they are planted, especially in places where the climate ranges from very hot to very cold. In parts of the country where the temperatures stay within a much smaller range, planting seasons are less meaningful.

Most plants will fall into one of three categories: cold weather, cool weather, and warm weather. This refers to the time frame in which to plant them whether as seeds or as seedlings, sets, crowns, or divisions.

Cold weather plants should be planted in the early spring, as soon as the soil can be worked, in places like the Northeast, Midwest, and Northwest. In the South and the Pacific Southwest, many of these plants are planted in the late summer or early fall for late fall harvest.

Some plants to start in cold weather include the following:

- Onion
- Leek
- Pea
- Chive
- Garlic
- Shallot
- Radicchio

Cool weather plants are usually planted just before the last expected frost of the year. They don't like to be hit by frost, but they will survive a mild hit. These plants generally don't do as well in very hot weather. In places where it never frosts, plant these so they will grow during the coolest part of your year.

Some plants to start in cool weather include the following:

- Lettuce
- Parsley
- Coriander
- Broccoli
- Cabbage
- Radish
- Kale
- Spinach
- Arugula
- Swiss chard
- Turnip
- Chervil

Garden Guru Says

Fruit bushes, brambles, and canes along with grape vines can be planted in the early spring or in the fall in areas that experience cold winters. Rhubarb divisions prefer an early spring planting.

The majority of vegetables and annual herbs are warm weather plants in colder zones. These plants will not tolerate cold weather and shouldn't be put out until all danger of frost is past. Many of them like the soil to be nice and warm too. They might not die if you plant them too early, but their performance might suffer.

Some plants to start in warm weather include the following:

- Tomato
- Pepper
- Basil
- Sorrel

- Bean
- Eggplant
- Dill

Garden Guru Says

If in doubt about what to plant when in your area, call on your local County Extension Office or Farm Bureau for advice.

Support Systems

Most plants can grow with little help beyond regular watering, feeding, and weeding. But some plants want to climb, sprawl, or otherwise spread out and they need a support system to keep their foliage and fruits from winding up on the garden floor.

To keep plants tidy, to support their climbing habits and to protect ripening fruits, gardeners use a variety of support systems including stakes, trellises, netting, and old fashioned string.

String It Along

Lightweight twining plants like peas and beans will happily climb up trellises, fencing, or other structures, but you can also meet their needs by preparing a grid of twine strung between a few bamboo poles. This is a one-year at a time technique, as the twine will probably rot after one season. You can use plastic twine for a long-lived grid.

Cages

Tomato plants, especially the larger varieties, generally want to sprawl. This can become very untidy and often results in too many fruits lying on the ground where they will rot or pick up insects.

To support the tomatoes, place a wire tomato cage over the plant when it is still small. The tomato will grow up inside the cage and rest its stems on the wire, making it easy for you to harvest the tomatoes. Another advantage is that more of the plant is exposed to sunlight, which will encourage growth.

You can buy tomato cages at home and garden centers. Or you can fashion your own using fence wire or concrete reinforcing wire and heavy-duty metal stakes. Make sure the openings between the wires are large enough for a big tomato to grow through.

Stake Your Claim

Stakes made of bamboo, metal, or plastic are indispensable in the edible garden. You'll need them to support pepper or eggplant plants that are heavy with fruit. You can also stake smaller varieties of tomatoes, especially the grape and cherry types. And you'll want to stake up any plant that seems to need a little bit of help standing up straight. Use twist ties, twine, plastic plant ties, or foam-covered wire ties to attach the plant to the stake. Or place three stakes around the plant and wrap twine around the stakes to make a support all the way around.

Trellis

Grape vines and bramble fruits require the strong support of a trellis or fence. Usually made of wood but sometimes of metal and even plastic, a trellis or fence is the most expensive kind of plant support. Do some independent research to find out what material and configuration will work best for you.

The Least You Need to Know

- Plant seeds indoors to have an earlier harvest.
- Find unusual varieties of your favorite vegetables and herbs by buying seed.
- Use a light, airy, sterile potting mix.
- Select healthy seedlings with no signs of yellow, browning, or curling leaves and without insect damage.
- Harden off young seedlings before planting them in the garden.
- Use a cold frame to extend the growing season in the spring and in the fall.
- Use stakes, cages, netting, twine, or trellises to support plants.

Part 4

What to Plant

Here's where we talk about what we will be cooking in a few weeks when all this stuff is ready for harvesting. In the next six chapters we take a look at all the different kinds of plants you might consider growing in your edible garden.

The hardest part of putting this part together was having to leave out so many interesting and wonderful vegetables. There just wasn't room, but if you go to some of the websites or books listed in Appendix B, you might find the ones we had to leave out.

Chapter 12

How to Plant

In This Chapter

◆ Follow the steps for making neat planting rows

◆ Find out how hills and mounds are used

◆ Learn how to make a furrow

◆ Get into square-foot gardening

◆ Discover the best methods for planting seeds and seedlings

Now we get to the really fun part. Planting outside! If you are like me, you can't wait to get your hands in the dirt, whoops, I mean soil. In this chapter, we will have lots of opportunity to dig in and get our hands dirty. We look at various planting methods including how to create rows, hills, mounds, and furrows. I tell you how to plant seeds and transplant seedlings. And you learn all about square foot and intensive gardening.

All in a Row

My favorite vision of a vegetable garden is a tidy rectangle divided by neat rows of plants. Rows are orderly. They keep everything in place. They make sense. When your plants are set up in rows, you know what's a weed and what's supposed to be growing there. It's not hard to make garden

Compost Pile

Try to walk on your prepared garden beds as little as possible. If you walk back and forth you risk compacting the soil that will inhibit good root growth and proper drainage.

Garden Guru Says

To avoid compacting the soil while you are in the row-making and planting stage of gardening, lay long, flat boards between the rows and walk and kneel on them so that you never actually set foot on the planting areas.

rows, but it helps if you go back to your original garden plan. How many rows are you going to have? Will they run the length or the width of the garden? Or both ways? How wide will each row be? And how much space will you put between each row?

The answers to these questions will depend on what plants you intend to grow. Once you have made your selections, you'll figure out how much space each plant needs, and then create rows to accommodate that amount of space.

Now with a little sketch plan, you can lay out the rows. Measure out the length of each row and use stakes and string to mark them. You could also use spray paint but it doesn't stick as well to soil as it does to grass. Chalk string that you snap against the soil so it will leave a mark is another approach.

Leave the stake and string in place until you have finished planting each row. This will help you keep your rows straight and your spacing the way you want it.

Hills and Mounds

In addition to planting seeds and seedlings in little holes in nice straight rows, you will probably plant some things in hills and mounds.

Hill Country

Crops like beans and sunflowers, and any other large seed, can be planted in small hills that you space evenly along a row. To create a hill, just scoop up a handful of soil in each hand, pull the handfuls together in one pile, and smooth it down. Then it's ready for planting one big seed right in the center. Be sure you pull the soil evenly from all around the hill. You can make a tiny moat around the base of the hill to trap water during dry weather. A hill might be as small as six inches or as high as about a foot.

Mounds and Mounds

A planting mound is a large hill of soil pulled up from the surrounding area to create a raised planting environment. Traditionally, mounds are used for growing big and sprawling vegetable plants like zucchini, cucumber, summer and winter squash, pumpkins, and melons. A mound might be anywhere from about 18 to 24 inches high.

A group of mounds with big vegetables like pumpkins and watermelons can take up a lot of space in a garden. If your space is limited, stagger the mounds in a zigzag pattern so you can fit more in.

To form the mounds, start with a well-prepared garden bed. Determine the spacing for your mounds based on the distances for the plant you will be putting in the mounds. Mark a midpoint for each mound. Then, using a garden rake or a hoe, pull soil from the surrounding ground until it forms a pile. Make sure you take soil away evenly so there are no big dips around the mound, although a shallow moat at the base of each mound will help retain water in dry weather.

Flatten the pile a little on top and smooth the sides so the soil is evenly spread all the way around. Then follow the planting directions for each type of vegetable. Seeds or seedlings are generally planted in a circle or a triangle on a mound.

Prof. Price's Pointers

An advantage of growing on mounds is that the loose soil they are formed of allows for very good drainage. Planting on mounds will also help to deter insects and protect against disease to some extent.

Furrows

A furrow is a shallow trench—a long, narrow hole with a flat bottom. Using furrows makes sense when you are planting a lot of one kind of plant that requires a little more depth. These furrows are used for plants like asparagus, rhubarb, turnips, and potatoes.

Make a furrow using a hoe. Mound the soil up on one side of the furrow to make it easier to push back in on top of the seeds or roots you put in the furrow.

Irrigation furrows are another story. These are trenches that are used to move water through the garden.

One by One

Planting seeds one at a time can either be very satisfying or unbelievably tedious. I guess it has to do with your frame of mind. There is something really basic and reassuring about making a little hole, dropping in a seed, filling the hole back up with soil, and firming it down with your hand.

Some seeds—beans, corn, cucumbers, melons, and squash most notably—are quite large so handling them one at a time is easy to do.

Food for Thought

Some seed sellers prepare seed tapes to make the job of planting even easier than it already is. These tapes are long strips of a biodegradable material. Strung out along the tape are little pockets with a seed inside each one. To plant, all you do is dig a tiny trench, gently bury the tape, water, and wait. This is so easy—a great way for kids to plant.

When you plant one seed at a time, you have a lot of control over your spacing. But if many of the seeds don't germinate or fail to grow well, you will need to replant in those spaces. This isn't necessarily a bad thing. It's just a kind of forced succession planting (succession planting is discussed later in this chapter).

Scatter Method

You've probably seen old paintings or prints of a charming rural scene with a farmer scattering seed across a field. This is a perfectly good method of sowing seed if you have lots of space and want large quantities of one kind of plant. It is also called broadcasting. Keep in mind that broadcasted seed will not necessarily space itself evenly in the garden, but you can thin out young seedlings that are too close together.

Garden Guru Says

Some very tiny seeds, like carrots and radishes, can be sowed by the scatter method. But because the seeds are so small, it's difficult to get an even coverage. If you mix the seed with a little bit of dry sand and then scatter the seed, you'll probably have more success.

You can also scatter seeds in very confined spaces like a large pot or planting box. This is a great way to grow mixed lettuce varieties. Just fill your planting box, tray, or pot with soil and scatter a handful of seeds as evenly as possible across the surface of the soil. That's it. You can thin any that are poorly spaced as you harvest young seedlings for your salad bowl.

The scatter method won't work for seeds that need a soil cover. Be sure to check the information on individual seed packets before you start throwing seeds around your garden.

A Little Extra Help

To ensure the health of your plants, try to transplant seedlings on an overcast day. If you live near Prof. Price in San Diego where there never seems to be a cloudy day, do your transplanting in the late afternoon or early evening when the sun is low in the sky. The point is to protect tender, new plants from a heavy dose of sunlight when they are at a very vulnerable stage.

Water all the seedlings well before transplanting. Some gardeners dunk the plant, pot and all, in a big bucket of cool water. Just don't leave them there for too long or the roots won't have access to air.

While you are planting seedlings, pick off dead or damaged leaves, flowers, and any tiny fruits. This allows the plants to put all their energy into producing thick, healthy foliage that will, in turn, help the plant make plenty of its own food for later fruit production.

Food for Thought

My dear friend Pat McKearn (who is also my former partner in our landscaping business) has a nifty way of avoiding working in the garden during the heat of the day. She wears a miner's helmet which has a battery-powered headlight so she can work anywhere in the garden well into the night without having to set up floodlights.

Bush Country

Planting a bush is a very different task than planting a seedling or a seed. If you follow these steps, you should wind up with a happy bush.

First, dig a hole that is twice as wide as the root ball. It should be as deep as the root ball is high. Measure with the handle of your spade. Next, mix some good organic matter like compost with the soil in the hole. Carefully place the bush in the hole, making sure it is not too deep. The stem or trunk of the bush should be level or just slightly above the firm soil at the edges of the hole. Untie and remove any twine or stem wrapping around the trunk. Fold back the burlap about halfway.

CAUTION Compost Pile

Some growers are now using burlap made of plastic to cover the root balls of trees and shrubs. This kind of burlap does not degrade so the roots are forever confined. Eventually the plant will die, or at the very least, fail to thrive. Test the burlap on your fruit bushes by touching it with a lit match. If it melts, it's plastic. Take it all off before planting.

Begin to fill in the hole with soil, pushing it down into the hole and under the root ball with the handle of your spade. Keep adding soil and pressing it in until the hole is filled. You are trying to fill in any air pockets that could fill with water. Tamp down the earth around the hole with your feet, pressing firmly. Water thoroughly. You can make a little moat around the planting hole to help keep water from rushing off. Mulch if you want to.

Some for Now, Some for Later

Before the advent of railroads and interstate highways, consumers didn't have access to fresh fruits and vegetables all year long. They could buy what was grown locally and had to accept the fact that strawberries were only available for a couple of weeks in June or that once the beets were harvested, that was it. Everything is different now. We can have anything we want just about anytime of year thanks to the global marketplace.

If we want to grow our own food, we are still limited to the nuances of the growing season where we live and garden. But, with some ingenuity, we can stretch the harvest time. With repetitive planting of the same vegetable over the course of several weeks, you can have a staggered and drawn-out harvest. This method is also called relay planting.

> **⚠ CAUTION**
>
> **Compost Pile**
>
> Plants with a long growing season, such as tomatoes, melons, and pumpkins aren't good candidates for repetitive planting. To extend your harvest period, plant several varieties with different growing times instead.

For example, in early spring, you might plant a row of lettuces. A week later, plant another row, and then another row a week after that. As one row matures and is harvested, the other two are continuing to grow. So instead of all your lettuce maturing at once, it is stretched over many weeks. Some plants, like lettuce and spinach, can also be planted in the spring and then again in the fall.

Some of the plants that work well with repetitive planting include the following:

- Lettuce
- Basil
- Parsley
- Pea
- Corn
- Dill
- Bean
- Spinach

Success with Succession Planting

Even with lots of effort and many repetitive plantings, some plants just peter out and are finished early in the growing season. Then you are left with empty space in the garden. It's a shame to waste that space. That's where *succession planting* comes into play.

Native Americans were the first to practice this method of planting. They planted "the three sisters"—corn, beans, and squash—together on the same hill. The corn grows up at about the same rate as the beans, and the beans use the corn as a kind of living trellis. The squash grows at the base of both the beans and corn, keeping the soil cool and shading out weeds. The beans mature quickly and the plant dies back as the corn begins to ripen. The squash continues to grow happily below. It's a beautiful relationship!

For successful succession planting be sure that the plants you use have the same requirements for nutrients, pH, and moisture.

Prof. Price's Pointers

Succession planting is the practice of planting different crops with differing rates of maturation in the same spaces.

Interplanting is a similar concept. This method allows you to plant one kind of plant with another because they are compatible and won't get in each other's way. A good example is planting beans with peas. The peas go in very early in the spring. While they are growing, you can plant beans among them. By the time the beans begin to grow, the peas are finished for the season and the beans climb up over the poles or netting. Onion sets planted among larger, slower-growing plants can be harvested young as scallions before they start to interfere with their larger neighbors.

Square-Foot Gardening

We looked at square-foot gardening briefly in Chapter 2. Here are a few more details. This type of garden is frequently done as a raised bed, though that is not a requirement. The garden is laid out in 4 × 4 feet sections. Each of these sections is then further divided into one foot squares. The sections are best marked with string and little stakes (Popsicle sticks work well).

Each square is designated for a plant or type of plant. For example, lettuce might go in one square with a mixture of radishes and carrots in another. A third square would provide space for a few onion sets and the fourth one could be planted with three or four basil plants. You could devote four squares for one tomato plant.

Square-foot gardening has the following characteristics:

◆ Provides efficient use of space

◆ Requires careful planning

◆ Requires loose, fluffy, rich soil

◆ Requires regular fertilizing

◆ Results in cooler soil due to intensive planting

♦ Requires less watering than gardens with exposed soils

♦ Has fewer weeds

This approach to gardening is ideal for gardeners with limited space and time.

Planting in Mulch Cloth

Mulch cloth is a layer of plastic fiber material used to create a planting environment that warms the soil, retains moisture, and deters weeds. The cloth creates a barrier that plants can't break through, which is how it keeps weeds from growing. But if weeds can't grow there, how will your vegetable plants? Here's how.

> **Garden Guru Says**
>
> It's easiest to plant seedlings, as opposed to seeds, in mulch cloth. Small mounds with a couple seeds, like zucchini or melons, work well with mulch cloth, too. But rows of seeds would require a long slit in the cloth, which is not ideal.

Use a measuring tape, or your own good estimation, to measure your spacing. Then with stakes, spray paint, chalk, or stones, mark the spots where each planting hole will go. Using a utility knife, cut an X in the cloth, fold back the cloth, dig a planting hole with a trowel or your hand, insert the seedling, and tamp down the soil. Fold the flaps of mulch cloth back down around the seedling, but just away from the stem.

Later in the season, when the weather has warmed up considerably, spread mulch on top of the mulch cloth to help keep the soil temperature from rising too high and "cooking" your plants.

The Least You Need to Know

♦ Make neat garden rows to keep track of what's a vegetable and what's a weed.

♦ Plant vining and sprawling plants in mounds.

♦ Make furrows for rows of plants that require a deeper planting hole.

♦ Transplant seedlings after the sun goes down.

♦ Use square-foot gardening in small spaces.

♦ Maximize garden efficiency with succession planting.

The Basics

In This Chapter

- ◆ Get up to speed on growing salad greens
- ◆ Clear up any misconceptions about cucumbers
- ◆ Test your knowledge of tomatoes
- ◆ Secure your knowledge of squash and pumpkins
- ◆ Be sure about beans
- ◆ Clear up any confusion about corn

Your idea of basic vegetables might differ from mine. It all has to do with what you grew up on and what you have become used to. But, we can try to make some kind of generalizations. I think salad fixings are about as basic as you can get. And, quite frankly, I can't imagine a garden without at least one tomato plant. Corn and beans are also right up there as first-tier basic foods, as are squash varieties. In this chapter, we look at the art and science of growing these vegetables.

We also talk about soil requirements, planting techniques, and some of the idiosyncrasies that make growing these edibles so much fun.

Salad Stuff

Salad expert Karan Davis Cutler, a guest editor for the Brooklyn Botanic Garden's publication *Salad Gardens*, discovered that salads have been around for a long time. She found a reference to an English salad recipe dating to 1390 that called for herbs, greens, onions, and leeks dressed with oil, vinegar, and salt. That sounds pretty familiar. Other recipes include even more raw ingredients like lettuce, sorrel, purslane, mustard, flower petals, and turnip greens.

Today we take our salads very seriously. Think about it. Most grocery stores and restaurants, even McDonald's, feature salad bars. Basic salad ingredients including lettuce, cucumbers, and radishes are in this section. But tomatoes deserve an entire section of their own.

Let Us Grow Lettuce

Food historians (by the way, I think that would be a great job!) have found that lettuce was grown by the Babylonians more than 3,000 years ago. It might have been big with the Pharaohs and it was certainly a popular vegetable with the ancient Greeks. It's even more popular today. On average, Americans eat more than 30 pounds of lettuce per person each year. If you grow it yourself, you might wind up eating even more than that.

Lettuce, whose Latin name is *Lactuca sativa*, falls into four general categories:

◆ Leaf or loose-leaf

◆ Semi-heading or soft-heading

◆ Heading or crisp-head

◆ Cos

Leaf lettuces are the easiest to grow. They are quick to germinate and fast to mature. Some varieties can go from seed to salad bowl in as little as three weeks. Diverse varieties range from pale green to dark red and can be frilly, crinkly, knubbly, or smooth.

The most common varieties of soft-heading lettuces are Bibb, Boston, and butter-crunch that have small, loosely formed heads. Soft-heading lettuces are almost as easy to grow as loose-leaf varieties.

Iceberg lettuce is the best known crisp-head lettuce. It's the one you see most in the grocery store and in plain-Jane salads. Finally, Cos lettuces include Romaine and endive.

Dozens of varieties of lettuce fall into these categories, including the following:

- Iceberg
- Romaine
- Curly endive or escarole
- Chicory
- Belgian or French endive (a.k.a. witloof chicory)
- Black-seeded Simpson
- Oak leaf
- Mache (a.k.a. corn salad)
- Four seasons
- Winter red

- Purslane
- Mesclun
- Watercress
- Butterhead
- Boston
- Bibb
- Italian chicory
- Speckled troutback
- Blush Batavia
- Deer tongue

Grow a few different ones, or sow a mix of varieties together. You'll want to grow like varieties together so that planting, maintenance, and harvesting are easier.

Large head lettuces like iceberg and romaine should be grown about 12 inches apart in rows that are two to three feet apart. Smaller head lettuces such as bibb, Boston, and butterhead, and looseleaf lettuces should also have about a foot between each plant. But the rows can be closer together, perhaps a foot or so. Looseleaf lettuces can also be planted intensively with little or no spacing. Harvesting young, tender leaves will provide room for the remaining leaves to grow.

Although seedlings are readily available at nurseries and garden centers, growing lettuce from seed is really easy. It also gives you the opportunity to experiment with many different varieties, especially the ones you would never find at the grocery store.

Because lettuce seeds require light to germinate, you'll need to sow them on the surface of a prepared bed of loose, rich soil with plenty of organic matter. Gently pat the seeds down. Water with a fine mist. Don't allow the soil to dry out, but avoid letting it become soggy.

Garden Guru Says

To harvest loose-leaf lettuce, simply pick the largest leaves, breaking them off right at the base. You can also harvest individual leaves from soft-heading lettuces, taking just a few outer leaves at a time. Or pick the entire head by slicing it off at the base of the stem. Use the same procedure for harvesting crisp-heading varieties.

Sow new lettuce seeds every week or so until the weather gets very hot, and again when it starts to cool off. That way you'll have a nearly continuous supply.

Food for Thought

Belgian or French endive (also known as witloof chicory) is a small pale green Cos lettuce that costs a lot at the grocery store. The reason it's so expensive is that it requires special treatment to attain that color; it is blanched. Blanching is a gardening technique—also used for celery, cauliflower, and asparagus—that robs the leaves of chlorophyll. To blanch endive, pull the outer leaves of a nearly mature plant up over the head and secure at the top with twine. Leave it for three weeks, and then harvest and discard the outer leaves. Alternatively, cover the plant with a terra cotta cloche (special bell-shaped crocks). Make sure the cloche doesn't touch the leaves. Blanching tends to reduce bitterness and produces a milder flavor.

You Say Tomato, I Say Tomahto

Tomatoes (*Lycopersicon lypersicum*) might very well be the favorite vegetable of American gardeners. Yet as late as 1820, many people believed tomatoes were poisonous. Thomas Jefferson was one of the first people to grow tomatoes as an edible rather than an ornamental. If I could grow only one vegetable in my garden it would be a tomato plant. There is nothing like picking a ripe tomato on a hot day and eating it right there in the garden.

Plant breeders have been messing around with tomatoes for years. They have managed to make faster growing, uniformly shaped, and pest resistant varieties; but they've also become less and less tasty. This is particularly true of commercially grown tomatoes. Fortunately, many of the tomatoes available for home gardeners still retain the flavors we like so much, including some of the rediscovered *heirloom* varieties.

Prof. Price's Pointers

An **heirloom** plant is an open-pollinated variety introduced more than 50 years ago. Some heirloom varieties have been reintroduced and are again available commercially. Others are traded among aficionados.

Burpee has at least 24 varieties of heirloom tomatoes sold as seeds or plants including Jubilee (developed in 1943), the Rutgers or Jersey (introduced in 1943), Mortgage Lifter (1930s), and Marglobe (1917).

Tomatoes fall into a number of categories. They are described more or less by use (slicing, plum or paste, and cherry or grape), by season (early, mid, and late), and by vine type (determinate or indeterminate).

The characteristics for determinate and interdeterminate varieties are as follows:

Determinate	Indeterminate
Vine ends in fruit	Keeps forming new vine
No new fruit after first	Keeps forming new fruit
Fruit ripens	Bigger plants
Smaller plants	Needs lots of space
Grows in smaller spaces	Needs staking or caging
Doesn't always need staking	Produces later in season
Produces early in season	

Tomatoes are also differentiated by color, ranging from yellow to orange, and pink to burgundy. When selecting tomatoes to grow in your garden, you'll want to consider all these factors.

To start tomatoes indoors, sow seeds about 8 to 10 weeks before the last predicted frost date in your area. Then harden off for about two weeks.

Plant seedlings, whether your own or store-bought plants, with two or three inches of stem under the soil. The stem will soon sprout roots that will help stabilize the plant and make it stronger. Place the plants from 1½ to 3 feet apart, depending on the variety.

Days from planting to maturity can range from a short 59 days (Early Girl) to as long as 95 (Aunt Ruby's Green). Maturation times for other popular varieties include 78 (Big Boy), 70 (Super Sweet 100), and 80 days (Viva Italia).

Tomatoes are heavy feeders and will need fertilizer every two or three weeks. Use the formula suggested on the fertilizer packaging.

Food for Thought

Plant tomato seedlings in a well-prepared garden enriched with compost or well-rotted manure. Water well. Then place cages over the seedlings. If you prefer to stake the tomatoes, use three heavy stakes and wind twine around them at various heights to create a support. Or use one tall stake and loosely attach the stem to the stake.

Cool as a Cucumber

Cucumbers are members of the cucurbit family, whose relatives include melons, squash, chayote, and gourds. A native of India, cucumbers arrived in the New World with Christopher Columbus and are now, of course, a salad staple. In fact, according to a report by the U.S. Department of Agriculture, Americans eat more than three billion pounds of cucumbers a year!

Though popular with backyard gardeners, cukes aren't the easiest veggie to grow. They are a bit fussy about soil, need a lot of water, and are susceptible to pests and disease problems. Even though there are a few negatives, growing cucumbers can be very satisfying.

Prof. Price's Pointers

Cucumber vines produce both male and female flowers. The first flowers are staminate or male. These simply fall from the plant without becoming fruit. The second kind of flowers are both staminate and pistillate or female, allowing pollination to occur. Some newer varieties are gynoecious or only female. These plants will require some staminate plants planted nearby in order for pollination to occur.

Garden Guru Says

Thicker skins contribute to the "burp" factor of cucumbers. Some gardeners favor the "burpless" varieties, which are usually longer and thinner than standard cukes, and they have a thinner skin.

There are three basic types of cucumbers: slicing, pickling (both *Cucumis sativus*), and gherkin (*Cucumis anguria*). Slicing and pickling varieties are available in bush and vining form, though vines are far more common. Slicing varieties tend to have thicker skins than the pickling types and are generally larger.

Plant cucumber seeds or seedlings outdoors after all danger of frost has passed. They like very rich, well-cultivated soil with a pH in the 6.0 to 7.0 range. Cucumbers don't take kindly to transplanting. If you start seeds indoors, use biodegradable planting pots so you don't disturb the tiny roots when it's time to set them out.

Sow cucumbers in hills with about four or five seeds or plants per hill. Seeds should be planted about ½ to ¾ inch deep. Allow four to six feet between hills. If you prefer row planting, allow the same distance between rows with about two or three feet between each plant. Cukes can also be trained to grow up a trellis or netting. Or you can use tomato cages in which case you will want to make smaller hills with just one plant per hill. Expect cucumbers to take about 40 to 60 days from seed to maturity, depending on the variety.

Plan on a fertilizing program beginning with an application about one week after the first flowers appear and continuing every three or four weeks. Keep your cucumbers well irrigated and never let them dry out. A thick mulch around the roots will help hold moisture in and will keep the soil a little cooler when the weather gets steamy.

CAUTION **Compost Pile**

Be sure to harvest your cucumbers as they mature. If you leave ripe fruit on the vine, the plants will stop producing.

Rows and Rows of Radishes

One of the fastest growing vegetables, and great for introducing kids to the joys of gardening, radishes are also among the easiest of edibles to grow.

Radishes are almost always grown from seed. They prefer cool weather, so it's best to plant them as soon as you can work the soil in the spring. The soil should have a pH of 5.8 to 6.8 and it should be well cultivated and well drained. If you plan to grow the long varieties like Daikon, white icicle, salad rose, or Chinese white, be sure to cultivate the soil down at least 8 or 10 inches.

Prof. Price's Pointers

Originating in Asia, most likely in China where they were thought to have aphrodisiac powers, radishes are a member of the Crucifer or mustard family and are related to cabbage, broccoli, and kale.

The bright red, round radish we put in our everyday salads (*Raphanus sativus*) is the most commonly grown, but there are many other types including long, narrow varieties, turnip-shaped ones, black-skinned forms, all white and yellow types, and the exotic Japanese Daikon (*Raphanus sativus var. longipinnatus*).

Plant seeds in shallow furrows, about ¼ to ½ inch deep. If you plant more than one row, make the rows about one to two feet apart. Radish seeds are very small and are usually sold in large quantities (Burpee packs about 300 to 400 seeds per packet, for example), so you can sow them in a slow dribble along the furrow. Then when the seeds begin to sprout (it usually takes less than a week), you can thin the seedlings to about 8 to 10 inches apart.

Sow additional radish seeds every week until the weather gets hot. Then start again in the late summer or early fall for fall harvesting.

CAUTION **Compost Pile**

Radishes will become woody and unpleasantly hot if left in the ground too long. Traditional salad radishes usually take about 25 days from seed to harvest. Daikon types will take 45 to 60 days.

The Three Sisters

In Chapter 12, we talked a little about the three sisters, the Native American concept of growing squash, beans, and corn together. In this section, we'll take a closer look at these plants.

Squish, Squash

Pumpkins and all kinds of squash are members of the cucurbit family and relatives of melons and cucumbers. They are generally vining plants and tend to grow very large. Just about all squash (and we'll use that term to include pumpkins for our purposes here) require a fair amount of growing room.

The most commonly grown squash types in American gardens include summer and winter varieties. The summer types mature earlier in the season and tend to have thinner skins than the winter varieties. Many of the winter varieties, including pumpkins, can be stored for several weeks or even months, which is one of the reasons they were an essential staple of Native Americans and early settlers in America. The following should help you understand the summer/winter types.

Summer	Winter
Zucchini	Pumpkin
Crooked neck	Butternut
Straight neck	Spaghetti
	Lakota
	Buttercup
	Acorn
	Patty Pan

Prof. Price's Pointers

Knowing the Latin names of ornamental plants is part of the basic knowledge most gardeners work to acquire. But it's a little different with many of the edible plants. Instead of helping the gardener identify exactly what the plant is, the Latin names of many edibles sometimes causes more confusion. For example, *Curcurbita pepo* is the Latin name for spaghetti squash, zucchini, and pumpkins. It's actually easier to identify these plants by their common names.

Squash are relatively easy plants to grow; many varieties are downright prolific. The vines will grow from 6 to 15 feet long, depending on the variety. Though many of the summer varieties grow in bush form, they still need a lot of space.

Squash are generally grown on large hills with two or three seeds or seedlings per hill. Give each hill about six to eight feet of space all the way around the hill. Water thoroughly and regularly. Then follow up with a good feeding every two to three weeks. Summer squash will need about 40 to 50 days from seed to maturity. The winter varieties take much longer, with maturation times of 70 to 100 days depending on the variety. The soil must be nice and warm when seeds or plants are first planted.

Food for Thought

You can allow vines to trail on the ground or train them up a sturdy trellis tying the vine loosely to the support. This will help keep ripening squash from rotting where it touches the ground. If maturing squash look like they are becoming too heavy for the vine, make a sling with a pantyhose leg. Ease the stocking over the fruit, cut off a section and make slits to form a pair of ties. Then tie the sling to the trellis. The material will expand with the growing fruit.

All types of squash require regular watering and should never be allowed to dry out. About a month after planting, feed the plants with a low nitrogen fertilizer. Then follow up with a feeding every two or three weeks.

Beans

Beans are another one of those really easy vegetables to grow. No garden should be without a crop of them. There are three types of beans: snap beans, shell beans, and dry beans.

Beans probably originated in South America and have become a staple all over the world. The dry beans—like kidney, pinto, great northern, navy, and black eye—are fully mature bean seeds that are harvested and dried for future use. They are not generally grown in home gardens but rather as crops on farms. Snap beans are young beans harvested before their seeds mature, whereas shell beans are harvested when the seeds are almost mature but still tender. We'll limit our discussion here to snap and shell beans.

Prof. Price's Pointers

Snap beans are the newer name for what we used to call string beans. Plant breeders have bred beans without the strings that used to run along the "seam" between the two halves of the beans, so now they are more or less stringless and have a new name.

Both shell and snap beans are available in bush or pole (climbing) varieties. They aren't particularly fussy about soil, as long as the drainage is good. The pH should be in the 5.8 to 6.3 range. Sow the bean seeds in shallow furrows about one inch deep and two or three inches apart. Water gently. Don't worry about fertilizing unless the leaves begin to yellow or if the plants don't seem to prosper.

It's a Snap

Snap beans include what we think of as green or string beans, wax beans, Italian snap beans, filet beans, and scarlet runner beans. Though you could start them indoors, there really is no need to. Snap beans are incredibly quick to germinate, emerging in a week to 10 days after planting. Just be sure to wait a week or two after your last predicted frost to plant. These beans take about 40 to 50 days from seed to harvest.

> **Garden Guru Says**
>
> Beans will produce more if you harvest them diligently. The more you pick, the more prolific they become.

Beans have a tendency to mature all at once, so it's a good idea to plant several varieties with varying maturation rates, or to sow new seeds every week for a month or so. This will prolong the harvest.

> **Food for Thought**
>
> In their charming book *The Family Garden: Clever Things to Do in, Around and Under the Garden*, Jan and Michael Gertley suggest using a no-longer-used metal swing set as a trellis for climbing beans. Cultivate the soil under the swing set (it might be pretty compacted if it's had years of use). Run a wire or sturdy twine just above ground level connecting the two front legs of the set and another wire connecting the two back legs. Then string wire from the top cross bar to each of the bottom wires, spacing the wire about a foot apart. Plant at the base of each wire and watch the beans sprawl up the wire. Alternatively, lay chicken wire or plastic mesh over the swing set frame as a trellis for all kinds of climbing plants.

Shell Game

The most commonly grown shell beans are limas and favas. They are grown the same way snap beans are, though their maturation time is considerably longer—about 70 to 85 days depending on the variety.

Can-Do Corn

An all-American meal isn't complete without corn on the cob. And I don't mean just modern America. Corn was the main staple for Native Americans going back centuries. It is thought to have originated in Central America some 80,000 years ago and was one of the first crops to be cultivated in the New World.

Today's corn is very different from that early native, which by the way, is a member of the grass family. Plant breeders have developed new varieties that are sweeter, bigger, more prolific, and more resistant to pests and diseases than ever before.

Generally speaking, home gardeners prefer the sugary enhancer hybrids because of their high sugar content and the pleasing texture and tenderness of the kernels, and because they don't need to be isolated from other types of corn.

Corn will grow in just about any kind of soil. It's not very fussy. Good drainage is important though. Plant seed corn in furrows about one inch deep when the soil has reached at least 60 degrees Fahrenheit. This is one plant that doesn't mind really hot weather, so you can keep planting every week or so well into the summer. Just keep in mind that you'll need 60 to 90 days until the corn is ready to harvest.

Prof. Price's Pointers

Corn is grown as three types that are genetically different: normal sugary, sugary enhancer, and supersweet. They each contain genes that control the sugar content and texture, tenderness, and color of the kernels. Many varieties must be isolated from each other so that cross-pollination doesn't cause the plants to revert to undesirable characteristics.

Garden Guru Says

Most corn is wind pollinated. To make sure the pollen blows onto all the tassels of your corn crop, make short rows in a block rather than just a few long rows.

Though corn will survive dryer weather than many vegetables, it will be happier with regular irrigation. Weed control is also important, but use care when cultivating around corn plants—the roots damage easily.

The Least You Need to Know

- ◆ Sow new leaf lettuce seeds every week or so as long as the weather isn't hot for a long harvest season.
- ◆ Provide tomato plants with a soil rich in organic matter.
- ◆ Keep cucumbers well watered.

- Harvest radishes before they become woody and overly hot.

- Give squash plants plenty of room to spread out, and be sure to select an appropriate variety of sweet corn.

- Keep up with bean harvesting to encourage the plants to continue production.

Chapter 14

More Great Veggies

In This Chapter

- ◆ Corner the market on cabbage family concerns
- ◆ Leaf through material on leafy greens
- ◆ Master the art of growing melons
- ◆ Perfect your pepper and pea presence
- ◆ Extend your eggplant expertise

In this chapter, we look at a few more great vegetables. These could easily have been in an earlier chapter on basic vegetables but there just wasn't enough room to put them there and do them justice. In the next few pages, we look at members of the cabbage family including broccoli and Brussels sprouts. And there are sections on peas, peppers, eggplant, leafy greens, and melons.

The Cole Family Album

Let me introduce you to the cole family, also known as *Brassica oleracea* (and just to confuse things, also sometimes known as the Cruciferae family or Crucifers for short), whose members include cabbage, broccoli, cauliflower, kale, Brussels sprouts, Chinese cabbage, and kohlrabi. Brassicas originated as Old World plants, with some, like cabbage, beloved by ancient Egyptians and Romans, Russians, and many others for the past 2,000 years. In this section we talk about these family members except kale (which is discussed later in this chapter) and Chinese cabbage and kohlrabi (discussed in the next chapter).

All the Brassicas, which are sometimes referred to generically as the cabbage family, prefer rich, well-drained soil with lots of organic matter like compost or well-rotted manure worked in thoroughly. They are all cool weather plants (except cauliflower) and they are pretty tolerant of a fairly broad pH range (except cauliflower) of 5.5 to 7.0.

> **⚠ CAUTION**
>
> **Compost Pile** _____
>
> Cabbage family plants are prone to quite a few ailments, many of which are carried in the soil. Try to change their location in the garden every couple of years to avoid disease. This is called crop rotation.

You can start most Brassicas from seed indoors about four to six weeks before setting out, or directly in the garden about one inch deep, but why bother? Unless you are planning on growing heirloom or specialty varieties, young plants are readily available.

Give the plants a good feeding when you set them out, and then again every three weeks or so after that.

Cabbage

Cabbage (*Brassica oleracea capitata*) is sort of the mother of all Brassicas. They are very easy to grow, and I think their big, fat heads look beautiful in rows in the garden. Be prepared though. If you have a large crop, you might find that they have a certain, well, stink.

Cabbage seedlings should have four complete sets of leaves before they are transplanted. Set them out, or plant seeds, as early as the soil can be worked for a summer harvest, or in early summer for fall harvest. Plant them deep, with the stem buried right up to the first set of leaves to encourage root development along the stem. Plant cabbages 1½ to 2 feet apart, or more if you are growing any of the giant varieties.

Choose from green, red, Chinese, and Savoy varieties.

To harvest, use a sharp knife to slice straight across the base of the stem.

Food for Thought _____

After a heavy rain or if the plants have been watered irregularly, cabbage heads will sometimes split open. To avoid this, first, keep your watering to a regular schedule, if possible. And second, try pruning the roots when the cabbage heads are nearly full size. To do this, take a sharp spade and push it straight down along one side of the cabbage plant. This severs the roots. If the head splits anyway, harvest it immediately.

Cauliflower

Cauliflower (*Brassica oleracea botrytis*) used to be the wimp of the cole family. It didn't like cold weather and couldn't take the heat, either. Plant breeders have taken cauliflower to new levels with weather-tolerant early and late varieties, and some that are bred to overwinter in the ground for spring harvest. Cauliflower produces old-fashioned white "curds" (heads) as well as purple and green ones.

> **Garden Guru Says**
>
> To make white cauliflower heads whiter, blanch them by gathering up the big side leaves and tying them gently on top of the head with a piece of twine. You can also blanch with a cloche or even with a salvaged cabbage leaf. Just lay it over the cauliflower head like a big sun hat. Or look for self-blanching varieties with big leaves that grow up over the head, though they might need a little assistance with twine to stay put.

Even with the newer varieties, cauliflower isn't the easiest plant to grow. It prefers a pH of 6.5 to 7 and requires lots of rich organic matter in the soil. Cauliflower has trouble setting its curds if irrigation is irregular.

Set out cauliflower plants about 1½ to 2½ feet apart in rows that are about 2½ feet apart. Feed with a high nitrogen fertilizer when you plant and then again every couple weeks. With overwintering varieties, stop the feeding program at first frost and pick up again when the weather warms.

To harvest, use a sharp knife to slice through the stem at the base.

Former President George Bush's Least Favorite Vegetable

When my older daughter was little, she would eat an entire head of broccoli for dinner. It's one of our family's favorite vegetables. Broccoli has a delicious flavor to begin with, and the homegrown stuff is fabulous. Though not as fussy as cauliflower, it's still not the easiest vegetable in the world to grow.

Set out plants with at least one full set of leaves after the last frost allowing about 1½ feet between plants. If you start from seed, plant them about one inch deep. Feed transplants with a high nitrogen liquid fertilizer, and then repeat every three weeks or so.

We eat the unopened flower buds of the broccoli plants. Harvesting should be done when the buds are still tightly closed. If they start to open or produce little yellow flowers, you've waited too long. Cut the buds with a bit of stem using a sharp knife. The broccoli plants will send out new bonus stems with buds a little later.

Brussels Sprouts

How Brussels sprouts got their name is a little murky. It seems they were popular in Belgium in the 1700s. There's surely more to it than that, but no one seems to be able to come up with the final answer. There is pretty good documentation, however, that Thomas Jefferson imported some seeds from Europe to grow at Monticello in 1812. Today, American vegetable farmers produce about 70 million pounds of Brussels sprouts each year.

You can add to that poundage by growing them in your garden, too. It's not very difficult. Give them a soil pH of about 6.5, lots of organic matter and a long, cool growing season. Plant seeds indoors about four or five weeks before setting them out in late spring or early summer. Or plant them directly in the garden. Brussels sprouts require 70 to 110 days to mature and are best when harvested in cool or even cold weather. Some varieties over-winter for a spring harvest.

Leafy Greens

Health experts tell us to eat plenty of leafy green vegetables. If you grow your own, eating them will be a pleasure. We discussed salad greens in Chapter 13. Here we look at kale, spinach, and chard.

Kale

As we mentioned earlier, kale is a member of the Brassica family (*Brassica oleracea sabellica*). It is one of the most cold-hardy leafy vegetables we grow in North America. Kale is typically grown in very rich, well-drained soil with lots of organic matter and a pH of 7.5 to 8.0. Seed are planted individually about ½ inch deep or are broadcast for intensive planting. Do this as soon as the soil can be worked for spring harvest and in early fall for a late fall harvest. In warm areas, kale is a winter crop.

Kale requires regular, thorough irrigation. It should also be fed every two weeks or so with a high nitrogen fertilizer.

Food for Thought

Years ago in my New Jersey garden, I harvested some incredibly delicious kale in February from under at least six inches of snow. The flavor of kale actually improves when it is harvested after a frost.

Popeye's Favorite

Popeye scarfed down a can of spinach when he needed to supersize his muscles. Though I don't think canned spinach has much of a market share these days, the popularity of fresh spinach is on the rise because of its amazing nutritional benefits.

Spinach (*Spinacea oleracea*) is a relatively easy vegetable to grow as long as you keep it cool and well fed and provide it with a rich soil with plenty of organic matter and a pH of 6.4 to 7.0. Sow seeds about ½ inch deep and 2 inches apart as soon as the soil can be worked. You can also broadcast seed in a small area for intensive planting, covering them with a light layer of soil. Some gardeners even broadcast spinach seed over frozen ground; it germinates when the snow thaws.

Water spinach regularly and thoroughly, and feed the spinach every couple weeks with a high nitrogen fertilizer. Harvest by thinning the plants to about four to six inches apart and by picking individual leaves of larger plants. You can also harvest whole plants by pulling them, roots and all, from the row.

Spinach is one of the few vegetables that will tolerate some shade.

Prof. Price's Pointers

Spinach has a tendency to bolt. This is an undesirable early maturity of leafy plants whereby they rush through their life cycle to the flowering and seed producing stage. This is typical of spinach, lettuce, and radishes and usually happens when the weather gets too warm for them. Once the plants have bolted, they are inedible.

Swiss Chard

One of the prettiest of all vegetables, chard is often overlooked for anything more than a garnish. What a mistake. When picked nice and young, chard leaves are a delicious addition to a salad. And more mature leaves are a tasty alternative to spinach.

Chard has thick celery-like stems and large, thick leaves. Some varieties are very colorful with red, yellow, burgundy, white, or green stems and veins. Chard, whose Latin name is *Beta vulgaris var. cicla*, is a relative of the beet. It's easy to see the resemblance in the red veined varieties.

Chard prefers a high pH, in the 6.5 to 7.0 range, and rich soil with plenty of organic matter. This is a cool weather plant so you can sow seeds outdoors two to four weeks before the last predicted frost date. Plant the seeds ½ to ¾ inch deep and just a couple inches apart.

As new chard plants appear, you can harvest them for salads by thinning the plants to about six or eight inches apart. Later, harvest outer leaves as they grow. Chard will wilt in really hot summer weather, but will do well in cool fall temperatures.

Get a Load of Those Melons

Melons come right after tomatoes on my list of favorite summer garden crops. These sweet, juicy fruits can be a challenge to grow because they need a lot of room, warm temperatures, and plenty of water. But they are also great fun, especially for kids.

Melons are members of the Curcubitacea family and are relatives of cucumbers and squash. They originated in the Middle East where they remain a very important part of the agricultural scene.

In addition to cantaloupe and watermelon, the two most commonly grown melons in the United States, some gardeners enjoy growing the following:

- Crenshaw
- French Charentais
- Muskmelon
- Butterscotch
- Persian
- Ogen
- Dudaim

- Casaba
- Honeydew
- Galia
- Canary
- Prince
- Santa Claus

Garden Guru Says

To warm up soil temperatures early and to keep it warm, use black plastic mulch in your melon patch.

Prof. Price's Pointers

Watermelons, unlike their close relatives, do best in soil that has not been amended with compost or manure. They actually prefer a poorer soil and will thank you for not fertilizing them during the growing season.

Most melons are vining plants that can take up to six square feet or more of garden space per plant. In order to grow them, you'll need to have lots of room to let them sprawl. That said, plant breeders have been developing more compact bush varieties. Look for these if your space is somewhat limited.

If your garden is really small, you could try growing melons on a sturdy trellis or in a wire cage. But because melons are pretty heavy, you'll need to support the fruit as it matures. Try the pantyhose sling trick described in Chapter 13 in the section on squash.

Melon seedlings are planted on large hills well after all danger of frost has passed. They need warm weather in order to germinate. If you live in a warm weather zone, you can start your melons from seed. If not, stick with seedlings.

Food for Thought

An article in *Garden Gate* magazine outlined a novel way to grow melons. Cut off one side of an old tire and place it cut side down in a prepared bed. Fill the center of the tire with compost and plant your melon seeds or seedlings. Water well, feed regularly, and watch the melons grow. The tire creates a raised bed and the black rubber soaks up the sun and warms the soil just the way melons like it.

Watermelons

These giant, improbable fruits are the essence of summer. They don't ask for too much besides plenty of space, lots of sun, warm weather, and loads of water.

Plant one watermelon on top of each planting hill, and allow six or eight feet in every direction.

Watermelons generally take from 75 to 100 days to mature, so be sure to leave them on the vine long enough to ripen. In zones with short summer seasons, leave the melon on the vine until just before the first frost. Harvest by cutting the stem with a sharp knife or garden shears.

Cantaloupe

You can plant as many as three cantaloupe seedlings on a large hill. Give them plenty of organic matter in the soil, and feed them every two or three weeks with a high nitrogen liquid fertilizer. To avoid having the fruit rot before it is ripe, some gardeners put a small piece of plywood under each fruit to keep it off the soil.

Pick a Peck of Peppers

Christopher Columbus, bless his exploring ways, gave peppers their name when he first bit into a hot chili pepper on arrival in the New World. (Remember, he thought he had found a new route to the Spice Islands, and he believed he had discovered a brand new kind of spice pepper.)

Peppers, hot and sweet, originated in South or Central America, found their way to Europe via Columbus, and eventually were exported to Asia where they caught on big time.

Prof. Price's Pointers

Capsaicin is a special substance peculiar to peppers that we taste as pungent (hot). The level of capsaicin is controlled by several genetic factors that determine the level of hotness of specific varieties.

Peppers fall into two general categories: sweet and hot. And there are dozens of varieties, including the following:

- Green sweet bell
- Yellow, orange, or red sweet bell
- Sweet banana
- Jalapeño
- Cayenne
- Poblano
- Huasteco
- Serrano
- Chiltepin
- Thai dragon
- Habanero
- Hungarian wax
- Anaheim
- Cherry
- Pepperoncini

Peppers prefer well-drained and well-cultivated soil that is slightly alkaline, with a pH of 6.0 to 6.8 being ideal, though you won't see much difference with more acidic soil. Space pepper plants from 1½ to 2 feet apart. Peppers should be well irrigated but will do poorly in soggy conditions.

As soon as the pepper plants begin to set tiny fruits, apply a high nitrogen fertilizer according to the package directions. Then feed every two or three weeks. Mulching around pepper plants is also a good idea; it will keep moisture in and weeds out. Peppers will take 60 to 80 days from the plant set out date to first harvest. Then you'll want to pick the peppers as soon as the fruits are ripe, to encourage more production. Do it gently, using garden snips. Most peppers will keep producing until frost.

Garden Guru Says

You can also plant pepper seeds indoors 8 to 10 weeks before the last predicted frost date. But that's a long time to tend seeds indoors. Most people prefer using seedlings.

Sweet pepper varieties include green, red, orange, and yellow varieties. The green types stay green even as they mature. The colored varieties, which have high levels of carotenoids (the same ingredient that makes carrots orange), are green in their immature form, then take on the bright color at maturity.

Eggplants

Eggplants (*Solanum melongena*) used to be considered a fairly exotic plant, but they've become much more commonplace in the last 20 years or so. Old World natives, eggplants are members of the nightshade family (Solanaceae) whose relatives include New World plants like tomatoes, potatoes, and peppers.

These are very tender plants with no tolerance for cold weather, which isn't surprising considering they probably originated in India. Eggplants need lots of long, hot days in order to thrive. They also like a soil with a pH of 6.0 to 6.8.

Most gardeners start with seedlings, setting them out a week or two after the last predicted frost. If you have the patience, you can start seeds indoors about 8 to 10 weeks before the set-out date. Be sure to use biodegradable planting pots to avoid disrupting the roots during transplantation. Give eggplants a foot or two of space between plants.

If you like eggplant, you might want to experiment with several different varieties. You can choose from the varieties shown in the following table.

Food for Thought

Although black plastic mulch isn't my favorite product, eggplants seem to do really well with it. The black plastic absorbs the sun's heat and keeps the soil temperature high which is right up an eggplant's alley. The plastic also keeps moisture in and weeds out.

Variety	Shape	Color	Skin
American	globular and/or elongated	dark purple	thick skin
Japanese	thin, elongated	light to dark purple	thin skin
Chinese	long, thin	pale purple	thin skin
Italian	short, wide or elongated	dark purple	thick skin
Mini	small, elongated	shades of purple	
White	egg shaped or round	white	thin skin
Filipino	elongated	green to purple	thin skin
Indian	small, round	purple	
Green	elongated	green	
Thai	tiny, round	green, yellow, or white	
Heirloom	various shapes	green, white, or shades of purple	

Eggplants require regular irrigation, particularly when the weather gets very hot. A dose of high nitrogen fertilizer at planting time should be followed up with another

Compost Pile

Eggplants have sharp thorny growths on their stems and calyx (the little green "cap" at the top of the fruit) that can prick your fingers. Wear gloves when you harvest.

feeding when the first fruits appear, and then every two or three weeks. Use the formula on the packaging.

Begin harvesting your eggplants when they are at least one third their mature size (these are baby eggplants which cost a fortune in gourmet stores) up to fully ripe. If you leave them on the vine too long, they will become bitter. Keep up with harvesting to encourage production, and use garden snips to avoid breaking the stems.

Peas, Please

Peas, natives of China (or maybe the Middle East), have been an important staple for thousands of years. But for most of that time, peas have been dried after harvest for later use. It wasn't until sometime in the 1600s that a clever European snacked on some raw peas and started a whole new culinary trend. And the rest is history.

Peas fall into three categories:

◆ Snow peas

◆ Snap or edible-podded peas

◆ Garden, shelling, or English peas

Each of these types is relatively easy to grow and makes few demands on the home gardener. Peas prefer a well-cultivated, neutral to slightly alkaline soil with a pH of 6.0 to 6.7 being ideal. But if your soil is more acid than that, the peas won't mind too much. What is far more important is that the soil be well-drained. Though they must be watered well and regularly, peas hate to have wet feet.

Sow pea seeds outdoors in the early spring. St. Patrick's Day is the traditional pea-planting time in northern zones. In Zones 9 through 11, peas are a winter crop. The seeds, which are tiny, should go in a shallow furrow about one inch deep, and about two to three inches apart.

Snow Peas

Snow peas are the delicious edible pods so familiar in Asian stir-fry dishes. They require anywhere from 55 to 70 days from seed to harvest and should be picked when they are still young, small, and flat. Snow peas will climb pea netting or a small trellis about two to four feet tall depending on the variety. Look for one of the newer stringless varieties when you buy seed.

Prof. Price's Pointers

Along with other legumes, peas have the unusual ability to take nitrogen from the atmosphere and turn it into ammonium, a form they can metabolize. This is called *fixing* nitrogen. But to perform this trick, they need to negotiate a deal (symbiosis) with a certain kind of bacteria called Rhizobium: The plant provides a home for the bacteria in the form of root nodules, and the bacteria proceed to fix nitrogen. Neither plant nor bacteria can do it alone. Gardeners can help out by "inoculating" the soil with the bacteria before planting.

It's a Snap

These are more or less a cross between snow peas and garden peas and are grown for their edible pods. But the big difference between snap peas and snow peas is that the snap peas develop little peas in the pod. They are usually eaten raw in salads or cooked in stir fry. Some varieties of snap peas are bushy and don't require a support, whereas others will climb a bit up netting or a trellis. Snap peas should be picked just as the little peas develop. If the harvesting gets ahead of you, you can shell the snap peas just like garden peas, but they won't have that sweet, delicate flavor.

Garden of Pea Delights

There are dozens of varieties of garden peas from which to choose. These peas are also called English or shelling peas. They've been bred for early or late season harvest, so you might want to mix up several varieties to stretch out the picking time. Most garden peas grow from 1½ to 3 feet tall and will need some support. Most prefer cool weather and will rapidly die back when the weather gets hot. Some newer varieties have been bred to be more heat tolerant.

The Least You Need to Know

- The cabbage family includes cabbages, cauliflower, broccoli, Brussels sprouts, kale, and kohlrabi.
- Cauliflower heads become white when they are blanched.

- Kale can be harvested very late, even after a snowfall.

- Spinach will bolt once the weather gets hot so you'll want to plant a second crop for fall harvest.

- Melons take a long time to reach maturity so they should be started early.

Chapter 15

Back to Your Roots

In This Chapter

- Get a basic spud education
- Learn how to grow onions and their relatives
- Find out the differences between rutabagas and turnips
- Distinguish between sweet potatoes and yams

In this chapter, it's time to get back to our roots and learn all about root vegetables. These are, for the most part, the solid, basic starch vegetables that play such a big part in our old-fashioned image of a holiday dinner. Think Thanksgiving. Potatoes, turnips, rutabagas, parsnips, beets, carrots, sweet potatoes, and onions. They are all here. All that's missing is the turkey.

One Potato, Two Potato

Potatoes (*Solanum tuberosum*) are an ancient food, dating back thousands of years to their roots (if you will) with the Incas in Peru around 200 B.C.E. From there they traveled with the Spanish conquistadors back to Europe in the fifteenth century. Potatoes have become the world's largest food crop, beating out rice and corn (at least according to a potato trade association). The United States produces 35 billion pounds of potatoes every year, and we eat them in prodigious quantities.

Potatoes are classified in a number of ways based on their size, skin color, flesh color, harvest time, starch level, use, and shape.

Some of the descriptions include the following:

- Early, second-early, and main crop

- Round, long, oval, and oblong

- Yellow and white flesh

- Thin and thick skin

- White, red, russet, brown, pink, yellow, blue, and purple skin

- High-, medium-, and low-starch

- Baking, chip, french fries, mashing, and all-purpose

You might want to grow several different kinds, especially the unusual varieties that are so expensive to buy in stores.

Home gardeners generally start their spuds from seed potatoes, which are very small tubers with several eyes on each one. Be sure to buy only certified seed potatoes. Lots of serious diseases plague potato crops, so you want to avoid spreading any of them. Get seed potatoes ready to sprout by warming them up a bit and exposing them to sunlight for a few days. A bright window in a warm part of the house will do.

> **Garden Guru Says**
>
> Move your potato patch each year to a different part of the garden to avoid introducing or spreading diseases or pests.

Plant potatoes in the spring when the soil has warmed to about 45 degrees F or just before the last predicted frost. But if tender young plants have appeared and a heavy frost is predicted, they won't stand up to a heavy frost; be prepared to run out with newspapers, blankets, row covers, or straw to protect them.

Give your potatoes a well-drained, well-cultivated bed with loamy soil, rich with organic matter. They like a pH of 5.8 to 6.5, but they will tolerate 4.7 to 7.0.

You can grow potatoes in mounds or in rows. If you choose rows, make a furrow about four inches wide and six inches deep. Plant the seed potatoes, which you should cut into 1½-inch chunks with at least one eye per chunk, spaced according to the size of the potato you plan to harvest. For example, if you want full size potatoes, plant the seeds 10 to 15 inches apart. If you're planning on harvesting a lot of baby potatoes, you can place them every four inches.

Put the seed potatoes cut side down in the hole, and then fill it halfway with soil. Once you see little plants push through the soil, add more. Keep on doing this as the plant grows. But don't cover the foliage once it develops. Just keep adding soil to cover the stem.

Potatoes grow just under the soil, but they should never be exposed to the sun. So that's why you need to keep adding soil as the spuds grow.

Give the potatoes a regular, thorough watering, but never allow the soil to become soggy or you'll wind up with rotten potatoes. They will manage better with too little water than with too much. As for feeding, give them a low-nitrogen fertilizer so they don't put too much energy into their leaves.

Food for Thought

Remember the tire trick for growing melons we described in Chapter 14? You can do the same thing with potatoes. The only difference is you add a tire on top of the first one as you mound the soil over the stem.

Compost Pile

When young potatoes are exposed to sunlight, they produce a toxic substance. You'll know if this has happened because they turn green. Dispose of them.

Harvest potatoes a few at a time, beginning about two to three weeks after the flowers have fallen off. The remaining potatoes will continue to grow so you can keep harvesting as long as there are potatoes. Do this by hand without pulling up the plants. Or wait until all the leaves have died back, and then carefully pull the spuds out of the soil—take care because they damage easily.

Sweet Potato and Yam

Sweet potatoes aren't really potatoes and yams aren't really yams. Confused? Let me explain. Sweet potatoes (*Ipomoea batatas*), though they look a lot like potatoes, belong to the morning glory family. They are native to Central and South America. Yams are another species all together, hail from Africa, and aren't grown in the United States. The confusion came when sweet potato growers introduced the orange-fleshed varieties and began calling them yams to distinguish them from the more familiar pale yellow-fleshed earlier varieties.

Sweet potatoes are a warm weather crop that requires a long, hot growing period. They like well-drained loamy or sandy soil that has been well tilled. Many sweet potato growers create raised hills to grow them in.

Start with seedlings (called slips) that have been certified as disease free. Once all danger of frost has passed, plant the slips about 4 inches deep and 8 to 12 inches apart in the raised rows. Feed with a liquid fertilizer. Water regularly. Sweet potatoes will take from 100 to 150 days to mature, so if you live in a cooler climate, you might want to hurry things along a bit by using a black plastic mulch. It will raise the soil temperatures substantially. It will also keep the weeds down.

Garden Guru Says

Rotate the sweet potato crop to another part of the garden every two years to avoid introducing or spreading diseases and pests.

Weeding is important in the early stages of the sweet potato's life, but eventually the vines will sprawl all over the place and crowd out any interlopers.

Harvest the sweet potatoes before the first frost. First cut back the stems and leaves, and then gently sift through the soil with a garden fork. Sweet potatoes are fragile, so if you have a small crop, do this task by hand.

Turnips and Rutabagas

Turnips and rutabagas are members of the Brassica clan, cousins of cabbages and kale. The Latin name for turnip is *Brassica rapa*. Rutabagas go by *Brassica napus*. They are very similar plants, with many of the same growing requirements and preferences.

They both prefer a loose, well-prepared soil with a pH of about 5.5 to 6.8. Raised beds provide an excellent environment for turnips and rutabagas because they do best when the soil is prepared to a depth of at least a foot. You might also consider working in some superphosphate a few months before planting to promote strong root growth.

Turnip

Plant turnip seeds indoors three to four weeks before the last predicted frost date. Outdoors, seeds can go in four to six weeks before that date. Place them in holes ½ inch deep and a couple of inches apart. Thin to about four inches apart when the seedlings are a few inches tall. You can use the thinnings as greens. Successive sowings two weeks apart will give you a longer harvest season for both the tops and the roots.

Food for Thought

According to Irish folklore, the first jack-o'-lantern wasn't carved out of a pumpkin; some fellow named Jack put his candle in a hollowed out turnip.

A second planting in late summer will provide you with a fall crop as long as you can allow about 80 days for them to grow. A late crop might actually have an improved taste, though the flavor will not get better with exposure to frost.

Turnips will appreciate a layer of mulch to keep weeds down and moisture in.

You can harvest individual turnip leaves without jeopardizing the root as long as you don't injure the crown. Harvest the roots any time after they mature. There aren't too many varieties, but each one will have a slightly different maturity time. Remember that smaller roots have a better flavor and more pleasing texture.

If you are more interested in the turnip greens than the roots, add a bit more nitrogen to the soil to promote leaf growth.

Rutabaga

If you've read many English novels you might have seen a mention or two of people eating swedes for dinner. These aren't stories about cannibals! Europeans refer to what we in the United States call rutabagas as swedes, which is a shortened version of the full name, Swedish turnips. Rutabagas are actually a cross between a cabbage and a turnip. The differences between a rutabaga and a turnip are as follows:

Turnip	Rutabaga
Small, round, or elongated root; rough, hairy leaves; white flesh; tinge of purple at neck	Large, round root, smooth, blue-green leaves, yellow flesh

Rutabagas are cool weather plants with a very long growing period. They require 80 to 100 days from seed to harvest, depending on the variety and the growing conditions. Generally, rutabagas are planted in early summer for a fall harvest. They are grown from seed planted ¼ to ½ inches deep about 6 or so inches apart.

The flavor of rutabagas is improved when the plants have been exposed to a light frost or two. And you can leave them in the ground well into the winter if you give them a light blanket of mulch.

Better Beets

Cultivated since prehistoric times, *Beta vulgares*, better known as beets, were originally grown for their green tops. It was the Romans who began eating the round, red roots.

Today, there are many types of beets, including:

- White
- Striped red and white
- Cylindrical
- Gold
- Round
- Baby

Beets like a well-drained, well-cultivated soil with plenty of organic matter and a neutral pH (6.0 to 6.8 is best). To help with root development, mix in some superphosphate well before planting. Beets prefer cooler weather and tend to bolt quickly if temperatures get too hot for their tastes. There are some heat-tolerant varieties for southern gardens.

Start beets from seeds right in the garden as soon as the soil can be worked in the spring. You can plant again in the late summer for a fall harvest. Plant the seeds evenly in a shallow furrow, about ½ inch deep. When the new plants have a few leaves, thin the seedlings to about two or four inches apart and use the thinnings as greens for salad.

Sow beet seeds successively to extend the harvest period. Plant some in late summer for a fall harvest too. Beets are ready to harvest whenever you think they are large enough. Don't let them get oversized, even the larger varieties, because they will be woody and tough.

Parsnips

Pastinaca sativa, parsnips to you non-Latin speakers, is part of the Umbelliferae family whose relatives include carrots, celery, fennel, parsley, and chervil. No one seems to be exactly sure where they came from, but they were around for the ancient Romans to enjoy way back when.

Parsnips look a little like thick, white carrots. They are another cool weather crop that takes a long time—16 to 20 weeks—to mature.

As with all the root vegetables, parsnips prefer their growing environment to be well drained and deeply cultivated. Many gardeners grow parsnips in an area of the garden with soil that was improved the previous year. Parsnips do best with a pH of 6.5 to 7.0.

Plant seeds in the garden in early spring to early summer and be prepared to wait a long time for the new seedlings to appear—it might take a couple of weeks. In fact, parsnips are notoriously slow to germinate. Many gardeners grow radishes in among the parsnips so they know where the parsnips are. Radishes germinate quickly and are harvested well before the parsnips need the space. Plant the parsnip seeds about ¼ inch deep, 2 to 4 inches apart in rows that are from 1½ to 2 feet apart.

Parsnips are ready to harvest when the foliage has died back. Let them stand through a few hard frosts

> **Garden Guru Says**
>
> Parsnips have an aversion to too much nitrogen, so don't add any to the soil where you plan to plant them. If the soil is too rich, parsnip will produce poor quality roots that might split, fork, or grow unappetizing hairs.

to improve the flavor. You can also keep them in the ground over the winter if you cover them with a layer of mulch. Because parsnips are biannual plants (see Chapter 16 for an explanation), they will push out new growth in the spring. If you overwinter your parsnips, harvest them before any new growth appears or they will lose all their flavor.

> **Food for Thought**
>
> Parsnips were used as a meat substitute during Lent in the Middle Ages. Although they don't taste a bit like meat, they do have a heavy, satisfying quality to them that might have felt like meat to serfs. After all, who knows what kind of meat they were used to!

Uh, What's Up Doc?

Bugs Bunny's penchant for carrots (*Daucus carota*) is a latter-day thing in the history of food. Carrots have been around for 5,000 years, though in colors and forms we might not recognize. The orange thing Bugs loves was developed, legend has it, in the sixteenth century by Dutch horticulturists who wanted to honor the royal House of Orange.

> **Prof. Price's Pointers**
>
> Parsnips and turnips have a sweeter flavor when they have been through a heavy frost or two. The reason for this is that the plants respond to the cold by storing more sugar in their roots.

After potatoes and onions, carrots are probably the most popular root vegetable in the United States. And they are grown in gardens everywhere. As with all the root veggies, carrots like well-drained, deeply cultivated soil.

Carrot seeds are tiny, so they are a bit of a challenge to grow. Try mixing the seed with some sand to help with the sowing. Carrots are usually planted in the spring, and sometimes again for a fall crop. Scatter the seeds over a prepared bed and cover with a light layer of soil. You will have to thin them so plant way more than you think you'll need. Keep carrots well watered. Then harvest when they are the size you want.

The Allium Family Album

Onions, leeks, garlic, chives, and shallots are all members of the Allium family and are also distant relatives of lilies. We've already learned (in Chapter 10) that the bulb part of the onion and its cousins are not actually bulbs at all but are in fact a collection of modified leaves that live underground in the form of a bulb. For the purposes of this section, we'll call them bulbs. It's just easier.

Onions

Humans have been eating onions for thousands of years. And every year they seem to want more. According to the National Onion Association, 105 billion pounds of onions are produced worldwide each year. Americans, on average, eat 18.8 pounds per person annually. But that's nothing compared to Libyans, who consume a whopping 66.8 pounds per capita each year!

Prof. Price's Pointers

Plant scientists and agriculture experts call the length of the day or the number of daylight hours in the day the photoperiod. Knowing the photoperiod requirements of the plants you want to grow will help you determine when and what to plant.

Onions prefer a slightly alkaline soil pH of 6.5 to 6.8. They tend to suffer in more acidic soils but will tolerate a pH level of 5.5. As with most of the plants we've been looking at, onions like the soil to be well-drained with plenty of organic matter to help with moisture retention and to boost fertility. Onions are also heavy feeders requiring a feeding of 10-10-10 or 5-10-10 fertilizer, or the equivalent, when the young plants are a few weeks old, then again in a month or so.

The common, everyday onion (*Allium cepa*) is classified in several ways:

Characteristic	Description
Color	White, yellow, or red
Photoperiod	Long-day or short-day
Flavor	Sweet or strong
Bunching	Small, green stems
Use	Fresh or storage
Growth habit	Perennial (Egyptian) or annual/piennial
Shape	Round globe or flat globe

Onions are grown from seeds, sets, or seedlings generally in the early spring as soon as the soil can be worked. Scallions, which are also called green onions, can also be planted in the late summer or early fall for additional harvests.

Plant seeds about ½ inch deep or place sets about two inches below the soil. Allow three to five inches between plants, depending on the variety you are planting.

You can harvest onions at almost any time after the bulb has formed to use fresh. Onions harvested for storage are left in the ground until the leaves have dried up. Then they must be "cured" or dried. Get instructions for curing onions from your County Extension.

Garlic

If you have any experience with Italian, French, Mexican, or Chinese cooking, you've worked with garlic. It originated somewhere in Asia, but people from all over the world claim it as their own.

The biggest difference between garlic and its onion cousins is that the bulb (which, as we know isn't really a bulb) is actually a grouping of cloves that fit together forming the shape we recognize so easily. The other difference is in the leaves. The leaves of onions, leeks, scallions, chives, and shallots are hollow like straws. But the garlic leaf is flat.

> **Garden Guru Says**
>
> Scallions or green onions can be grown as simply immature white onions or from seeds or seedlings specifically designated as scallions. Burpee, for example, offers a variety called Evergreen Long White Bunching Scallion that takes 60 to 120 days to mature from seed sown in spring or summer for harvest in fall through the winter.

There are three basic kinds of garlic—common or softneck (*Allium sativum*), stiffneck (*Allium sativum ophioscorodon*), and elephant (*Allium ampeloprasum*).

As with other onions, garlic is a heavy feeder and will appreciate a rich soil enhanced with organic matter and fertilizer. Plant seed cloves in early spring in northern zones or as a fall or winter crop where the weather is warmer. The small cloves should be at a depth of ½ to 1 inch, spaced 3 to 5 inches apart.

Harvest the garlic when the green tops have dried up and fallen off.

Shallot

These elegant little members of the onion clan are de rigueur in French cuisine and add a delicate flavor to all kinds of dishes. They aren't grown all that often in the home garden, but they should be—they aren't particularly difficult and they don't take up much space.

Shallots (*Allium ascalonicum*) have the same basic requirements as the other onions. New plants are grown from sets and planted as early as the soil can be worked in cool zones or as a fall or winter crop in warm parts of the country. The sets are placed pointy end up about ½ to 1 inch deep and 3 to 5 inches apart.

Shallots are harvested when the foliage begins to die back.

Leek

The leek (*Allium porrum*) is the national symbol of Wales, but in France it's known as the poor man's asparagus. Though still not an everyday vegetable in the United States, their popularity is growing as Americans become more adventuresome.

Leeks look like scallions on steroids. They have thick stems that are white at the bulb end and become increasingly green toward the leaf part. The bulb never actually develops but stays about the same width as the rest of the stem. The stem must be blanched in order for it to be white.

Leeks are generally grown from seed, which can be planted indoors about 10 to 14 weeks before they are set out in early spring.

To plant the seedlings, dig a narrow trench about six inches wide and a foot deep. Place each leek transplant upright in the trench, spacing them about four inches apart, and add just enough soil to hold them upright. Water thoroughly, but don't fill in the trench. As the leeks grow, add more soil so that the stem is nearly covered. Keep on filling the trench as the plants grow, eventually hilling the soil up so that just a couple of inches of green stem show.

Allow anywhere from 12 to 15 weeks for leeks to mature for harvest. Try growing a few extra plants to harvest early as baby leeks.

The Least You Need to Know

- Don't allow young potato tubers to be exposed to the sun. If they are, and they turn green, throw them out.
- Blanch leek stems to give them their distinctive white stem.
- Harvest rutabagas after they've experienced a light frost or two for enhanced flavor.
- Don't give parsnips a very rich soil.

Chapter 16

Herbs

In This Chapter

◆ Easy-to-grow essential culinary herbs

◆ Annual herbs to grow from seeds or seedlings

◆ Perennial favorites

◆ Some delicate herbs to bring inside in cold weather

◆ Exotic and esoteric herbs to try

◆ Growing herbs with medicinal powers

It didn't take long for our ancestors to figure out that certain plants taste good or satisfy hunger, some plants improve the taste of food, others make folks feel sick, and still others make them feel better when they were under the weather. Obviously this sequence of discovery didn't happen in a week, but instead took several thousand years. Eventually, someone developed the bright idea of growing all those feel-better and taste-better plants, and the concept of the herb garden was born.

Today, herb gardening is one of the most popular forms of edible gardening—and one of the easiest. *Herbs* will grow in poor soils, will thrive with a minimum of care, and generally take up far less space than most vegetables. In this chapter, we'll explore growing a wide variety of edible herbs, from the culinary basics to exotic specialty types, as well as those known for their curative powers.

An early American herb garden might have looked like the one shown in this drawing. Typically, the herb garden would contain a mix of culinary, medicinal, and fragrant herbs including thyme, sage, parsley, lavender, hyssop, chamomile, and horehound.

Easy and Essential Herbs

There are a few herbs that no good cook can do without. Can you imagine a world without basil or parsley? And what's a baked potato without a few snips of fresh chives? I can't bear the thought of ice tea without sprigs of fresh mint to liven it up. These four essential herbs are among the easiest of all herbs to grow.

Partial to Parsley

Parsley (*petroselinum crispum*) is the number one essential herb. Cooks of every persuasion use both the curly variety and the flat-leafed Italian type to enhance just about any foods you can imagine. This *biannual* plant is easy to start from seed especially if you soak the seeds overnight. In cooler zones, start the seeds inside about seven weeks before the last predicted frost.

Food for Thought

Here's an herbal primer—from monks to mothers:

Starting in the Middle Ages, monks added the practice of medicine and the production of herbal remedies to their religious responsibilities. Elaborate herb gardens (called "physick" gardens in the British Isles) sprouted up within the stone walls of monasteries. Later, growing herbs became women's work as these culinary and medicinal plants were incorporated into kitchen gardens. In colonial America, herbs were usually grown just outside the kitchen door in gardens like the one in the drawing here. Many herbs had both culinary and medicinal uses, while some had nonedible functions including as insect repellants (artemisia and tansy) and simply to make a room smell good (lavender and sweet woodruff).

In recent years, the "country" lifestyle trend promoted in shelter magazines and how-to books spawned enormous interest in herb gardening. That interest continues to be widespread.

In warm areas, sow outside directly in the garden. Once the seedlings are a couple inches tall, you can thin them to about three inches apart. If you are pressed for time or just plain lazy, buy young plants.

With its two-year life span, parsley can survive in cold conditions. I actually picked parsley in the snow in my Zone 5 vegetable garden, though it can become a little bitter and tough in its second season. Because parsley is so easy to grow from seeds or seedlings, most gardeners treat it as an annual.

Prof. Price's Pointers

A smaller group of plants, including a few herbs, belongs to the **biannual** category. (They are also sometimes called biennial.) These plants take two years to go through their growth cycle. In the first year, they germinate and produce leaves. Then in the second season, they produce flowers and seeds.

Basil Is Best

Known officially as sweet basil or *Ocimum basillicum*, this easy-to-grow annual herb is essential in Italian cooking. Several varieties are available, including a very pretty purple type. But the medium-green classic variety is the one to grow for making pesto and spaghetti sauce and to serve with fresh tomatoes and mozzarella cheese. I begin to drool just thinking about it.

Sow basil seeds thinly (about 8 or 10 seeds per inch) indoors in mid-spring in cold climates. Plant seeds directly in the garden as soon as temperatures are reliably over 50 degrees.

Food for Thought

Aside from having the opportunity to be a botanical smarty pants, there's really no other reason to know about biannuals, except when it comes to caraway. Caraway leaves can be used in salads and the root is sometimes cooked or even eaten raw like a radish, but the seeds are the main attraction. And caraway plants don't produce seeds until their second year.

Angelica is another biannual. Its leaves should be picked in the second year for use as a condiment, and the two-year-old stems can be candied like orange peel. Parsley is the most common of the biannuals. In fact, it's probably the most well known and most-used of all herbs.

Set out seedlings when they have four leaves and after all danger of frost. As plants grow, pinch back the top to make them bushier.

Also pinch back any flower buds as they form to encourage the basil to keep on producing all those tasty leaves. And always grow lots of it. You'll need handfuls to make fresh pesto.

Much Ado About Mint

I'm including mint in this selection of easy and essential herbs mostly because mint is easier to grow than just about any plant I can think of. Mint is a perennial herb. In fact, we can include mint in the "invasive plant" category, meaning that you can't get rid of it even if you want to. Think "the eggplant that ate Chicago." But a little bit of mint is, as Martha would say, "a good thing." The two most common varieties are spearmint and peppermint. There are also apple, pineapple, and orange flavored mints for gardeners who like to show off. All are available as seedlings.

Garden Guru Says

To prevent mint from taking over the entire garden, place plants in plastic or terracotta pots and plant the pots. Leave a bit of pot rim (about an inch or two) above the surface of the soil. Every few years, dig it up and replace the pot with a larger one, adding more soil. Or unpot the mint, trim back the roots and repot with fresh soil.

Another method for growing mint is from a root cutting (anyone with mint growing in his yard will be delighted to give you a handful of roots). Just stick a bit of the root (with some stem and leaves attached) into a pot with some soil, water it, and stand back.

Crazy About Chives

Think of chives as itty, bitty onions, because that is exactly what they are. Chives are especially easy to grow, unless you insist on starting them from seed. But why bother? Chive plants are easy to find. And once you have a mature clump or two growing in your herb garden, you can divide them to produce more (see Chapter 23). Actually, you'll need to divide them every three to four years to keep the clumps healthy. Place chive plants about a foot apart as soon as the soil can be worked. To harvest, snip the hollow stems at their base.

Chives produce pretty, papery, pink blooms, which are very decorative in the herb garden, in pots, or among other perennials. They are also edible. This is one herb plant you can allow to bloom without sacrificing flavor.

One at a Time

As you've most likely figured out by now, some herbs are annual plants: They go through their entire life cycle from germination to flowering and seed production in one year. The following annual herbs are among gardeners' favorites.

Delightful Dill

One of the tallest herbs we'll look at in this chapter, dill can reach four feet, though there are dwarf varieties. Feathery dill leaves are used to flavor pickles and fatty fish like salmon. The seeds are also used as a flavoring. I love cucumber and onion salad with sour cream and lots of dill.

Growing dill from seed is a bit of a pain in cold zones. The seeds can't be planted outside until the last frost, but they need about three weeks to germinate, so you wind up waiting well into the summer season to harvest. And since it doesn't transplant very well, starting the seeds indoors is iffy unless you start the seeds in peat pots, eggshells, or homemade paper starting cups. The seeds need light to germinate, so lay them directly on top of the soil.

Be sure to do successive plantings every couple of weeks until the weather gets too hot. Dill hates hot weather. I prefer to buy dill as seedlings so I can start harvesting it early. I also like to use it as a decorative addition to pots of flowers on the terrace.

Coriander (a.k.a. Chinese Parsley)

Unless you've been living in a cave for the last 10 years, you already know about coriander. It's an essential ingredient for Mexican and Chinese cooking, and another relatively easy-to-grow annual herb. I say relatively easy because it does have one little quirk—coriander hates hot weather. The seeds will germinate in about 10 days, so there's no need to start them indoors. Instead plant outdoors after the last frost, and then start a new crop every couple weeks. The plants will grow quickly until the heat gets to them. They will either stop growing and look awful, or die. Not to worry. As soon as the weather cools a little in the early fall, start another crop. In places like Arizona, Florida, or South Texas where summer temperatures soar, consider coriander a winter herb.

Summer Savory

More gardeners should grow this great herb. It's easy to start from seed indoors (about two months before the last frost), though it will take up to a month to sprout. The seeds need light to germinate, so place them on top of the soil. You can also grow this herb from cuttings. The easiest way to add summer savory to your herb garden is to buy small plants, though you aren't likely to find them everywhere. Plant seeds and plants in a good potting soil with some compost added because this is one herb that likes a richer soil than most.

Summer savory is very versatile in the kitchen. It tastes a little like thyme but a bit spicier. Use it to add flavor to meat, fish, poultry, beans, eggs, and potatoes.

Summer Savory will grow to almost two feet and might need to be supported (see Chapter 11).

Fabulous Fennel

There are two types of fennel, and it's the annual bronze variety that is usually found in an herb garden—though not often enough for my tastes. It is a gorgeous, feathery plant that can reach four feet in height and is often grown just for its good looks. But its leaves and seeds, with their licorice flavor, are used to enhance fish, sausages, salads, and cookies.

Bronze fennel will grow easily from seed in ordinary, or even sandy, garden soil. Plant it after the last frost and it will germinate in about two weeks. To keep the leaves looking their best, pinch out flower buds regularly. A few weeks before the first frost of fall you can allow the flowers to bloom, and then collect the seeds to use for winter cooking.

In warmer zones (though not where it's really hot), bronze fennel will behave like a perennial.

Chic as Chervil

No French chef could survive without a source of fresh chervil to use in salads, and as a flavoring for meat, poultry, fish, vegetables, eggs, and vinegar. It's also an essential ingredient for "herbes fines."

But it's still not a household herb in the United States, even though it is so easy to grow. Start the seeds outdoors in spring as soon as the soil is workable. Like dill seeds, chervil seeds need light to germinate. New sprouts will appear in about two weeks. If you find you like using chervil in your cooking, plan on making successive plantings so you'll have a steady supply.

Like coriander and dill, chervil hates the heat, so avoid new plantings in very hot weather. Unlike most herbs, chervil will tolerate shade. In fact, it prefers a shady location, and it doesn't like to dry out.

Perennial Favorites

One of the most beautiful herb gardens I have ever seen is at Sissinghurst Castle in the south of England. It's a huge square intersected by flagstone paths and surrounded by a tall hedge. And it is filled with perennial herbs—including such culinary varieties as thyme, rosemary, and sage—that form a gorgeous tapestry of colors, shapes, and textures.

Perennial herbs are the aristocrats of the herb world. As important as parsley and basil are, somehow the perennials described in this section are a step above. They are also a boon for thrifty souls. Buy a few of these plants (or start them from seed) and enjoy the harvest for years.

> **Garden Guru Says**
>
> To help herb plants produce the tastiest and most aromatic leaves, use fertilizer sparingly. It's better to under fertilize than to use too much. You can follow mixing directions on the product label, but don't use it as often as prescribed. Or mix the fertilizer at half-strength and use it according to the suggested schedule.

Oregano

You can't make spaghetti sauce, pizza, or an Italian hoagie without this pungent perennial herb. Oregano (*Origanum onites*) is easy to grow from seed, germinating in just 8 to 10 days. But it needs a pretty long growing season before the leaves are ready to harvest. So in cold areas, seeds should be started indoors six to eight weeks before the soil can be worked. In warmer zones, they can go directly in the garden. Plants are also easy to find.

Oregano is a low-growing herb, never reaching more than about 18 inches tall. It will spread rapidly but doesn't become invasive like mint. Divide oregano plants every three or four years to keep them full. Frequent harvesting will also encourage lots of new growth. Oregano might need a little bit of protective mulch in very cold climates, unless there is continuous snow cover.

You will find several varieties of oregano available in seed catalogs and nurseries including Spanish, Mexican, and Cuban. But when cooking Italian, use the Greek type (go figure!).

Sage Savvy

For the past four years I've been neglecting a large sage plant that just refuses to die. Originally I planted it so that its silvery color would complement the bright annuals in a large container. The savory, mint-flavored leaves were just a bonus for flavoring poultry and fish dishes. After three years in the pot, I pulled it out because it had become too large. Now it sits in a corner of the garden, where I had dumped it without any sort of proper planting. I feel a little guilty when I yank off handfuls of its leaves. I don't recommend this kind of treatment. But it does prove just how tough sage is.

Sage, whose Latin name is *Salvia officinalis*, prefers dry conditions with a slightly alkaline soil, but don't go out of your way to meet these needs. You can sow sage seeds outside as soon as the soil is workable, or start them indoors about a month earlier. The seeds will sprout in a week or two. Young plants are readily available, too.

Sage produces spikes of pretty purplish-pink blooms that are very attractive to bees. Pinching out buds will force the plant to put more energy into its leaves. Or you can look for one of the bloomless varieties ("Dalmatian" and "Berggarten") though they might not be easy to find.

Time for Thyme

Sissinghurst Castle (which is sort of a Mecca for gardeners), has another herbal wonder—a large walkway completely carpeted with thyme plants. The concept is that when you walk on the springy, low-growing lawn of thyme plants, the fabulous scent will be released. It's quite a romantic, though impractical, design.

Thyme (*Thymus vulgaris*) is a really important herb for French cuisine. And though it is usually used sparingly because of its strong flavor, no herb garden should be without at least one plant. Look for English or French thyme for the basic flavor.

Specialty nurseries sell orange, lemon, caraway, and even coconut-flavored thymes for the gardener who has everything.

Grow thyme from cuttings or buy small plants. They like dry conditions and will require a light soil. Pinch a few sprigs regularly to encourage healthy new growth and be prepared to replace tired plants after three or four years.

King Tarragon

The French call tarragon the king of herbs, and we should be paying attention. It is used to flavor poultry, fish, and cheeses and is essential for creating béarnaise sauce.

Creative cooks also make flavored mayonnaise, butter, vinegar, oils, and mustard with tarragon, which is called *Artemisia dracuinculus* in Latin. But it's important to use only French tarragon for these things. The very common Russian form of the herb is all but flavorless.

Tarragon is a bushy herb that will grow to two or three feet in height and width. It doesn't mind very poor soil and likes dry conditions. It is hardy even in very cold climates as long as there is excellent drainage.

Be prepared to divide or replace tarragon every few years.

Food for Thought

These little bundles of herbs are used to flavor all kinds of soups, stews, roasts, and casseroles. Depending on what French cooking expert you talk to, a bouquet garni is made of three sprigs of thyme, four sprigs of parsley, and one bay leaf; or three springs of parsley, one spring of thyme, and one bay leaf; or five springs of thyme, two bay leaves, and three sprigs of parsley. You can either make little bouquets of the herbs and tie the stems together with a piece of string, or place the bundle in a square or circle of cheesecloth folded up to form a pouch, and then tie the pouch closed with string.

Another French herbal traditional is called *herbes fines*, which just means fine herbs. This is the same concept as the bouquet garni, but these are usually tied as a bundle without the cheesecloth, or they are finely chopped. The most common combination is equal amounts of chives, tarragon, parsley, and chervil.

Tender and Tasty

Among the most-often used culinary herbs are a few that are part of a class of plants known as tender perennials. This means that that they will live for several years as long as they are protected from cold weather. Some are more tender than others.

Rosemary

If tarragon is the king of herbs, rosemary must be the queen. There are more than a few cooks who would select this exquisitely aromatic herb if they could choose only one to grow. Rosemary is used to flavor poultry and meats, especially lamb and pork, and vegetables.

Don't even attempt to grow rosemary from seed. It's way too hard. You can buy young plants at any good garden center. If you like to make things difficult, start new plants from cuttings. Rosemary isn't too fussy about soil as long as it's well drained. What's really important to remember is that this plant will not survive winters in any place cooler than Zone 8. But if you live where it's warm, you can have rosemary shrubs up to six feet tall.

Be diligent about not overwatering and give your rosemary plants plenty of room and good air circulation—they are prone to mildew.

To grow rosemary in cool places, keep it in pots so you can bring it inside easily. Put the pot in your sunniest window, or even consider using a grow light during the short winter days. Water your rosemary sparingly, letting it dry out between waterings, and never let the pot sit in standing water. Use a mister to keep humidity levels high.

The Noble Bay

Another of the herb world's aristocrats, bay leaf (a.k.a. sweet bay or bay laurel) has a long history, going back to ancient Rome and Greece (think of the laurel wreath around Caesar's head). In warm areas (Zones 8 to 10), it grows as an evergreen tree that can reach 10 feet or so. Everywhere else it's grown as a potted plant. Bay grows slowly and can be kept to a manageable size with root pruning.

Don't bother trying to start a bay plant on your own. Buy an established one and be prepared to baby it for a long time. This means a slightly acidic soil (a pH of 6.2 or so), full sun indoors, afternoon shade outdoors, careful attention to watering (don't let it dry out but don't let roots become water logged), and moderate amounts of fertilizer.

Bay leaf is used to flavor soups, stews, shellfish dishes, and a variety of sauces.

Sweet as Marjoram

A close relative of oregano, sweet marjoram has a slightly stronger flavor and is less hardy (except for another cousin, pot marjoram). It grows in nice, neat clumps to about a foot or two high and is evergreen in Zones 8 to 10. Marjoram can be grown from seeds started about six weeks before the last hard frost, or from cuttings. Plants are easy to find too. This herb prefers a slightly alkaline soil in the pH range of 7 to 8.

For the best flavor, pinch back flower buds as they form. And to keep the plant nice and bushy, harvest small sprigs of leaves frequently.

Windowsill Herb Gardens

Fresh herbs are an essential ingredient of fine cooking year round, but I hate to pay grocery store prices for a bunch of rosemary, basil, or tarragon. And even more annoying, I have to buy a whole bunch even when I only need a few sprigs. The rest winds up rotting in the vegetable drawer of the fridge—an expensive mess. Instead of overpaying and wasting, grow a few frequently used herbs on a sunny windowsill right in the kitchen.

You might have to replace indoor plants more often than the ones you have outside because they might not like the conditions in the house. But your chances of success will improve with plenty of sun and a relatively cool temperature.

Food for Thought _____

The following are good candidates for a windowsill herb garden:

- ◆ Parsley (both flat-leafed or curly)
- ◆ Rosemary
- ◆ Coriander
- ◆ Sage
- ◆ Thyme
- ◆ French tarragon
- ◆ Mint

Not Your Everyday Herb

Dedicated foodies as well as ambitious gardeners might enjoy experimenting with some other herbs that might not be as well known or as often grown as the traditional parsley, sage, rosemary, and thyme.

Thai One on with Lemongrass

If you like to cook Thai or Southeast Asian food, lemongrass is a must. A tropical perennial, lemongrass is grown as an annual everywhere except in the hottest climates. Start new plants by dividing existing ones or look for young plants to buy.

Lemongrass plants tend to need a richer soil than most herbs and they like slightly more moist conditions. You can bring these plants indoors before the weather gets cold and they will do pretty well. A grow light and regular misting will help. I have heard that cats like to chew on lemongrass leaves which could be a plus or a minus depending on your point of view.

High on Hyssop

Hyssop is a really old-fashioned herb, one that was grown by the ancient Hebrews and perhaps even earlier. Known mostly for its medicinal properties, the fresh leaves of the hyssop plant are also used to flavor salads and soups, and to make tea.

Hyssop is a very hardy perennial that can stay evergreen even in severe cold climates. Where winter temperatures regularly drop below zero degrees Fahrenheit, you might need to use a thick layer of mulch. It will grow to about three feet high and about half as wide. Start seeds indoors about two months or so before the last predicted frost. Hyssop can also be grown from cuttings or by dividing existing plants. Expect to replace hyssop plants every four years or when they become very woody and rangy.

Borage Is Not Boring

Borage is an annual herb with cucumber flavored leaves which are used in salads or to flavor meats and vegetables. The crunchy stems and the beautiful blue flowers are also edible. Plant seeds or seedlings outdoors after the last predicted frost. New sprouts will appear in a week or so. Do successive sowings every two or three weeks for a steady supply until it gets very hot.

Exotic or Esoteric Herbs to Grow

Herb	Usages	Annual or Perennial
Lovage	Celery flavored seeds and leaves	Perennial
Horehound	Used for teas and candy	Tender perennial
Mexican mint marigold	Substitute for tarragon	Tender perennial
Curry plant	Curry flavor	Tender perennial
Winter savory	Spicy seasoning for meat, fish, poultry	Perennial
Anise	Licorice-flavored leaves, seed, and flower	Annual
Shiso	Tastes like mix of cilantro, cumin, and parsley	Annual
Mitsuba	Japanese wild parsley	Perennial

A Taste of Your Own Medicine

Before herbs were stirred into the cook pot to flavor foods, they were used to cure every kind of ill from headache to insomnia. Some medicinal uses were nothing more than quackery, but many continue to be reliable alternatives to what we now consider traditional medical practice. The following list contains just a few of the many herbs used for medicinal purposes.

Herb	Medicinal Use
Comfrey	Skin care
Rosemary	Headache cure
Sage	Reduces fever
Chamomile	Encourages sleep; cures upset stomach
Lemon verbena	Encourages sleep
Italian parsley	Diuretic
Hyssop	Expectorant; cough suppressant
Horehound	Cures sore throat; helps with digestion
Feverfew	Stops migraine; helps with digestion
Clary sage	Treats eye ailments
Thyme	Helps with digestion; antiseptic
Tarragon	Anti-bacterial
Valerian	Sedative; pain relief
Chicory	Diuretic; laxative
Lovage	Eases intestinal gas
Calendula	Heals wounds
Tansy	Treats worms
Chervil	Skin freshener

CAUTION

Compost Pile

While traditional folk medicine makes wide use of herbal concoctions and recipes, one should proceed with a great deal of caution. The strength of homemade remedies might vary widely, presenting the risk of allergic reaction, overdose, or even the potential of life-threatening poisoning. If this aspect of growing and using herbs appeals to you, you should take the time to read some of the many books on the topic. You might also look for classes, seminars, or workshops on medicinal herbs. Visit the website for the Herb Society of America (www.herbsociety.org) to find an herb group in your area.

The Least You Need to Know

◆ Herbs are annual, perennial, and biannual plants with culinary, medicinal, or aromatic qualities.

◆ Grow herbs in a spot that is convenient to the kitchen for easy harvesting.

- Provide herb plants with well-drained soil and at least six hours of sunlight a day.

- Avoid overfertilizing herb plants to ensure the best flavor.

- Pay close attention to the cultural requirements of each herb you plan to grow so that you can adequately meet their needs.

- Be careful when using herbs to create your own remedies.

Chapter 17

Exotic, Unusual, and Esoteric Edibles

In This Chapter

- ◆ Get a taste for Asian vegetables
- ◆ Find out about growing artichokes and asparagus
- ◆ Look into some of the world's more esoteric vegetables
- ◆ Heirloom vegetables

In some parts of the country, plants elsewhere considered exotic are every-day fare. Okra is almost ubiquitous in Deep South gardens, for example, but might be rarely seen in Maine or Michigan. Artichokes are common along the central coast of California but an uncommon sight almost every-where else. Bok choy, mitsuba, and mizuna are staples in gardens tended by Koreans, Chinese, Vietnamese, and others of Asian descent, but are still far from standard in mainstream backyard gardens. And specialty roots like kohlrabi, horseradish, and fennel have devoted followings, but aren't in everyone's garden vocabulary.

In this chapter, we broaden our gardening horizons a little and perhaps help bring a little more diversity to our dinner tables.

Asian Specialties

As the number of Asian Americans increases, so does our awareness of the specialty vegetables many people of that community consider everyday fare. Most grocery stores now carry bok choy and Chinese cabbage. We look at some of these basics, and suggest a few more you might want to try.

Bok Choy

An essential for stir-fried vegetable dishes, bok choy has become more or less a mainstream vegetable in many markets. Bok Choy is a cool weather green that grows in rich, well-cultivated soil, and will bolt when the temperature rises. It's becoming an important fall and winter farm crop in parts of the Southwest where winters are warm.

Bok Choy, whose Latin name is *Brassica rapa sp. Chinensia*, goes by many names, depending on the heritage of the person who is growing or buying it:

- Pak choy
- Baak choi
- Chongee
- Joi choy
- Pai tsa
- Tak tsai

Sow bok choy seeds about a foot apart in well-prepared beds as soon as the soil can be worked. Keep them well watered. The seeds will germinate in a week or so, especially if the soil is nice and warm. You can begin harvesting individual leaves as soon as they are a few inches long. Small heads of bok choy can be cut at the soil line when they are as little as six inches high—then it's baby bok choy which is really expensive to buy. You can continue to harvest individual leaves or wait to pick nice big heads later in the season.

Mitsuba

Also known as Japanese parsley, *Cryptotaenia japonica* or mitsuba is a hardy perennial that grows in USDA Zones 4 through 9. In colder places it's grown as an annual. Sow seeds in late spring and again in late summer for an abundant harvest. You can make additional sowings every month or so throughout the summer. Mitsuba will grow in the shade and prefers rich soil with plenty of organic matter worked into it. Harvest about 50 days from seed planting by cutting individual stems.

Mizuna

Mizuna is a loose-heading lettuce-type green with curly leaves that look a little like endive, but are very dark green. It is sometimes called Kyoto greens. Mizuna tolerates more heat than most lettuces and is grown much the same way.

Prepare the soil so that it is rich and light with lots of organic matter. Sow the seeds on top of the soil (they need light to germinate), and pat them gently into the soil. Keep the seeds well watered using a fine mist. The seeds will germinate quickly, and you might actually begin to harvest tiny, baby greens just a couple weeks after sowing.

Some other Asian favorites include the following.

Name	Type of Plant
Malabar spinach	Leafy green
Hon-Tsai-Tai	Leafy green
Gai Choy	Chinese mustard green
Komatsuna	Chinese mustard spinach grown for leaves, stalks, and flowers
Dau gok	Chinese long bean, like a snap bean
Nira	Chinese chives
Een Choi	Amaranth spinach
Kintsai	Asian celery
Kailaan	Chinese kale
Shiso	Leaf and stalk vegetable
Santoh	Chinese cilantro
Kobu Takana	Horned mustard
Gai lum	Chinese broccoli
Choy Sum	Chinese flowering cabbage

Specialty of the House

The vegetables profiled in the next few sections might be completely unfamiliar to you, or they might be things you grew up on. Most of these are not available everywhere all the time, making them special to many of us.

Growing Oysters in the Garden

Salsify, also known as oyster plant, is an old root vegetable that, according to his garden diaries, was a favorite of Thomas Jefferson, who imported the seeds from Europe. It looks a little like a parsnip only longer and thinner. Salsify got it's oyster plant name because it does actually taste like oysters. Some gourmet food markets will occasionally offer salsify for sale, but generally if you crave this unusual root vegetable, you'll have to grow it yourself. Look for seeds from specialty companies. It goes by several names:

- Salsify
- Oyster plant
- Vegetable oyster
- Tragopogon porrifolius

Salsify is grown much the same way other tap-rooted root vegetables including parsnips and Daikon radishes are. They need the soil to be deeply cultivated, well-drained, with a pH of 6.0 to 6.5, and rich with organic matter. Salsify takes up to 150 days from seed to harvest, and should be planted as early as the soil can be worked. Sow seeds one or two inches apart, and then thin out the weaker seedlings leaving a spacing of three or four inches. You can use the green leaves of the thinnings for salad or cook them like beet greens. You can also plant salsify as a fall crop in warm zones. Salsify is very cold tolerant, and some gardeners say it tastes better if the plant experiences a heavy frost. Harvest by pulling up the entire plant.

Not a Green Tomato

Nearly 30 years ago when I lived in Mexico, I was introduced to the tomatillo (*Physalis philadelphica*) or husk tomato, an essential for salsa and enchiladas verdes. Today, tomatillos can be found in many grocery stores in areas with a large Latino population. But they still aren't universally available, so you might want to consider growing your own.

It is not a tomato, or even a close relative, but a completely different plant. The tomatillo does look a lot like a tiny green tomato, but it is more firm, has a thicker skin and is covered in a husk that has the thickness and texture of tracing paper. Start tomatillo from seeds using the same methods you would for tomatoes. These are warm weather plants, so you'll need to wait until all danger of frost has past. Allow about 100 days from seed to harvest, though some varieties require less growing time. Tomatillos are large plants that have a tendency to sprawl all over the place. Using tomato cages might help keep them under control. Harvest tomatillos when the outer husk splits open.

Broccoli Raab

Say hello to yet another *Brassica*, this one *B. rapa*, sometimes known as *B. ruvo*. Broccoli raab is a cool weather plant popular with those who like Italian cuisine. The stems, leaves, and tiny unopened flower buds are the parts we eat.

Broccoli raab, which is also called rapini, likes well-drained, rich soil with lots of organic matter mixed in and a pH of 6.5 to 8.0. It can be direct seeded in beds or grown from transplants. Place plants about 6 to 12 inches apart. This fast growing plant will bolt if exposed to hot weather, so get it going in early spring for a late spring harvest or in late summer for a fall harvest. In places like California and Arizona, broccoli raab is a winter crop.

Okra

This is yet another plant known by more than one name: *Abelmoschus esculentus* or *Hibiscus esculentus*. It is a relative of the ornamental hibiscus, and interestingly enough, cotton. Okra is pretty easy to grow requiring a neutral soil, lots of sun, and warm temperatures. You can start seeds outdoors about two weeks after the last frost or start them indoors about six to eight weeks before that date. To give the seeds a head start, place them between a couple wet paper towels overnight before planting. Sow the seeds about ½ inch deep in medium-size hills placed about 2 feet apart. Okra gets pretty tall, sometimes up to about five feet.

While most vegetable plants like well-drained soil, okra is particularly picky about it. It's better to underwater than to overwater this plant.

The edible part of okra is the immature seed pod. Harvest when the pods are no more than six inches long.

> **Garden Guru Says**
>
> With its big white flowers, okra can be a very pretty plant. Try using it in an ornamental bed as well as the vegetable patch.

Heirlooms

In Chapter 13, we defined heirloom plants as an open-pollinated variety introduced more than 50 years ago. More specifically, heirloom varieties are the resurrected varieties of plants that were grown by farmers and gardeners before the mass production and mass distribution of seed, and before farming became big business. Here, we'll look at some specific heirlooms that are particularly interesting and fun to grow, including tomatoes, corn, squash, and peppers.

Tomatoes

Among the most fascinating heirloom plants are tomatoes, many of them throwbacks to the turn of the century. One of the joys of these old-fashioned plants is that they retain the true tomato flavor that is often lacking in the new varieties which have been bred for disease resistant, uniform size, ripening qualities, and long shelf life often at the expense of flavor.

Food for Thought

In Prof. Price's 1942 Victory Garden in Long Beach, California, he grew the relatively new Rutgers tomato that had been introduced in 1934. That tomato became the standard for decades until plant scientists developed newer varieties to meet the demands of the canned food industry.

Heirloom tomatoes are grown using the same techniques as modern tomatoes. Some might need careful staking, others are not particularly prolific and a few might be a bit more susceptible to diseases. But if true tomato flavor is one of your favorite things, growing heirloom varieties will be worth the effort.

Check the following tables for a few varieties to look for.

Variety	Color	Fruit	Size
Big Rainbow	Gold with red highlights	Very large fruit	Tall
Aunt Ruby's Green	Green with gold centers	Very large fruit	Tall
Green Grape	Gold-green	Cherry type	
Brandywine	Pink-red	Beefsteak-type fruit	Upright plant
Rutgers	Tomato red	Traditional shape	Tall
Cherokee Purple	Purple-red	Extra large fruit	Large plant
Yellow Pear	Bright yellow	Pear-shape, small fruit	Prolific
Super Italian Paste	Red-orange	Elongated, lumpy fruit	Large plant

Corn

Corn is another one of those vegetables that has been extensively hybridized to the point that some purists find ridiculous. Today, mass-produced corn has been bred to stay sweet days after picking which is a boon for those who can't grow their own and don't live near enough to a farm to buy it fresh. But that sweet taste, some would argue, is a far cry from the true corn taste that is so dear to our American heritage. Heirloom varieties, including some hybrids developed around the turn of the century and even earlier, allow gardeners to step back in time.

Prof. Price's Pointers

Burpee has done a lot with corn heirlooms. For example, they now offer Golden Bantam, which they first introduced in 1902. At that time, most Americans preferred white corn because it was thought to be a higher quality. Golden Bantam changed people's opinion of yellow corn because it was easy to grow and matured earlier than other varieties. Other Burpee corn heirlooms include Country Gentleman, a white corn with shoe-peg kernels (they are irregular along the cob, rather than in rows), and Stowell's Evergreen, an early relative of the ubiquitous Silver Queen, that was first developed in 1848.

Heirloom corn is grown the same way new varieties are. The big difference is that these old varieties will tend to lose their flavor soon after picking, so get that pot boiling before you head to the corn field.

Squash

Old-fashioned squash varieties are, for the most part, a pretty funny looking bunch. Many of them are winter types, including pumpkins, and a lot of them have strange shapes and lots of lumps and warts. One particularly interesting one is Long Island Cheese squash. It is shaped sort of like a wheel of cheese, is tan on the outside like a butternut squash, and bright orange inside. And each fruit can weigh as much as 20 pounds! Another old beauty is the True Hubbard. The Burpee heirloom catalog says it might have originated somewhere in the Caribbean and was brought to Massachusetts in 1798.

Heirloom squash are grown using the same planting methods as modern varieties of squash.

Baby Vegetables

Some of what we call baby vegetables are just that. They are the plant's fruit picked when it is still in its early stage of development—far enough along to look and taste like that vegetable but with a milder flavor and tender texture. Other so-called baby vegetables are actually varieties that have been bred to be tiny versions of the original.

Harvesting baby vegetables is done using the same techniques as for mature vegetables that are described in Chapter 24; it's just done earlier. You'll also find some hints about when to harvest baby vegetables. Among the vegetables that can be harvested when very young and tender are as follows:

- Bok choy
- Zucchini
- Beets
- Potatoes
- Carrots
- Artichoke
- Eggplant
- Fennel
- Crooked neck squash
- Spinach
- Scallions
- String beans
- Asparagus

Vegetable plants with varieties that are bred specifically for their mini size include the following:

- Beets
- Eggplant
- Tomatoes
- Squash
- Carrots
- Potatoes
- Pumpkin
- Watermelon

Perennials—They Keeping Coming Back

Most vegetables are grown as annual plants. We harvest them when they fruit and generally the plant dies and we replant the next year. A few vegetables are biennials (plants that develop roots, leaves, and stems in their first year, but do not flower and produce fruit or seed until the second season).

But we still harvest them in the first year and ignore their two-year life cycle. But a few vegetables are true perennials that go through the fruit production cycle year in and year out. Artichokes and asparagus are the best-known and most-often grown perennial vegetable plants. Another plant, cardoons, are popular in Europe but still don't have a large following in this country.

Globe Artichoke

Globe artichokes are huge, beautiful plants (Latin name *Cynara scolymus*) that produce flower buds treasured by gourmets and gourmands all over the world. And though they are considered a delicacy, artichokes aren't all that difficult to grow, as long as you provide them with a hospitable environment. For the most part, artichokes prefer relatively cool weather. According to the Reimer Seed Company, they need 250 hours of below 50 degrees Fahrenheit to set their buds. That's only about 10½ days. If you grow artichokes from seed, you should start them indoors about six to eight weeks before the setout time that is after the last predicted frost. In warmer climates, plant artichokes in the late fall for a spring harvest. But be advised, artichokes really don't like very hot weather. And they do require regular irrigation. Globe artichokes are reliably hardy in USDA Zones 8 to 10. In Zones 6 and 7, they might survive milder winters with a good layer of mulch.

Place artichoke plants about two or three feet apart. To harvest, pick the immature flower buds along with a couple of inches of stem using a sharp knife. Artichoke plants will die back in colder zones but will grow year round in places like Castroville, California, which is known as the artichoke capital of the world. California artichokes produce from March through May and again in October through December. Some artichoke growers cut plants back after the first harvest and allow them to send out new growth for the second harvest.

Garden Guru Says

Baby artichokes are harvested before they develop the prickly choke that must be removed from the mature flower bud before you eat. The baby form is ready to harvest when it is about three inches across, or about a third of the size of the mature bud.

Asparagus

Asparagus is another highly prized gourmet vegetable that is an essential for Easter dinner in our family. This is a relatively demanding plant to grow, only in that you have to wait a year after planting to get the first sparse harvest. Asparagus pays you back for your efforts, however, because the plants will continue to produce for 10 or even 15 years.

Home gardeners rarely grow asparagus from seed. Instead look for one-year-old crowns.

Compost Pile

Insist on male plants when you buy asparagus crowns. These are hybrids that have developed in recent years. The male plants don't produce seeds the way the female plants do. Plants that grow from these seeds could become a weed problem in your asparagus patch.

Reserve an area in your garden for your asparagus patch, keeping in mind that each asparagus crown will produce about a half pound of asparagus each year, and that crowns should be planted about 18 inches apart in rows that are about 5 feet apart. You can do the math to figure how many crowns and how much space you'll need. Dig furrows about 5 inches deep and add a dose of triple superphosphate to the soil at the bottom of the furrow, working it into the soil. Asparagus likes soil with a pH of 6.0 to 7.0. Then put the crowns in the furrow, cover lightly with soil and water well.

Though the asparagus will produce little spears its first year, leave them alone and let them die back. The second year, you'll have a small harvest, with a full harvest in the third year and after.

Asparagus will grow in USDA Zones 4 through 10.

Food for Thought

As if asparagus weren't special enough, some growers have "kicked it up a notch" by producing white asparagus. This is done by blanching, which is described in Chapter 14. Blanching asparagus is done a couple ways. One technique is to build up soil around each spear as it develops, allowing only the tiny tip to be exposed to the sun, a tedious, time-consuming task. In Belgium, growers of white asparagus bring portable sheds out into the asparagus field to shield the spears from the sun for the last few weeks of maturing. Home gardeners can use black mesh row covers to achieve the same result.

Cardoons

These Mediterranean favorites are a close relative of artichokes. And though cardoons still haven't made much of an inroad in the United States, adventuresome gardeners eager to try new things are beginning to give cardoons a small presence here, particularly in the Pacific Northwest where the climate conditions seem to be especially hospitable.

Garden Guru Says

According to a publication of the University of Oregon Extension Center, cardoons need to be blanched starting about a month before harvesting. This is usually done by tying the leaves up at the top and wrapping them with burlap or paper. The leaf stalks are the parts that are blanched.

Cardoons are very large perennial plants with massive leaves that can be as long as five feet. Young new leaves and the immature flower stalks are the edible part of the plant.

Cardoons do not tolerate frost and prefer moist, cool conditions. They like well-drained, rich soil that is deeply cultivated to ensure good root formation. They also require regular irrigation. Plant seeds outdoors after all danger of frost, spacing them about 1½ to 2 feet apart. Or purchase stem suckers and plant them with the same spacing.

Cardoons grow in USDA Zones 7a to 9b.

Exotic Roots

You might remember that some foods that we think of as root vegetables are actually the thickened stems of the plant rather than actual roots. Kohlrabi and fennel are two such exotic fat stem plants that we'll look at in this section. There is also information on Jerusalem artichokes and horseradish.

Kohlrabi

Kohlrabi is another member of the Brassicas (*Brassica oleracea var. caulo-rapa*), and one of the easiest of that family to grow. Kohlrabi, which means cabbage-turnip in German, is considered a root vegetable, though the round rootlike part we eat is actually a swollen stem that forms above the ground.

Food for Thought

Kohlrabi plants that have grown quickly are said to have the best flavor. In order for them to grow at a substantial rate, they require regular watering and every-other-week applications of a quick-release fertilizer.

As with many of the Brassicas, kohlrabi likes cool weather. You can sow seeds directly 1 to 1½ inches deep in the garden in early spring and in the late summer for a fall crop. In warm zones, plant in late fall for a winter crop. Provide them with a rich neutral soil that has been amended with plenty of organic matter. Allow four to eight inches between plants. You can also start seeds indoors allowing five or six weeks for seedlings to develop before setout time.

Food for Thought

Many flowers make very tasty edibles. Some, such as chive blossoms and violets are used as edible garnishes while others, such as nasturtiums and arugula flowers, are tossed into a salad or become part of a sauce. Squash blossoms can be stuffed with cheese, dipped in batter, and fried.

Here are some you might want to try:

- Roses
- Violets
- Calendula (also known as pot marigold)
- Beebalm
- Chamomile
- Borage
- Chives

- Nasturtium
- Angelica
- Dill
- Arugula
- Fennel
- Marigold
- Squash blossom

To find out more about growing flowers for eating, visit www.culinarycafe.com/Flowers/ or www.ent.iastate.edu/ipm/hortnews/995/7-21-1995/eatflow.html.

CAUTION

Compost Pile _____

Horseradish tends to run rampant in the garden. You might want to control its growth by planting it inside a big, commercial size can (the kind restaurants buy canned tomatoes in) with the top and bottom removed. This is the same concept as the suggestion for containing mint, but with a larger container.

It's very important to keep weeds out of the rows where you grow kohlrabi or risk misshapen, stunted vegetables. Take care when weeding because the kohlrabi has shallow roots. Mulch will help considerably; just keep it away from the round stems.

Harvest when the stems are about two or three inches across by cutting through the roots just below the stem.

Horseradish

Did you ever wonder where that white, grainy pickled stuff that you add to ketchup to make cocktail sauce comes from? It's horseradish, a wonderful root vegetable that's pretty easy to grow. Horseradish grows in cool to cold weather and is usually planted in the early spring or late fall. Plant roots in furrows one foot deep spacing the roots about a foot apart. Be sure the soil is well-drained and avoid overwatering.

Horesradish is harvested in the late fall, usually after a hard frost. This plant is a biennial that is generally grown as an annual. To collect seeds, leave one or two plants in the garden and allow them to die back. They will grow back the following spring. Allow them to mature and they will produce seeds. The root will probably be too tough and woody for consumption.

Fennel

It's important to differentiate between fennel, the herb, and fennel, the garden vegetable. Here we're talking about the vegetable, _Foeniculum vulgare var. dulce._ Fennel is generally grown from seed and planted outdoors after the last predicted frost. Space fennel about one every foot or so. It is a particularly beautiful plant and can be used as a decorative foliage plant in an ornamental garden, with an added bonus, because you can it eat it later. Fennel is harvested about 70 to 80 days after the seeds have been sown, usually when the bulb, which is actually thickened stems that grow in an overlapping pattern, is about three or four inches across. You can blanch the bulb, which sits up in the soil above a taproot, by mounding soil up around it for a couple of weeks before harvest.

Bulb fennel, which is sometimes called finocchio, prefers a pH of 5.0 to 6.8, frequent watering, and cool weather. Keep the soil moist but not soggy to avoid having the bulb split, which will ruin the flavor.

Celeriac

Celeriac, which is also called celery root, is far better known in Europe where it is served au gratin or julienned, than it is in the United States. If you would like to try growing this esoteric veggie, you will most likely have to start it from seed as it's not generally available as a seedling. Celery root takes 100 to 120 days from seed to harvest, so start the seeds early. Grow it as you would a turnip.

Jerusalem Artichoke

Jerusalem artichoke is a giant plant, Latin name *Heli-anthus tuberosus* (which tells you they are related to sunflowers), that grows up to eight feet tall. The fleshy tubers are another example of a swollen, underground stem; are eaten like potatoes; are harvested in the fall; and can remain in the ground until just before or just after the first frost.

Grow these plants starting with pieces of tuber in a rich sandy loam, planting them in early spring. They don't like hot weather. Allow at least two feet between each plant.

Prof. Price's Pointers

The Jerusalem artichoke has a peculiar trait. It stores carbohydrate as insulin, instead of starch, which is metabolized when people eat it as fructose instead of glucose. This quirk makes Jerusalem artichoke a starch substitute for diabetics.

The Least You Need to Know

◆ Don't be afraid to try new and unusual things. They are often as easy to grow as the basic stuff.

◆ Grow old-fashioned heirloom vegetables for authentic flavors.

◆ Grow enough carrots, potato, zucchini, eggplant, leeks, and other appropriate vegetables to harvest as baby vegetables.

◆ Try some specialized dwarf or mini varieties of your favorite vegetables.

Chapter 18

Growing Fruits

In This Chapter

- Uncover some of the tricks to raising strawberries
- Discover the differences between blackberries and raspberries
- Find out what one thing makes blueberries happy
- Learn all about rhubarb
- Get the juice on grapes

Many gardeners like to include small fruits among the edibles they grow. It's not hard to understand why. If you've ever picked blueberries in the morning to put on your cereal or harvested a basket of strawberries in the afternoon for your strawberry shortcake at dinner, you know the sublime pleasure of growing your own fruit.

In this chapter, we learn more about growing small fruits including strawberries, blueberries, brambleberries, grapes, and even currants and gooseberries.

Pruning fruit bushes is an important part of growing them. We'll cover that subject in Chapter 22.

Food for Thought

Curious to know the pH levels and zones best suited for the fruits discussed in this chapter? Be curious no longer!

Plant	pH	Zone
Strawberry	5.8 to 6.2	4 to 8
Blueberry	4.0 to 5.0	4 to 8
Brambleberries	5.6 to 7.0	4 to 8
Gooseberries and currants	5.5 to 7.0	3 to 8
Rhubarb	5.5 to 6.5	5 to 8
Grapes	5.5 to 6.5	3 to 9

The USDA Zone will depend on the specific varieties you select.

Strawberries

According to the U.S. Department of Agriculture, Americans consume 4.85 pounds of strawberries per person per year. California, which is the country's largest producer of strawberries, grows one billion pounds every year. Think about it. Strawberries are huge! I don't have enough room in my garden to grow my own, so I rely on a few pick-your-own farms in my neighborhood because the flavor of fresh-picked strawberries is unequaled.

Prof. Price's Pointers

To grow strawberries in very cold climates, follow the advice of the experts at the University of Maine Cooperative Extension. They suggest planting strawberries on a slight slope which will allow cold air to float away from plants rather than settling in with them. The slope also has the added advantage of improving drainage.

While strawberries are grown in every state in the country, they do best in places where they can have a full 90 days of warm days with full sun, cool nights, and regular watering.

Strawberries prefer well-drained, deeply cultivated sandy loam with a pH of 5.8 to 6.2 and plenty of organic material worked in thoroughly. Since they are heavy feeders, you'll be doing your strawberries a favor by adding a 10-10-10 fertilizer to the bed before planting. For about 250 square feet of strawberries (about enough room for 100 or so plants), you'll need about 5 pounds of fertilizer. (See Chapter 20 for more information about fertilizers.)

There are three basic types of strawberries:

♦ June or spring bearing

♦ Everbearing

♦ Day neutrals

Generally, home gardeners work with everbearing or day-neutral varieties, both of which produce over a longer period of time versus the June or spring-bearing types.

Strawberries are planted as seedlings as soon as the soil can be worked. The roots are just barely covered with soil and care must be taken not to cover the crown or it will rot. Three different spacing techniques are used, as noted in the following table.

Garden Guru Says

Weeds are a real problem for strawberries; they just don't do well with competition. So if you have turned a lawn into a planting bed, wait a year until you plant strawberries and be diligent about removing weeds during that time. If you are going to allow that extra year, why not bring in a truck load of manure to welcome those strawberry plants?

Plant Type Best Suited For	Spacing	Description
Matted row June/spring bearing	3 to 4 feet between rows; 18 to 20 inches between plants	Runners form 15 to 18 inches mat "daughter" plants spaced 4 to 6 inches apart
Space matted row all types	3 to 4 feet between rows; 18 to 20 inches between plants	Runners limited to 2 to 4 "daughter" plants spaced 6 to 12 inches apart
Hill best for everbearing and day-neutral rows	2 to 3 feet apart; 12 to 15 inches between plants	All runners removed

Strawberry plants will generally last several years, with the runners supplying new plants. The hill system of planting, however, will quickly tire the plant and you'll have to replant every couple years.

Strawberries can be grown in Zones 4 through 8 depending on the variety.

Blueberries

Many years ago I was a houseguest at an estate in New Hampshire. On the property were acres of wild blueberry bushes. Every day we picked pails full and at every meal we ate them: on cereal, in pancakes, in fruit salad, as jam with peanut butter, and in pies and cobblers for dessert. And all day long as a snack. By the end of my visit, my hands and my teeth were stained purple. But I never got tired of blueberries, and they remain one of my very favorite foods.

> **CAUTION**
>
> **Compost Pile**
>
> If you can't provide blueberries with a soil pH of 4.0 to 5.0, don't even bother trying to grow the plants. It just won't work.

> **Food for Thought**
>
> Blueberries are self-pollinating, but experienced growers find they have higher yields and better fruit when they plant two or more varieties together. If you select early, mid-season, and late cultivars, you could enjoy fresh blueberries for up to six weeks.

Blueberries (*Vaccinuim corynbosum*), North American natives, are long-lived shrubs that are relatively undemanding except for one rather important factor: They require a very acidic soil.

Blueberries like full sun, but Prof. Price grows them in partial shade at his home on Cape Cod, and they do just fine there. They like sandy loam but will manage in heavier soils that have been thoroughly worked and amended with organic matter.

Most blueberry growers buy two- or three-year-old plants in containers or with balled and burlapped (B&B) roots. Plant them in early spring following the instructions for planting shrubs found in Chapter 12. Try soaking the roots in a pail of water for a few hours first to give them a good start. If you buy your blueberries in containers, you'll need to prune the roots before planting. You'll find techniques for root pruning in Chapter 22. Allow four to six feet between plants.

Be sure to water your blueberries regularly. They have shallow roots and will dry out quickly, particularly in sandy soils. Feeding blueberries requires the gardener to have a little more information than for most garden plants. You might want to test the soil in your blueberry patch every few years to help you determine what, if anything, is missing. In between tests, sprinkle a coffee can full of Hollytone around each plant to keep the soil on the acid side and give the shrub a feeding. Avoid feeding new transplants because their root systems remain delicate for some time.

Blueberries can be grown in Zones 4 through 8 depending on the varieties.

Raspberries, Blackberries, and Other Brambles

Raspberries and blackberries and their various hybrids and relatives are known collectively as bramble fruits or bramble berries. The bramble refers to the thorny branches or canes that the original plants had. Many of the newer varieties of blackberries, and some raspberries, have been bred to be thornless, a boon to growers and pickers.

Other bramble fruits include the following:

- Loganberry
- Marionberry
- Tayberry
- Boysenberry
- Ollalaberry
- Dewberries

Most of these are close relatives of the blackberry but have distinctive traits that appeal to aficionados.

Bramble berries, like other fruits, will require space and time. If you have both, then growing them is a joy. Bramble fruits belong to the *Rubis rosaceae* family and are relatives of roses.

These fruits have perennial roots and biennial or perennial foliage and shoots, depending on the type. This means that the roots are long-lived, and the shoots, or canes, that develop each year from the crown require a one- or two-year cycle to produce fruit. Some grow only leaves the first year, then leaves and flowers the second year. Others produce flowers on the new canes. The flowers, of course, drop off and the fruit develops.

Garden Guru Says

Bramble berries do have a little quirk that puts them a bit higher up on the difficulty scale than some plants. It has to do with the weather. In order to set fruit, bramble berries must have a cool dormancy period, so they have a hard time in places that never get cold. But many varieties are susceptible to very cold weather and have serious die-back of new canes. And some varieties won't tolerate heat. So you have to know your varieties and know your weather.

Bramble berries are usually planted from dormant bare roots that are available from garden centers, nurseries, by mail order, and over the Internet. Place your bramble patch in a sunny spot that's out of the wind but gets good air circulation. Then provide the plants with a slightly acidic (pH 5.6 to 7.0) and sandy loam soil with organic matter worked in for moisture retention. Plant the roots in a shallow trench (maybe three inches deep and one foot wide). The spacing per plant varies from one variety to another.

Most bramble berries are grown more as a continuous row of plants that form a hedge, rather than as individual plants. These plants almost all require some kind of support. Many bramble growers build sturdy wooden trellises for the plants to grow up and over. The amount of support needed will also depend on the variety.

Compost Pile _____

Bramble berries should never be grown in soil that was previously home to potatoes, tomatoes, eggplant, or peppers because of the risk of contamination with the Verticillium virus that causes roots to rot.

Food for Thought _____

Generally, red raspberries are the most cold-hardy while yellow ones are the least. Yellow raspberries are best eaten fresh and tend to look yucky as jam.

Raspberries

The variety among raspberry plants is broad. The fruits can be red, dark pink, purple, black, or yellow. The plants can be floricanes (fruit grows on one year old canes) or primocanes (fruit grows on new canes). There are summer or fall producers and early, mid and late season varieties. Growing several of each variety gives gardeners the opportunity to extend the growing season significantly.

Raspberries can be grown in Zones 4 through 8, depending on the variety.

Blackberries

Most blackberry varieties are a tad more delicate than their raspberry cousins. Generally, they won't tolerate temperatures that drop below 20 degrees F. The good news is that they don't mind the heat as much. That's why some people think of raspberries as more of a northern fruit and blackberries might have a southern reputation.

Blackberries are classified a number of ways including with thorns and thornless, erect or semi-erect Eastern, or trailing Western. Typically, thorny varieties are sweeter and more cold tolerant, so many gardeners are willing to put up with scratches all over their arms because the plants are more rewarding.

Blackberries can be grown in Zones 5 through 8 depending on the variety.

Gooseberries and Currants

Gooseberries and currants are perennial shrubs with a larger following in Europe than in the Unites States. They were popular in the eighteenth and nineteenth centuries, but then they got into some trouble with the law.

But if you decide to give these fruits a try, you'll probably enjoy the way they look and their wonderful flavors. Gooseberries and currants are members of the *Ribes* family and have a long history in this country, going back to the early colonists who brought cuttings with them from Europe.

Both gooseberries and currants prefer a cold dormancy period, a cool growing season, well-drained clay loam soil with plenty of organic matter for moisture retention, a sunny location (though they will tolerate some shade), and good air circulation. The only thing they aren't particularly fussy about is pH; they tolerate from about 5.5 to 7.0.

CAUTION

Compost Pile

In the early part of the twentieth century, there was a federal ban on growing gooseberries and currants in the United States because these plants can be a host to white pine blister rust, a serious fungus that destroys white pines. The restriction was lifted in 1966, but some states still have the ban in effect. Plant breeders have developed cultivars that are resistant to the fungus, but you should check with your County Extension before growing gooseberries or currants to make sure you are allowed to grow them.

Gooseberries and currants should be planted in the early spring, about four to five feet apart and just a little deeper than you would other shrubs. You can grow them in rows, orchard style, or use them in among ornamental shrubs in a mixed border.

Food for Thought

What do you get when you cross a gooseberry with a black currant? This isn't a trick question. You get a newcomer called jostaberry (*Ribes nidigrolaria*). They produce very sweet fruit on thornless, disease-resistant plants that are hardy in Zones 3 through 8.

Gooseberries

Two types of gooseberries are generally cultivated: American and European. Though the European varieties are treasured for their juicy fruits, they are prone to diseases. The American varieties, though less tasty, are easier to grow. Both types usually have thorns, though newer varieties have fewer thorns.

Currants

Three types of currants are grown in the United States. These are as follows:

- ◆ Red
- ◆ White
- ◆ Black

As with blueberries, currants are self-pollinating, so you can grow just one variety and still have a decent crop. But if you grow several different cultivars, you will probably have more and better fruit.

Rhubarb

Have you ever tasted pie made from fresh rhubarb? It's one of those old-fashioned treats that stays vivid in your memory. Rhubarb does seem like an old-fashioned fruit. But many up-to-date gardeners grow it with enthusiasm and success. As with most fruits, rhubarb requires some patience on the part of the gardener because it can't be harvested until the second or even third year after planting.

Compost Pile

The leaves of the rhubarb plant contain oxalic acid, which is poisonous. Although a few bites of leaf aren't likely to kill a healthy adult, it can still make you quite sick. And someone in ill health, or small children, might become very sick indeed from ingesting even a small amount. Remove the leaves immediately upon harvesting the rhubarb stalks.

Food for Thought

Rhubarb plants are usually divided every three or four years, unless the plants aren't thriving. To make divisions, use a sharp spade to cut straight down through the crown. Dig up the two halves and, using a sharp, clean knife, further divide the crowns, making sure that each small piece has one bud, or eye. Plant the divisions as individual new rhubarb plants.

Rhubarb, which originated in Asia, is grown for its green, red, or pink stalks which are shaped like celery, only longer. They are used to make pies, jams and jellies, stewed desserts, and sometimes punch (that's really old-fashioned!).

Rhubarb likes well-drained soil with plenty of organic matter worked in thoroughly. Though it's not all that fussy about pH, a range of 5.6 to 6.5 is best. Plant crown divisions, which are available from garden centers, nurseries, and online vendors, in the early spring or late fall, placing the crowns about 2½ to 3½ inches below the soil. Allow about three to four square feet per plant. Rhubarb is a heavy feeder, so you'll want to plan on a regular schedule of fertilization. Apply a high nitrogen fertilizer a month after the leaves first appear, then about every three weeks after that.

To harvest, cut individual stalks a few at a time, over the course of a month or two, usually starting around mid-May.

Rhubarb is grown in Zones 5 through 8.

Growing Grapes

Le Creasy, a professor of pomology (fruit science), at Cornell University, has written that grapes are the most widely grown fruit in the world. Growing grapes for wine and for the table dates back thousands of years and is certainly part of the agricultural history of the United States.

In addition to use as table food and for wine, grapes are made into juice, jams, jellies, and raisins. It's important to decide what you want to do with your grapes before you grow them, because that will help you determine what type and variety to select and how many vines you'll want to plant. For example, to make wine you might need 20 or more vines, while a small family might only plant two vines for table use with a little left over to make a few jars of jelly. You will also want to make your choice based on local climate, disease and pest resistance, and soil conditions. Contact your local County Extension office for information on the best varieties to grow in your area for the uses you have in mind.

Grape vines require full sun, warm weather, well-drained soil that has been deeply tilled, and a soil pH of about 5.5 to 6.5.

Plant grape vines in the spring as early as the soil can be worked or in the fall, based on the variety. Set the plants about 6 to 24 feet apart, again depending on the variety. The planting hole should be wide enough to accommodate the spread-out roots. Cut off all but the largest cane (branch), leaving two good buds, and then water well.

Grapes must have support in order to produce harvestable fruit. There are many ways to train grapes on trellises, but we just don't have the room to cover all the details here. You'll want to contact your County Extension for more information about methods for trellising grapes. There are also several excellent websites, including www.extension.umn.edu, www.agweb.okstate.edu, and ohioline.osu.edu.

Regular watering is a must for healthy grape production, but you should avoid saturating the soil or you will wind up with rotten roots. Fertilizer amounts and application schedules should be based on the results of soil tests, on the varieties you have selected, and the growing conditions in your garden. Again, consult your County Extension office.

Grapes can be grown in Zones 3 through 9, depending on the variety.

Prof. Price's Pointers

Grapes are frequently sold as grafted plants. This means that the roots of one kind of grape are attached, or grafted, to the stem of another type of grape. This is usually done to avoid having disease-prone roots. The desired vine is grafted to disease-resistant roots.

Garden Guru Says

A little trick used by serious grape growers is to place rows running north to south. This positions the vines to receive the maximum amount of sunlight.

The Least You Need to Know

◆ Provide backyard fruit plants with good drainage.

◆ Don't grow blueberries if you can't provide them with a soil pH of 4.0 to 5.0.

◆ Remember that rhubarb leaves are poisonous.

◆ Consult with your local County Extension office for more information about specific growing requirements and cultivars to choose for homegrown fruits, especially grapes.

Part 5

Keeping It Going

The next few chapters aren't about any of the fun stuff. Let's face it. There are chores to be done. Someone has to water and weed. Pests and diseases won't go away just because you don't want to deal with bugs. You can skip this part if you really are a lazy slug, but if you do want to make the most of your garden, read on.

Go ahead, plow on in. It's good for you, and your garden, to know these things.

Chapter 19

Weeding and Watering

In This Chapter

♦ Learn to identify weeds and to develop strategies for removing them from the garden

♦ Find out how certain weeds indicate potential soil problems

♦ Discover the science behind a plant's tremendous thirst for water

♦ Develop strategies for water conservation

♦ Plan an irrigation system for your garden

This is the decidedly dreary part of gardening. Weeding and watering are time consuming, boring, tedious tasks. Weeding is particularly onerous, especially when it's hot and buggy. It's a lot like housework (which I loathe) because it never ends. Just as there are always dirty dishes and laundry, unmade beds, and dust and dirt in the house, there are always weeds in the garden. These are dirty jobs, but someone has to do them.

In this chapter, we analyze this essential garden work and look at ways to make it easier. Along the way, we'll try to identify the worst weeds and talk about mulch and herbicides. We'll also explore various irrigation systems.

What's Wrong with a Few Weeds?

You've probably heard the expression "one man's trash is another man's treasure." That's sort of the case with weeds. One gardener's *weed* is another's wildflower. Many of the worst noxious weeds were introduced at some point by gardeners who thought they were pretty.

Native wildflowers can be beautiful in a meadow but a royal pain in the neck in the vegetable patch. Some really invasive plants like kudzu and purple loosestrife were initially planted because someone liked the way they look. But then they ran amok with sometimes devastating results.

Although a few weeds in the garden are inevitable, gardeners should strive to eliminate as many of them as possible. Weeds will compete with your edibles for water, nutrients, growing space, and sunlight. They also provide hiding places for insects and can be a contributing factor in the spread of disease. Weeds can, and will, reduce the quality and quantity of your harvest.

Even though we hate weeds, they can serve an interesting purpose for the home gardener. Some are known as indicator weeds because they start to appear with certain soil conditions. If you begin to see a big crop of chickweed, for example, it might indicate that your garden has a problem with poor drainage. The following soil conditions might be indicated by the appearance of these plants.

Compacted Soil	Low Fertility	Poor Drainage	
Crabgrass	Red sorrel	Chickweed	
Chickweed	Henbit	Goosegrass	
Goosegrass	Johnson grass	Dock	
Knotweed	Peppergrass	Thistle	
Dandelion	Crabgrass	Hedge bindweed	
Quack grass	Smartweed	Bindweed	
High Acidity	**Highly Alkaline**	**High Nitrogen**	**High Salt**
Horsetail	Peppergrass	Horse nettle	
Dandelion			
Sorrel			
Dock			
Knotweed			
			Creeping Jenny
			Crabgrass

Weed ID

There are far too many weed plants that plague American gardens to allow us to profile all of them in this limited space. Fortunately, a number of excellent websites with well-designed weed identification formats allow you to look at photos of the plants, and identify then by name, type, and growth habit. Some of the sites also provide eradication advice.

Look for these websites:

- www.rce.rutgers.edu
- www.weeds.iastate.edu
- www.uwyo.edu/plants/weeds
- www.mtweed.org/identification
- pi.cdfa.ca.gov/weedinfo
- www.fmc.com/agweedbug
- www.wssa.net
- www.landscaping.about.com/cs/weedid

> **Prof. Price's Pointers**
>
> A **weed** is a plant that grows in a place where it is unwanted or a plant with unacceptable qualities. A noxious weed is one that grows rampant in places it is unwanted and is resistant to efforts to remove it.

Look for others, too. Just use your favorite search engine, type "garden weed identification," and see what comes up. Some of the sites are specific to regions, states, or even counties.

There are a few very common weeds that appear in gardens all over the country. These are a few of them:

Weed	Species	Description
Bedstraw (clingers)	*Galium* species	B, P
Bitter cress	*Cardamine* species	B, A; prolific seeds that pop out of pods and spread like crazy; often infiltrate the garden via nursery pots
Canada thistle (creeping thistle)	*Cirsium arvense*	B, P; very invasive; aggressive root system
Dandelion	*Taraxacum officinale*	B, P; flowers distract bees from pollinating less showy vegetable and fruit flowers; deep tap root
Cut-leaf evening primrose	*Oenothera laciniata*	B, P

continues

continued

Weed	Species	Description
Dodder	*Cuscuta* species	P; parasitic annual; sucks out chlorophyll; problem for blueberries
Bindweed (creeping Jenny)	*Convolvulus arvensis*	B, P; invasive vine with aggressive root system
Quickweed	*Galinsoga*	B, P; very quick to germinate; reseeds many times during growing season
Carpetweed	*Mollugo verticillata*	B, A; shallow root system; easy to remove with light cultivation
Crabgrass, hairy	*Digitaria sanguinalis*	G, A
Crabgrass, smooth	*D. ischaeum*	G, A; grows close to ground; spreads with runners
Roundleaf mallow	*Malva neglecta*	B, P
Smartweed	*Polygonum* species	B, A; many types; some a problem for blueberries
Mexican bamboo (Japanese bamboo)	*Polygonum cuspidatum*	B, A
Pennsylvania smartweed	*Polygonum pensylvanicum*	B, A; extremely invasive
Wirestem muhly	*Muhlenbergia frondosa*	G, P
Witchgrass	*Panicum capillare*	G, P
Henbit	*Lamium amplexicaule*	B, A
Prickly lettuce	*Lactuca serriola*	B, A
Shattercane (wildcane)	*Sorghum bicolor*	G, A; tall; looks a little like corn
Shepherd's purse	*Capsella bursa-pastoris*	B, A
Goosegrass	*Eleusine indica*	G, A; grows close to ground; difficult to pull out
Hedge bindweed	*Calystegia sepium*	B, P; aggressive vine; problem with corn
Horse nettle	*Solanum carolinense*	B, P; sharp, nasty spines; difficult to control; aggressive roots; poisonous berries; related to potatoes
Johnsongrass	*Sorghum halepense*	G, P; very tall; aggressive roots
Jimsonweed	*Datura stramonium*	B, A; toxic hallucinogen in seeds and leaves

Weed	Species	Description
Kudzu	*Pueraria lobata*	B, P; very aggressive vine in southern zones
Sorrelwood (sourgrass)	*Oxalis stricta, O. cornicula*	B, P; spreads by popping seeds
Mugwort (wild chrysanthemum)	*Artemisia vulgaris*	B, P; very invasive; spreads with rhizomes
Ivy-leafed morning glory	*Ipomoea hederacea*	B, P; vine; looks like bindweed
Blackgrass	*Alopecurus myosuroides*	G, A
Lamb's-quarter	*Chenopodium album*	Might have medicinal properties
Quack grass (couchgrass)	*Bytrigia repens*	G, P; very invasive; spreads by rhizomes
Purslane	*Portulaca oleracea*	A, B; fleshy stems
Prickly sida	*Sida spinosa*	B, P; sharp spines
Pineapple weed	*Matricaria matricarioides*	B, A; particular problem for spinach and other vegetables
Pepperweed	*Lepidium* species	Particular problem for strawberries
Poison ivy	*Toxicodendron radicans*	B, P; vine; invasive creeping stem and seeds; causes rashes
Common chickweed	*Stellaria media*	B, A; problem for strawberries

Key: B = broadleaf, G = grass, P = perennial, A = annual

Not every one of these weeds will appear in your garden. But some inevitably will. Be prepared.

Food for Thought

Weeds aren't a huge problem in my small Pennsylvania garden. That's because the beds were established a long time ago, and I spent a lot of time, early on, preparing the beds and keeping them weed free. What happened is I removed unwanted plants (weeds) before they had a chance to go to seed so new crops never became established. A few weed seeds will blow in on the wind or will be deposited by a visiting bird, but these are incidental and don't require much effort to keep under control. The only time I have real weed problems is when I reclaim a bit more lawn for a new bed.

Weed Between the Lines

The best defense against weeds is a good offense. Gardeners gain the upper hand by starting out with a well-prepared bed. If the bed is thoroughly and deeply tilled, with all the old vegetation removed, there will be fewer seeds to start with.

That having been said, you still have to deal with the weeds that crop up. Weeding is an age-old chore that doesn't take a lot of skill. Just effort. In a small garden, you can probably manage by hand-pulling weeds. This isn't such an awful task if you do it in the cool of the early morning or in the evening. Wear your gloves and pull the invaders out. Or scratch lightly along the surface of the soil with a hand-cultivator. But be wary of taprooted weeds. You'll want to get out your weeder tool for them (this is the one that has the V-shaped point on the end).

> **CAUTION**
>
> **Compost Pile** _____
>
> Don't put weeds that have gone to seed on your compost pile. There's a good chance that they will survive. When you add the compost to your garden soil, you'll simply reintroduce the weeds, only more of them.

In a larger garden, weeding by hand just isn't a practical option, unless you don't do anything but garden all day and night. Instead, you'll probably want to use some kind of cultivating tool like one of the hoes described in Chapter 4.

Attack weeds between rows as well as in the rows, but you'll use different techniques for each space. Between rows you can be pretty aggressive and just whack away at the weeds. But when you are working around plants, you have to be really careful. Overzealous weeding with a cultivating tool can damage vulnerable roots and stems. Just scratch the surface lightly to loosen the weed and pull it away from the planted row. For good garden hygiene, take the uprooted weeds away.

The Beauty of Mulch

Mulch goes a long way toward reducing weeding chores. It provides a barrier over the surface of the soil that prevents seeds from working their way into the soil, and also keeps out light, which is essential for any seeds that have somehow managed to germinate. Mulch has the added benefits of keeping moisture in the soil and preventing soil from overheating.

Generally mulches are inorganic or organic. Organic mulches are those that are or are made of plant material. Some examples include the following:

- Wood chips
- Sawdust
- Straw
- Shredded or chunked bark
- Grass clippings
- Hay (without seeds)

- Pine needles
- Shredded newspaper
- Seaweed
- Compost

- Ground corn cobs
- Leaves
- Manure
- Peat moss

The most common inorganic mulches are plastic sheeting and mulch cloth. Black plastic mulch has been used successfully by thousands, if not millions, of gardeners, including Prof. Price. Recent research by plant scientists at Pennsylvania State, Montana State, Auburn, and Iowa State, among other places, has been done with colored plastic mulch with promising results for the red, blue, and silver products. Though not available everywhere, some gardeners are beginning to use these new colored plastic mulches to boost production and hasten ripening. You might want to visit the websites for these institutions to find out how their research is progressing.

> **Garden Guru Says**
>
> Some vegetables work in the garden as a sort of living mulch. These are the plants that sprawl across the ground and wind up shading and crowding out weeds. Melons, squash, potatoes, sweet potatoes, pumpkins, and large tomatoes will do this.

When applying organic mulch, lay it on thick but don't let it touch stems or leaves. Always leave a little space around the stem and be sure to lift any leaves that are laying on the ground so that you put the mulch on top of the soil, not on top of the leaf.

When using organic mulches, you might risk lowering the nitrogen levels in your soil. This is because the soil will use existing nitrogen in the decomposition process. You might have to add more nitrogen to compensate.

Kill Weeds with Chemicals

There are some gardeners who won't touch herbicides with a 10-foot pole. I'm not one of them. If it weren't for Brush-B-Gon Poison Ivy Killer, I would be an itchy wreck all summer.

Herbicides have their place. When used properly, they do not have a negative impact on the environment, and they can greatly reduce the time you need to remove unwanted vegetation. The most important role herbicides play is in the development of new beds. You can use a herbicide to kill a large section of grass before you till it. And spot applications on really difficult-to-remove weeds, especially those with taproots, is sometimes the only way to be sure you really kill the blasted things.

Three basic kinds of herbicides are used by home gardeners: all-purpose herbicides designed to kill any plant they touch, selective herbicides that kill specific plants, and pre-emergents designed to prevent germination.

CAUTION **Compost Pile** _____

Always read herbicide labels carefully and follow directions exactly. Keep out of the way of children and pets. Don't get it on your skin or in your eyes. If you do, be sure to follow the caution directions on the label exactly. When in doubt, call a poison control hotline or go to the emergency room. In other words, be careful with chemicals and don't take risks.

Roundup, Kleenup, and Kleeraway are three of the better-known all-purpose herbicides. The active ingredient in many of the all-purpose herbicides is glyphosate. According to a water conservation bulletin from the Arizona Cooperative Extension, glyphosate decomposes quickly, so you can use it in an area where you plan a new bed, and plant a week later.

Dacthal is one of the best-known selective herbicides, with clorthal-dimethyl (DCPA) as its active ingredient. This one is a pre-emergent designed to kill annual grasses and broadleaf weeds. It is used on planted beds, whether they are seeded or if seedlings have been planted. There are very specific usage instructions that spell out when to use, how much to use, where it can be used, and how far from vines, stems, and leaves it can be used. Follow the directions exactly.

Treflan is another one of the popular pre-emergents. It is used on prepared beds before planting. According to the label, it is a selective herbicide that will prevent the germination of specific broad-leaf and grass weed seeds including such pests as johnsongrass, crabgrass, carpetweed, chickweed, lamb's-quarters, and pigweed. It will also kill purslane, so if you plan to grow that particular type of fancy lettuce, don't use Treflan in your garden.

Why Plants Wilt

The simplistic answer to the question of why plants wilt is they don't have enough water! Duh! But the scientific answer is that they lose turgor. Prof. Price gives us a complete explanation.

Back to Plant Biology 101

Think of a tomato plant as a balloon filled with a salty solution and attached to a tube (roots) that is sitting in a bucket (soil). A filter (osmotic membranes) in the tube allows water but not salts to pass through.

Now the activity of the water is decreased by the presence of salts. Since the activity of the water in the bucket (soil) is greater than that in the balloon (plant), water will try to move from the bucket into the balloon. The result is an increase in water pressure (osmotic pressure) within the balloon (plant), causing it to fill up and stiffen (become turgid).

So if the balloon (plant) develops holes and leaks, the balloon collapses. This collapse would also happen if salt were to build up in the water in the bucket. The collapse is the loss of turgor, or wilting.

Let's Look a Little Closer

Now that you totally understand the science behind why plants wilt, you need to know why it is so devastating to a plant. It's not really that complicated. Remember in Chapter 10, you learned that in order to photosynthesize, plants had to be able to pull carbon dioxide from the atmosphere. And they did that through the tiny holes in the leaves called stomata. But these thousands of holes also lose water. It's like a catch-22 for plants. They need those holes in order to make chlorophyll (photosynthesize) which is essential for their growth. But they lose a lot of their precious moisture through those same holes. So in order to survive, plants must have a continuous supply of water.

Irrigation 101

Now we know that plants can't survive without a continuous supply of water. In a perfect world, we would have enough rainfall during the growing season to provide just the right amount of water to meet the needs of all our garden plants. Well, guess what? It almost never works out that way. Here in Pennsylvania, we have had a series of severe droughts for several summers in a row. Our droughts have been so bad that emergency water restrictions have been mandated on several occasions by local and state governments. So conscientious gardeners have had to develop strategies for irrigating their gardens while honoring the restrictions. This means careful attention to water conservation techniques.

Some very useful water conservation tips have been prepared by the University of Georgia Cooperative Extension office. Their recommendations, along with suggestions from other experts, include the following:

- Use mulch to hold moisture in.
- Add organic matter to the soil to aid in retaining moisture.
- Make individual plant waterers to direct water directly to plant roots using milk jugs or soda bottles (find directions for making these online).
- Remove weeds scrupulously.

> **CAUTION** **Compost Pile**
>
> Do not use gray water on edible plants. Gray water is the leftover water from laundry, bathing, and other household activities. While it is okay to use for short periods of time on most ornamental plants, garden and health experts advise against using it on vegetables and fruits.

Garden Guru Says

Avoid watering your garden with a light sprinkling. The water will do nothing more than moisten the surface of the soil—none will penetrate to the roots and the plants will die of thirst.

Food for Thought

Professor Price has been using this system for a long time; his old soaker hoses were flat green plastic things with lots of little holes that sprayed water rather than leaked it. I remember that they were always getting twisted up so that the holes sent little sprays of water in all directions. The new versions are far better designed and efficient.

◆ Use a drip irrigation system to avoid loss of water through evaporation of surface moisture.

◆ Settle newly tilled soil with a light application of water so that future waterings will conduct the moisture properly.

◆ Water before 8 A.M.

◆ Keep hoses, hose bibs, and nozzles in good repair.

◆ Pay attention to weather reports and turn off automatic timers if rain is predicted.

◆ Don't irrigate areas of the garden that have been harvested.

Drip Systems

A drip system is a relatively new technology that helps conserve water while providing garden plants with just the amount of moisture they need to thrive. Essentially, the system is a set of emitter hoses that are snaked through the garden. The emitters are set at intervals that match the spaces between plants. Usually drip systems are connected to timers. The initial investment is relatively high and there is a fair amount of effort needed to install a system. Look for excellent instructions for installing a drip irrigation system in your garden from the Colorado State University Cooperative Extension at www.ext.colostate.edu.

Soaker Hoses

This is Prof. Price's favorite method of irrigation. He has yards and yards of soaker hoses in both his California and his Massachusetts gardens. Soaker hoses look more or less like regular hoses except that they are usually black and they are made of a squishy porous material that allows water to seep out slowly. One end of the hose is attached to the hose bib and the other is capped.

Overhead Sprayers

Many gardeners rely on overhead sprayers. Some are as simple as a sprinkler head set up on a pole with a hose attached to it. Others are more elaborate systems with heads that pop up out of the ground. All can be attached to timers. You can use rotary heads, which require high water pressure, or spray heads that require less pressure.

Important considerations include the size and shape of the area you want to irrigate, your water pressure, and the patterns of irrigation you want to use. Visit the University of Georgia Agriculture and Environmental Sciences Co-operative Extension website at www.ces.uga.edu for excellent advice on spacing formulas, system designs, and more.

Do It By Hand

A very small garden or a container garden of edibles can be effectively watered by hand using a hose with a wand or with watering cans. The wand will help you reach farther in the garden and is usually fitted with a nozzle that allows you to adjust flow, and multiple spray options. Look for one with an on/off latch so you can have complete control of the flow.

If you like watering cans, be sure to use one with a good rose on it. The rose is the part of the spout that has little holes in it to form a fine spray of water. You don't want to water tender little plants with a blast of water from the can.

Prof. Price's Pointers

In warm weather most edible plants will require 1 to 1½ inches of water per week. In very hot weather, plants might need as much as 2 inches of water per week. A good rule of thumb is that 1 inch of water equals about 60 gallons per 100 square feet. Use this to help you plan your irrigation schedule.

The Least You Need to Know

◆ Keep garden beds well weeded to ensure healthy plants and a good harvest.

◆ Use mulch to conserve water and keep weeds at bay.

◆ Provide your plants with plenty of water.

◆ Don't use gray water on edibles.

◆ Explore your irrigation options and select one that allows you to conserve water while meeting the needs of your plants.

Chapter 20

Feeding

In This Chapter

◆ Familiarize yourself with the nutrients plants require to thrive

◆ Know about NKP

◆ Find out the difference between a side dressing and a top dressing

◆ Learn how to use organic materials to feed your garden

People have been fertilizing plants since the beginnings of agriculture, but we've only really known why we do what we do since the early nineteenth century with the first systematic studies on the requirements of plants for nutrients—nitrogen, phosphate, potassium, and so on.

In this chapter, we have another important science lesson. This time it's about the nourishment plants need in order to prosper and how gardeners can respond to those needs, including so-called organic approaches.

All the substances are essential for every cell in every plant. Having said that, there are certain plant organs and developmental processes for which a given nutrient might play a larger role.

In this chapter, we also take a close look at the famous NPK trio: nitrogen, phosphorus, and potassium. We'll get familiar with some of the other important macronutrients and micronutrients, and we'll find out about the best ways to deliver these essentials to our garden plants.

Prof. Price's Pointers

We can now name 17 elements essential to the growth of plants, starting with carbon, hydrogen, and oxygen (air and water); then nitrogen, phosphorus, and potassium (the famous *NPK*); followed by the familiar calcium, magnesium, and iron; through the lesser known nutrients, including boron, manganese, and zinc; also copper, cobalt, chlorine, molybdenum, and finally nickel, whose essentiality was confirmed only about a dozen years ago.

What Plants Want

Keeping plants properly fed is all about balance. Just as humans and animals need a balanced diet, so do plants. In addition to adequate supplies of water and air, plants require generous portions of nitrogen, phosphorus, and potassium in order to produce leaves, grow roots, set fruit, and make seeds. And they need these things in specific amounts.

As plants grow, they draw nutrients from the soil. Some of the nutrients are plentiful with more than enough to keep on providing what plants need indefinitely. Other nutrients will become depleted. In a natural setting, depleted nutrients are replenished when plants die off and decompose. But in a garden, the plants are harvested and dead plant material is generally cleaned up, so that natural process is short-circuited. So it becomes the gardener's job to replenish the supply of used-up nutrients.

A Short Course on Fertilizer or Knowing All About NPK

The trio of NPK are the basis of all fertilizers. After you commit the following information to memory, you can officially call yourself a gardener.

Prof. Price's Pointers

The percentages are equivalents because the nitrogen could be present as ammonium, nitrate, or urea, not as elemental N, which is nitrogen gas; the phosphorus as phosphate, bone meal, or other organic form; and the potassium would certainly not be present as potassium oxide, which is caustic.

Just about all commercial fertilizers will have labels that give a series of three numbers like 5-10-5 or 10-10-10. These numbers represent the percentages of N (nitrogen), P (phosphorus), and K (potassium), respectively. But the numerical representations are not consistent, logical, or universal. Bear with me. You need to know this stuff.

In the United States, the numbers represent the percentages of elemental nitrogen, phosphorus as phosphate, and potassium as potassium oxide. The fertilizer labeled 5-10-15 would contain the equivalent of 5 percent nitrogen, 10 percent phosphate, and 15 percent potassium oxide.

Are you thoroughly confused? Well, don't go away. It gets worse. The percentages of nutrients, and especially of nitrogen, are only part of the story. Plants regulate themselves in terms of the balance of vegetative growth and reproduction, but too much nitrogen in a readily available form—ammonium or urea—can cause "fertilizer burn" or even turn off fruit set and push excessive vegetative growth.

Give Me an N

Eventually every gardener must become familiar with nitrogen. The big N is one of those really important factors in the health and prosperity of most plants. Nitrogen comes in several common forms, as noted in the following table.

Nitrogen Forms

Form	Description
Nitrate	Occurs as the mineral sodium nitrate, is highly soluble, can be used immediately by plants, is the most expensive form of nitrogen (comes from mines in Chile), and can be taken up by the plant and stored harmlessly.
Ammonium (similar to household ammonia)	Is instantly available to the plant, and the plant must convert it to a storage form which requires an investment of starch (if the plant runs out of stored starch, the ammonium will kill it).
	Like nitrates, most ammonium salts are highly soluble and, like nitrates, ammonium nitrogen is readily available to the plant. In fact, the problem with ammonium salts is that they are too available to plants: If ammonium nitrogen is not converted to organic nitrogen, it can become highly toxic.
Urea	The most common nitrogenous constituent of urine. Most plants convert it rapidly to ammonium nitrogen, so it has the same dangers. Urea is relatively inexpensive.
Organic nitrogen	Complex organic compounds that contain nitrogen; are ideal in that the nitrogen only becomes available as it is slowly decomposed by soil microorganisms. Urea (which is itself organic) can be converted to less available forms by various chemical tricks.
Atmospheric nitrogen	Eighty percent of the atmosphere is N_2 or nitrogen gas; gaseous nitrogen is not normally available as a nutrient to plants, but nitrogen-fixing bacteria can convert gaseous nitrogen to ammonium, and certain of these bacteria live symbiotically with peas and a few other plants, supplying ammonium to their host in exchange for carbohydrates and other nutrients.

Give Me a *P*

The chemical symbol for phosphorus is P. Plants absorb this essential as phosphate ion (PO_4). Phosphorus is a significant factor in the storage and distribution of energy in plants, so it's especially important for root development.

Sometimes plant specialists will recommend a shot of superphosphate for some plants. This stuff (a mixture of calcium phosphate and calcium sulfate) is a less soluble form of phosphate, which makes it available for a longer period of time. It won't wash away when it rains or when the irrigation system is turned on.

Give Me a *K*

The chemical symbol for potassium is K. Potassium is the third number in the fertilizer formula. Unlike nitrogen and phosphate, potassium does not make strong bonds with other molecules, so it's always floating around as a free ion. It moves around inside plants to wherever it is needed most. And because it's a free ion in the soil, it leaches out easily, especially in sandy soil.

It is rare to have too much potassium in garden soils, but there can be deficiencies. This will often show up as problems with older leaves. Roots are also susceptible to potassium deficiencies. A soil test will also point out whether you need to add potassium.

Most of the K found in commercial fertilizers comes in the form of potassium chloride. Old-time gardeners might still refer to potassium as potash, though this term is somewhat outdated.

Macro and Micronutrients

N, P, and K are the nutrients plants require in the largest amounts. But plants need 11 other nutrients, too:

- Calcium
- Sulfur
- Manganese
- Boron
- Chlorine
- Cobalt
- Magnesium
- Iron
- Zinc
- Copper
- Molybdenum

It's important to understand that plants require only tiny amounts of these nutrients. But if one element is out of balance, it can affect the availability (the ability of the plant to take in or to use) of another one of the elements. For example, if there is too much magnesium, the plant might have difficulty with calcium uptake. This can result in poor growth, a reduction in seed production, and other symptoms. Conversely, too much calcium can interfere with magnesium absorption.

CAUTION **Compost Pile**

One of the leading causes of eutrophication, which is the overgrowth of algae in aquatic and marine environments, is fertilizer run-off. While the contribution from home gardeners is relatively insignificant when compared to that from agriculture, it is still really important that home gardeners use commercial fertilizers carefully and according to the directions given by the manufacturers. Gardeners who work in sandy soil should take extra care, as fertilizer run-off is generally worse from these soil types.

Most of the micronutrients plants need are present in soil in adequate quantities. However, the combination of high pH and high calcium levels can make a number of the heavy metals unavailable to plants. Where micronutrients and trace metal deficiencies are common, as in the Southwest, there are a couple of approaches to getting them delivered to plants. These are …

◆ Lower the soil pH with gypsum to about 6.0 to 7.0.

◆ Add or spray with chelates.

Many commercial fertilizers also include micronutrients.

Natural Foods for Plants (the Organic Approach)

Organic gardening can be a loosey-goosey sort of approach, with a lot of myth and hearsay evidence in its favor. But when it comes to organic fertilizer, the "natural" perspective has undeniable advantages. The nutrients from manure, compost, fish heads, and other organic matter are released slowly, which avoids some of the real dangers of overfertilization. There are a number of methods for feeding the garden organically. (Note the earlier cautionary point on urea, which is organic.)

CAUTION **Compost Pile**

There is some concern about a toxic form of the Escherichia coli (E. coli) bacteria that can be present in the manure of ruminating (cud chewing) animals. Some scientists have gone as far as to recommend that this manure not be used on vegetable and fruit crops. At the very least, all vegetables and fruits fertilized with manure should be washed carefully before they are eaten.

Manure Tea

This is clearly not the tea to serve the ladies. Manure tea is a concoction made, you guessed it, of manure that has been steeped in water to create a liquid plant fertilizer. The best recipe I have found for manure tea is from *The Victory Garden Kids' Book* published in 1988. (My good friend Alison Kennedy did the design for the book, and it's one of my favorite gardening books ever.)

Put a shovelful of manure in a five-gallon bucket, and fill the bucket with water. Let it stand for a few hours. Ta da. It's ready to use. You can make larger quantities in a big plastic garbage can. Just use the same proportions.

Manure tea is great as a starter food for new seedlings or as an all-purpose fertilizer for the regular feedings you do every two or three weeks.

Sounds Pretty Fishy

The Wampanoag Indians of Massachusetts, as well as many early Native Americans, followed the tradition of dropping a fish head in each planting hole when they sowed their corn, beans, and squash crops. They were following their age-old traditions that were most likely based on someone's observation that plants grown near dead fish grew better than ones without the fish.

> **Garden Guru Says**
>
> While most herbivores produce suitable manure for gardening purposes, purists say that stuff from horses works best. This is because the form of nitrogen found in horse manure (called hippuric acid) is released more slowly than that in, say, cow, or sheep manure.

The scientific reason why decomposing fish might be good for crops is because in the breakdown of organic matter like dead fish, there is the slow release of nutrients like ammonium, nitrogen, phosphate, and potassium that, of course, are the principal nutrients plants require.

Today, instead of stocking up on dead fish, we can use fish emulsion to feed our garden plants. Don't try making your own unless you have large quantities of fish guts hanging around the house. Instead, look for commercial preparations at garden centers and nurseries.

The Poop on Poop

Manure is one of the best, and of course one of the oldest, organic fertilizers known to man. Cow pies, were, after all, free for the taking down on the farm. Manure from cows, horses, goats, chickens, and rabbits is the most commonly used.

Try to use manure that is free of straw. The microorganisms that help decompose the straw will convert nitrogen to organic forms that would only become available over time.

This natural time-released nitrogen is a good thing for gardens, but sometimes there is just enough at once to meet plants' needs.

Avoid using fresh manure on your vegetable garden as the acids in it will actually burn the growing plants. You might remember reading earlier in this book that well-rotted manure can be used as a fertilizer. This means it's been allowed to sit and age for several months. If you don't have your own source of manure, look for bags of processed manure at garden centers and nurseries.

> **CAUTION**
>
> ### Compost Pile
>
> Never use waste from dogs, cats, or humans as a fertilizer. While human waste (sometimes referred to as night soil) is still commonly used in some parts of the world to fertilize crops, it's a dangerous practice contributing to some really ugly diseases. Also avoid the use of processed sewage sludge as a fertilizer for edibles. While it is a rich food for ornamental plants, it might contain heavy metals that are toxic.

Fresh manure can be added to garden beds in late fall or early winter after everything has died back. Use a pitchfork or a big shovel and pile it on. Then spread it out as evenly as possible. You can either leave it on the surface or give the whole bed a quick till. In the spring, till it thoroughly.

When you use large quantities of cow, sheep, or goat manure to fertilize your garden, keep in mind that, while your garden beds will be rich and friable, there might be a deficiency in phosphorus. This is because cud-chewing animals enlist the aid of microorganisms to extract phosphate from phytins and phytic acid which can represent most of the phosphate in the plants that cows and others eat. Do a soil test to be sure. If your soil is low in phosphorus, add some superphosphate (0-45-0 fertilizer). About 4 pounds per 1,000 square feet of garden should be enough to get the levels up to par.

Compost

If ever there were a product that warms my thrifty soul, it's compost. I love the way we can take otherwise useless kitchen garbage and garden debris and turn it into one of the richest plant foods possible. Refer to Chapter 8 for tips on making your own compost.

Leaf Mold

This kind of organic fertilizer is a little different from compost. Essentially it's the leftovers of big piles of leaves that have been left to rot. Eventually the leaves decompose leaving behind a rich, fluffy organic material that makes a terrific plant food. Leaf mold, especially from oak leaves, tends to have a very low pH (which means it's very acidic) so is best used on plants that prefer a more acidic than alkaline soil.

Here's an easy equation for converting commercial fertilizer to so-called organic types:

- 25 pounds of commercial 10-10-10 fertilizer roughly equals:
  - 50 pounds of cotton seed meal + 15 pounds of lambeinite + 50 pounds of rock phosphate
  - 60 bushels of cow or horse manure
  - 24 bushels of chicken, sheep, or rabbit manure

Lay It On

There are several methods for applying fertilizer including broadcasting, banding, side dressing, and foliar feeding. Each one has its place in the home gardener's repertoire.

Broadcasting

You know when you use one of those little spreader contraptions to fertilize or lime the lawn? That's broadcasting. In the garden it's the uniform spreading of fertilizer over the whole surface of soil. Usually this is done just before you till so that you can then turn the fertilizer into the soil.

Garden Guru Says

Most gardeners don't refer to an overall application of manure or compost as broadcasting, though technically, it probably is.

Generally, you don't want to apply commercial fertilizers until you have had your soil tested so that you know what formula to use.

Strike Up the Band

Applying fertilizer using the banding method is a highly reliable way to deliver nutrients to young plants, but it does require a fair amount of labor. Banding is done at the same time you plant seeds and at transplant time. The amount of fertilizer you use will depend on the results of your soil tests and what crop you plan to grow. Here's how to band fertilizer:

At seed planting:

- Dig two furrows parallel to, on either side of, and three to six inches from the seed furrow. Make them twice as deep as the seed furrow.
- Add the fertilizer in the furrows and cover with soil.

Or ...

♦ Dig a furrow three to six inches deep.

♦ Add the fertilizer and cover with soil.

♦ Plant the seed in the furrow.

At transplant time

♦ Make two furrows six inches long and three inches deep on either side of each transplant. The furrows should be four to six inches from the transplant.

♦ Add the fertilizer and cover with soil.

Or ...

♦ Dig a circular trench around each plant three inches deep and four to six inches away from the stem. Then cover with soil.

Or ...

♦ Dig a hole twice as deep as you need for the transplant.

♦ Add the fertilizer and work it into the soil at the bottom of the hole. Fill the hole with soil to the level needed for the transplant.

♦ Plant the transplant.

After all the furrows or holes are dug and filled and the seeds or transplants are planted, water thoroughly.

Banding fertilizer will allow plants to have easier access to the phosphorus they need for good root development.

I Like My Dressing on the Side

This application method is done when young plants have reached a certain size. It's done by taking a small amount (one or two tablespoons per plant) of a dry fertilizer and sprinkling on both sides of the row of vegetables or in a circle around individual plants. You should allow six to eight inches of space between the fertilizer and the plant. The fertilizer is then gently worked into the soil with a cultivating tool, followed by a thorough watering.

Not all vegetables like getting a side dressing of fertilizer. Those that do, like it at different times. The following information will help you know when to side dress some of your favorite vegetables.

Garden Guru Says

When a side dressing is not worked into the soil but simply left on top of the soil, it is called a top dressing.

Plant	When to Top Dress with Fertilizer
Broccoli	Three weeks after transplanting or when heads begin to form
Tomato	When first flowers appear or when first fruits appear
Pepper	When first flowers appear
Eggplant	When first flowers appear
Kale	Four weeks after transplanting
Onion	Four and six weeks after planting; or when six inches tall, then again every two weeks until bulb is nearly full size
Cabbage	Three weeks after transplanting or when head starts to form
Potato	Six to seven weeks after planting; do it before adding more soil
Leek	When plants are a foot tall
Corn	When two feet tall; again when silk forms
Cauliflower	Five to six weeks after transplanting
Squash	Just before plants starts to form vines
Spinach	Just before blooms appear

Some perennial plants, like asparagus and artichokes, as well as some fruit shrubs, like raspberries and blueberries, benefit from a side dressing of fertilizer, too.

Foliar Feeding Frenzy

You've probably figured out that foliar feeding is a way of applying fertilizer to the leaves of a plant. Applied as a spray, it is a quick fix for plants and helps them absorb the nutrients they need. Generally, foliar feeding is done when there hasn't been enough fertilizer added to the soil before planting; when micronutrients, especially iron and zinc, aren't being released adequately; or if the soil is too cold to allow the plants' roots from taking up the existing fertilizer in the soil.

A phosphorus foliar spray can also help new transplants get off to a good start in cold soil.

The Least You Need to Know

- Use well-rotted manure as an excellent alternative to commercial fertilizers. Never use waste from dogs, cats, or humans as manure.
- Avoid contributing to fertilizer runoff by only using the amounts recommended by the manufacturers.
- Water thoroughly after applying all fertilizers, except foliar types.
- Apply a foliar fertilizer spray to give plants a quick feeding, especially when the soil is too cold for the plants to take up fertilizer from the soil.

Chapter 21

Pests, Diseases, and Blight

In This Chapter

- ◆ Meet some of your garden's worst nightmares
- ◆ Find out which insects like what plants
- ◆ Explore "natural" and "organic" techniques for pest control
- ◆ Learn how to use plants to deter some pests

No matter how meticulous you are about planning, planting, and maintaining your garden, you are going to have problems with pests. It's inevitable. And it can be frustrating. In this chapter, I introduce you to some of the most common insect pests, along with a few of the predatory insects that eat them.

We'll also talk about some insecticides and pesticides that are effective against the invaders. But we'll consider some of the organic or natural approaches as well. And along the way, we will figure out what to do with warm-blooded pests who can make a mess of the garden.

And before we proceed, I'd like to suggest that you use common sense when dealing with pests in the garden. Most experienced gardeners put up with a certain amount of damage. They accept the fact that there will be losses and that some produce will be less than perfect. The most successful gardeners are smart enough to plant more of the most troublesome things in order to get at least a small harvest, or to give up that item altogether.

Bad Bugs

Maybe I should have called this section "Icky Insects" because educated gardeners try not to use the word *bug*. Anyway, the number and diversity of insects that can cause damage to a garden is staggering. Different insects are sometimes more of a problem in different parts of the country, and certainly create more difficulties with some plants more than others.

Some of the most common insect pests and their favorite meals include the ones in the following table.

Common Insect Pests

Pest	Plant
Cabbage root maggot	Cabbage, broccoli, cauliflower
Japanese beetle	Raspberry, grape, beans
Cabbage worm	Cabbage, broccoli, cauliflower, corn
Mexican bean beetle	Beans, pea
Cutworms	Corn, cucumber, onion
Cucumber beetle	Zucchini, summer squash, winter squash, cucumber, melon, beans, corn, eggplant
Vine borer	Zucchini, summer squash, winter squash, cucumber, melon
Whitefly	Beans, tomato, melon
Leafhopper	Beans, potato, carrots, pea
Corn earworm	Corn, beans, cabbage family plants, lettuce
Aphids	Corn, cucumber, beans, squash, melon, peppers, potato, eggplant, beet, pea, broccoli, cabbage, Brussels sprouts, cauliflower, kale, lettuce, melon, okra, parsley, peppers, spinach, chard, tomato
Red spider mite	Bean, leaf miners, cucumber, beet, spinach, turnip, cabbage family
Flea beetles	Corn, potato, eggplant, beet, carrot, beans, parsley, tomato
Carrot rust root maggot	Carrot, radish, parsnip
Squash bug	Squash, melon
Slugs	Lettuce

Pest	Plant
Colorado potato beetle	Potato, eggplant
Spider mites	Eggplant, carrot
Tomato hornworm	Tomato, beans, cabbage family plants, cucumber, lettuce, melon, spinach,
Thrips	Beans, corn, cucumber, melon, peppers
Stink bugs	Beans, beet, corn, cucumber, okra, pea, chard

As you can see, many insects are a problem for more than one type of plant. Frequently, the problems run in families. The *Brassicas* have trouble with cabbage root maggot and cabbage worm. Squashes and cucumbers, which are members of the *Cucurbita* family, are troubled by cucumber beetles and vine borers. When you know how plants are related to each other it can help you deal with their potential pests.

Food for Thought

One of the best sources for information on insect pests is a publication from the Texas A&M University Agricultural Extension Service called *Managing Insect and Mite Pests in Vegetable Gardens*. You can find the entire thing online at insects. tamu.edu/extension/bulletins/b-1300.html. In this amazingly thorough document are descriptions, including drawings, of a host of pests; lists of plants and the insects that attack them; and the pesticides that will kill these insects.

Although no garden will be completely pest-free, it is possible to keep the damage to a minimum. The best defense is good horticultural hygiene. This means removing any insects found on seedlings before transplanting, thorough and regular weeding, removal of damaged leaves and other plant parts, and on-time harvesting so that rotting fruits don't attract more insects.

Also, keep in mind that healthy plants are more able to withstand the occasional insect attack. Conversely, plants that are compromised because of poor soil, lack of water, or too much or too little fertilizer will be more susceptible.

Good Bugs

I know people who find all insects disgusting and frightening. That's not a good attitude for gardeners. Some insects are absolutely essential for the very survival of plant species (especially the pollinators), and others spend their entire lives devouring the insects that can cause so much damage in the garden (the predators).

Look for illustrations of many of these pollinator and predator insects in an article on beneficial insects at www.ces.uga.edu:

The pollinators:

- Bees
- Butterflies
- Wasps
- Moths

The aerators:

- Dirt mites
- Earthworms

The bad bug killers:

- Lady beetles (ladybugs)
- Damselflies
- Assassin bugs
- Predacious mites
- Hover fly maggots
- Minute pirate bugs
- Rove beetles
- Spined soldier bugs
- Dragonflies
- Praying mantis
- Braconid wasp larvae
- Bigeyed bugs
- Green lacewings
- Ichneumonid wasps
- Soldier beetles
- Spiders

As you can see, there are many beneficial insects, and unless you have studied them, you might have difficulty telling a good bug from a bad one. That's why it's just not a good idea to use insecticides and pesticides indiscriminately. If you just go out and spray like crazy, you'll wind up killing every insect out there.

Food for Thought

As helpful as praying mantis are at keeping aphids and other pests in check, they have voracious appetites and will be just as happy chomping on beneficial insects like ladybugs or lacewings. And praying mantis can deliver a nasty bite to unsuspecting humans as well. I found that out one day when a granddaddy mantis attached himself to the fleshy part of my ankle. Ouch! That really hurt.

Insecticides and Pesticides

Insecticides and pesticides are products that kill insects and other pests. To clarify, pesticides are products that kill pests; not all insects are pests and not all pests are insects.

Hundreds of chemical compounds are used as pesticides, some utterly lethal to everything and anything they touch. Their selection and use is too important and complicated an issue to be covered adequately in this small space. So before you use any commercial pesticide, read the labels carefully and thoroughly and follow the directions exactly. Be sure to identify the insects that are causing the damage so you can pinpoint the insecticide you need to use. If you have any doubts, consult your County Extension office. The sales staff at garden centers, nurseries, and hardware stores won't necessarily know enough to help you make the right choices.

When you do elect to use a pesticide to control an infestation, you will need to make a thorough application, especially to the undersides of the leaves, in order for it to be effective. Liquid pesticides are generally easier to apply than powders.

CAUTION

Compost Pile

Never apply pesticides when bees are around. They work during the day, so if you must spray with a pesticide, do it in the very early morning or late in the day after bees have returned to their hives. Better yet, look for products that are not toxic to bees.

Garden Guru Says

A few pesticides are available that have a relatively low environmental impact, including insecticidal soaps and vegetable oil–based sprays that use pyrethrins and other plant extracts to kill aphids, mites, whitefly, thrips, leafhoppers, and a few other pests. Milky spore, a bacterium, can be used against Japanese beetles, and iron phosphate–based baits will kill slugs.

The Argument for Organic

Many gardeners grow their own food expressly to reduce their exposure to pesticides. Naturally (cute pun, huh?), these gardeners will want to take an organic approach to dealing with insect pests. There are a number of options including barriers, natural repellents, and hand removing.

Floating Row Covers

Floating row covers are one of the best barrier methods for pest control in the edible garden. Also called agricultural fleece, floating row covers are lengths of lightweight fabric (usually spunbonded polyester) that are draped like a blanket over rows of plants. The fabric allows sun and water to penetrate, and even provides some frost protection, but it keeps insects out. The covers are held in place by burying the edges in soil.

Prof. Price's Pointers

Integrated Pest Management is an approach to disease and insect control that uses environment-friendly methods that reduce the use of chemical agents while maintaining and promoting a healthy garden. Other natural ways to prevent disease and pest infestation include mechanical and barrier controls, good garden hygiene, crop rotation, the use of resistant plant varieties, adequate irrigation, and good soil preparation.

Floating row covers are usually installed at seed planting or transplanting time and kept on during the early stages of growth. As soon as the first flowers appear, the row covers must be removed or pollinating insects will be unable to do their work. Floating row covers are particularly effective for protecting against the following:

- Leaf miners
- Cabbage worms
- Bean beetles
- Aphids
- Corn earworms
- Cabbage root maggots
- Cucumber beetles
- Squash bugs
- Cabbage loopers
- Whiteflies

If soil under the row covers is infested with plant-eating insects, the row covers might do more harm than good because you won't be able to see much of the damage until it's too late. Rotating crops every year will help prevent the soil infestation.

Cutworm Collars and Maggot Mats

Cutworm collars are insect barriers that I first learned about back in the late 1980s from the *Victory Garden Kids' Book*. You can make your own or buy commercial versions.

The collars form a circular barrier around the stem that prevents nasty chomping or boring insects from climbing up the stems of young seedlings. You can use a paper cup with the bottom half cut off for a small collar. Or use an empty tomato sauce can with the bottom removed. Plastic soda bottles and milk cartons with the bottoms and the narrow parts cut off will also make effective collars. The collars work best on young seedlings, but you can make larger versions. Put the collar in place when you plant the seed or seedling and leave it there as long as it doesn't interfere with the growth of the plant.

Maggot mats are like little carpets around the stem of young plants that prevent cabbage maggot flies from laying their eggs in the soil near the young plants. The *Victory Garden Kids' Book* gardeners used pieces of leftover carpet to make the maggot mats. The carpet is cut into 5 inch squares; a slit is made from one edge to the center with a small hole right at the center. When the seedling is planted, the maggot mat goes on top of the soil around the stem and then the slit is taped closed. If you don't have carpet remnants, use tar paper, cardboard, or even aluminum foil.

Pick a Peck of Pests

Removing the offenders by hand can be a very effective method of pest control. This works well for some and is almost impossible for others. Slugs, Japanese beetles, cabbage worms, tomato hornworms, and Mexican bean beetles are a few that are relatively easy to pick off plants by hand.

A hard spray of water is another way to remove insects from leaves and stems. Of course, you can't do this on tender young seedlings. And if you see suspicious-looking eggs on the backs of leaves, try to wipe them off with a paper towel or even scrape them off with your fingernail; then put them in an airtight bag in the trash.

> **Garden Guru Says**
>
> Slugs are nocturnal, so in order to catch them, you'll have to go into the garden at night. Use a flashlight, and follow their slimy trails. You can put them in a jar with alcohol, soapy water, or salt to kill them right away. You might want to wear gloves or use large tweezers. Otherwise you'll get their slime on your hands, and it's hard to get off.

Organic Sprays

Although not always helpful, some of the organic sprays do provide some relief from pests. Many of them are made from essential plant oils that allow the spray to adhere to the plants' leaves. Oil from mint, cedar, garlic, pepper, citronella, cloves, rosemary, tansy, and many more herbs are sometimes used to repel insects. For a wonderful and complete chart of organic pesticides and the insects they help control, go to www.geocities.com/Heartland/Meadows/1322/organic.

Plants Bugs Hate

Some plants have the ability to either attract or repel certain pests. By making the correct planting combinations, you might be able to reduce some of the pest problems in your garden. The following table provides a few of the plants you can use to repel, deter harmful insects, or attract beneficial insects.

Plant	Benefit
Chervil	Repels aphids near lettuce
Coriander	Deters aphids, potato beetles, carrot rust fly
Dill	Deters aphids; attracts tomato hornworm (use as bait)
Garlic	Deters rabbits
Marigolds	Attracts slugs (use as bait)
Onions, chives	Deters aphids
Parsley	Repels slugs; attracts hoverflies
Sage	Deters cabbage moth, ants, carrot rust fly, and slugs
Nasturtiums	Deters aphids, whitefly, squash bugs, cucumber beetle
Basil	Repels thrips
Catmint	Deters flea and Japanese beetles, squash bug, aphids
Mint	Deters flea beetles, cabbage worms, aphids; attracts predatory wasps and hoverflies

Moles, Voles, and Other Critters

First let me say that I am an animal lover. I still stop the car to gaze at a herd of deer at sunset; it's a beautiful sight. I get a kick out of watching young groundhogs standing on their hind legs as they survey the countryside. And there is something so gentle and sweet about a wild rabbit nibbling in the lawn.

> ### Garden Guru Says
>
> Birds can be a problem for fruit growers, especially with blueberries, brambles, grapes, and shrub fruits. Bird netting, available at garden centers and hardware stores, will help protect your harvest. Be sure to install the netting as soon as the first fruits appear.

But critters in the garden are anything but cute. I'll never forget the sense of rage I felt when, after waiting weeks for the tomatoes to ripen in my New Jersey garden, I ventured out to harvest the first beautiful fruits, and every one of them had huge gashes in them, courtesy of our neighborhood groundhog.

In this section, we talk about some of the worst warm-blooded pests, and look at ways to, well, dissuade them. We also discuss some lethal approaches, and I hope any animal rights activists among you will forgive me. Personally, I have always used the nonkill methods. (Except I do have cats that like to kill voles and the occasional mole.) But I wouldn't be doing my job if I didn't offer you as much information as possible.

Voles and Moles

Voles, also called meadow mice, are particularly insidious, and I might add, odious creatures. They are small rodents, ranging from about three to five inches in length. They feast on just about every part of plants, consuming several times their weight every day. Voles can girdle young trees (eat the bark all the way around—a death sentence), devour an entire row of tubers, polish off leaf crops, and generally decimate a garden in a matter of weeks.

Voles live underground but spend a lot of time carrying out their destructive marauding along little above-ground runways. They reproduce at prodigious rates, and the amount of damage they do will become worse as their numbers increase.

Moles are a different animal altogether, and they are nowhere near as hateful. They range from mouse-size to as much as a foot long, depending on the type. Moles are almost always carnivores. They eat worms, grubs, beetles, ants, and the larvae of other insects. They generally leave plants alone. In the edible garden, moles aren't much of a problem except for the tunnels they dig all over the place that can be used by voles and mice after the moles have left.

Although voles are a real nuisance in the garden, moles aren't usually such a big deal. Because they eat grubs that will mature into Japanese beetles and other pests, moles can actually perform a service to the gardener.

Food for Thought

I have had some success in discouraging voles and moles from sticking around my garden, though my technique is somewhat gross. I use very soggy and smelly non-clumping kitty litter (with the solids removed). Using a trowel, I pour the litter into the vole and mole holes until I can't add any more. You can never really fill the holes because the burrows go deep and far. I think the smell of cat pee is just too much for the voles and moles, and they take a hike. This is not a permanent solution, but can discourage them long enough to keep your crops safe until harvest. And if you're lucky, the voles will do their reproducing in a new location so you're spared the results of a population explosion.

Poison and kill traps are the only sure-fire way to eliminate moles and voles. If you have children or pets, or if your neighbors have children or pets, I would stay away from using poison. Mouse traps work pretty well on voles. Place unbaited traps in the runways, and you'll reduce the population pretty quickly. But again, you won't want to do this if there are pets or children that spend time in your yard. Special mole traps go deep inside their tunnels. They are gruesome but effective.

Groundhogs

I know people who think that the only good groundhog is a dead one. I don't belong to that group. I have nothing against groundhogs until they come into my garden. That's when I get out my Havahart trap. Groundhogs, which are also called woodchucks, marmots, and whistle pigs, are not very bright, so they are relatively easy to trap.

We trapped an entire family several years ago using a technique suggested by an old timer in the area. We located the main hole of the burrow (in this case it was under our neighbor's driveway), and placed an unbaited trap directly outside the hole. We set it up so that the trap was running in the same direction as the groundhogs when they left their burrow. We caught them one by one over the course of a few days. My husband carted them off to a large meadow a few miles away. (We probably unwittingly broke several laws doing that but I'm hoping the statute of limitations has passed by now.)

![CAUTION] **Compost Pile** _____

Before you set out to live-trap a wild animal, find out what the animal-control regulations are in your area.

By the way, groundhogs smell really bad. It took days for my husband's car to lose that pungent odor.

Other ways to deal with groundhogs include shooting them, using kill traps, and fumigating (carbon monoxide canisters are placed in the burrows). Most groundhogs do their damage during daylight hours, so some people leave their dogs outside to scare off intruders.

Cute as a Bunny

Admit it, rabbits are really cute. But when they attack your lettuces or go after the spinach, you want to wring their fragile little necks. If rabbits are the only pests in your garden, keeping them out is not such a difficult task. You will have to put up a fence, but it only needs to be about two feet high. Just use simple wooden stakes and chicken wire around the perimeter. Be sure to tack it down with steel pins, stones, or bricks, or Peter Cottontail and his relatives will find a way to go under.

Here Kitty, Kitty

We are a family of cat lovers. But even the most fanatic of feline fans might take issue when pussy cats poop in the garden. It's just plain disgusting. If neighborhood cats use your garden as a toilet, you have a couple options. First, keep the hose handy and give Kitty a shower when she sets paws in your space. Cats hate that and they learn quickly. If Pussy persists, sprinkle cayenne pepper on her favorite spot and she won't visit again. Neither method will hurt a cat, by the way.

Deer: In a Class of Their Own

My friend Ian McNeill wages a never-ending war against the deer that invade his backyard garden. On my most recent visit to see his intensively planted raised beds, Ian had just discovered a gaping hole in the netting he had installed. The deer were so desperate to get at the young beets that they tore into the netting with their hooves until it split open. Boy, does Ian hate those deer!

And so do most gardeners. At least gardeners who attempt to grow things in the same neighborhood a herd of deer calls home.

But there are solutions. One, of course, is to hunt them. That's not always an option in the case of suburban communities or in other places that don't allow hunting, or it might not be a solution that appeals to you. People have also tried …

♦ Tying aluminum pie pans to poles so they bang against each other in the wind.

♦ Placing net bags filled with shaved soap or human hair in strategic spots around the garden.

♦ Spraying the ground around plants or the perimeter of the garden with bobcat, lion, coyote, or fox urine. (I want to know whose job it is to collect that stuff!)

♦ Playing a recording of shotgun blasts.

♦ Installing motion detector–activated sprinklers.

♦ Playing a recording of the *1812 Overture*.

♦ Rigging huge spotlights to shine on the garden all night.

♦ Spraying a mixture of garlic, cayenne pepper, and canola oil on every last leaf.

♦ Spreading lion dung around the base of plants.

There are also some commercial products like hot pepper wax and garlic oil spray, along with special dispensers for the coyote and lion urine. Some of these strategies work some of the time. But the truth of the matter is if deer are hungry enough, they will put up with things that scare them like the noise and the predator urine, and with things that smell bad like the cayenne pepper and the garlic oil.

The only really good solution is a barrier, which is almost always in the form of a fence.

The key to a successful dear fence is height. Deer are remarkable jumpers, especially if they can get a running start. I remember a garden in Princeton, New Jersey, with a deer problem that has made national news. This garden had two chain link deer fences, one running parallel to the other but inside the perimeter. The owner of the estate found that a single fence wasn't enough to keep the local herd out, but that the deer couldn't cope with the second fence because they couldn't get that running start. Unfortunately, the place looked like a prison camp.

Compost Pile

Although the electric current that runs through electric deer fencing is not particularly high, it can hurt a young child. Keep that in mind before you have an electric fence installed.

Dave Benner, whose shade garden in Pennsylvania has been featured in many magazines and books, had such a problem with deer that he developed his own line of plastic mesh deer fencing. It can be up to 10 feet high and is strung between metal stakes. Combined with cattle gates at the driveway entrance, it has kept his garden deer free for a decade or more.

The other alternative is an electric fence. This really does keep Bambi and his family out of the garden. Electric fences have become less expensive as demand has increased.

The Least You Need to Know

- Identify the insects in your garden before you take any action.
- Encourage beneficial insects to take up residence in your garden.
- Give organic or natural approaches a try before using commercial pesticides.
- Use extreme caution with chemical pesticides.
- Use fencing to keep warm blooded animals from destroying your garden.

Chapter 22

Pruning and Trimming

In This Chapter

- ◆ Pick a pruning tool
- ◆ Find out how to prune bramble berries and grapes
- ◆ Learn how to put your garden to bed

In the next few pages, we look at the ways gardeners can keep plants healthy and productive by pruning and trimming, with some specific information on how to prune grapes and brambles. There is also a section on trimming herbs to maximize their potential.

You also learn a little about dividing plants to multiply them. And finally, we'll go through the steps you may want to take to put your garden to bed for the winter.

Pick a Pruning Tool

Gardeners get funny about tools. They may have a shed full of them, but they will reach for the same two or three every time. You won't need a big selection of *pruning* tools for your edible garden, but a couple basic items are essential, including a versatile hand pruning tool, small snips, and perhaps a lopper if you are doing lots of grapes, brambles, and shrub fruits.

Prof. Price's Pointers

Pruning is the cutting back of plant material to remove dead, diseased, or damaged parts; to alter the shape of the plant; to encourage new growth; and to improve the quality or quantity of the fruit or flowers.

Basic Pruners

The pruner, held in one hand, is used for cutting plant material up to about a half-inch in diameter.

Most hand pruners have metal blades and some sort of plastic-coated handles. A few have foam-covered or molded handles that have a comfortable feel. Blades can be chrome-plated steel, stainless steel, Teflon-coated steel, or carbon steel. The cutting mechanism is either a scissors action where a thin blade cuts against a thicker blade, or an anvil cut where a sharp upper blade cuts against a broad, flat blade.

Food for Thought

My favorite pruners are the Felco #7 bypass style with anvil blade, spring action, and signature bright red rotating handle. I've owned several pairs over the past 25 years (they don't wear out; I just lose them), and I have never found a style of hand pruners I like better. A few years ago, I gave Prof. Price a pair and he enjoys using them, too. What makes the #7s different is the way the rotating handle swivels in your hand—very comfortable and easy on the muscles, which is especially helpful when you have some big pruning jobs to do.

Garden Snips

Garden snips are handy little tools to have around for all kinds of garden tasks. You can use them to harvest herbs and vegetables that are cut from their stems (eggplants, peppers, some squash, and so on). They can also be used to trim out dead or diseased herbaceous (as opposed to woody) plant material. And once in a while you'll probably need them to cut twine or open a bag of mulch (but don't do that too often because it will dull the blade).

There are lots of different garden snips on the market. I have a pair that were given to me for my birthday 10 years ago, and I use them almost daily during the gardening season. I also sometimes use them when I can't find my kitchen scissors but don't tell my family that; they would think that's disgusting.

Loppers

This is the long-handled pruning tool you use to cut through thicker wood with a two-handed motion. You won't have too much need for this tool unless you are working with older grape vines and bramble berries with trunks that are more than a half-inch in diameter.

Grapes

Grapes must be pruned in order to promote strong growth and to simplify harvesting by forcing the grapes to grow where they can be reached. Pruning is essential for good grape culture, and is as important as the quality of the soil and the amount of irrigation.

There are a number of techniques, called systems, for pruning grapes, and they have somewhat unusual names:

- Umbrella Kniffen system
- Four-cane Kniffen system
- Six-cane Kniffen system
- Single curtain system

Though not actually complicated, the pruning systems require fairly precise work. For step-by-step directions visit one of the websites devoted to that topic, including mtvernon.wsu.edu/frt; www.ianr.unl.edu/pubs; www.ourgardengang.com; and www.extension.iastate.edu.

Grapes produce their fruit on one-year-old canes that are usually reddish-brown and about one third of an inch or so in diameter. Generally viticulturists (grape growers) prune before the buds on the canes open, and usually remove about 80 percent of the wood every year.

When pruning, you will want to select the strongest, but not necessarily the largest, canes to keep.

Garden Guru Says

All pruning tools should be kept well sharpened so that they deliver a clean, smooth cut every time. And if you have any suspicion that a plant you are pruning is infected with disease, wipe the blades clean with gauze soaked in alcohol between every cut.

Compost Pile

Prune too much of the grape vine, and you'll get too many leaves and not enough fruit. But, if you don't prune enough, you'll have wimpy vines that don't have enough strength to support the skimpy fruit that will grow.

Garden Guru Says

Dead wood is harder to cut than living wood unless it has begun to rot.

Bramble Berries

Of all the plants we have talked about in this book, bramble berries are probably the second most difficult to prune, but you can handle it. Raspberries produce on new canes, except everbearing varieties that produce a second time. The canes of noneverbearing raspberries die after they produce fruit, so they have to be removed by pruning.

Generally, you will prune out all damaged, diseased, misshapen, or puny canes leaving only the largest canes. They should be about four to six inches apart. Cut the remaining canes to five or six feet if you use trellises, or three to four feet if your brambles are free-standing.

For more detailed information about pruning bramble berries, go to www.inberry.com; www.utextension.utk.edu; or www.citygardening.org/raspinfo.

Herbs

Herbs are generally low maintenance plants. Most of them aren't too fussy about soil, and some can even survive with minimal watering. They are also pretty easy going when it comes to keeping trim. Only the perennials will need pruning, but some of the annuals will require an occasional "haircut" to prevent them from going to seed or to help renew growth.

Garden Guru Says

To pinch out a flower bud, gently squeeze the bud, just where it meets the stem, between your thumb and index finger and break it off with your fingernails.

When the weather gets hot and the plants have been around for a while, some herbs will be tempted to put out flowers. With most herbs, that's not a good thing. What you want to do with the basil, dill, mint, coriander, fennel, and most other herbs is to pinch out flower buds just as they appear.

If you have a lot of herbs growing in your garden, staying on top of this task will take some diligence.

Food for Thought

There are some herb flowers that you might want to allow to bloom because they are edible or because they are attractive. They include chives, rosemary, dill (to add to dill pickle jars as a garnish), nasturtiums (not technically an herb, but often grown with herbs), and chamomile. And if you want to collect herb seeds, you'll need to allow some of the herbs to go to seed in order to have them to collect!

If your herb plants get really scraggly looking, go after them with your garden snips. You'll want to do this anyway with your perennial herbs to keep them thick and compact. Just cut away, even up to half the plant. Do your cutting in the late afternoon when the sun isn't so strong, and give them a good watering. But don't do heavy pruning within a month of so of an expected frost. The new growth will be especially tender and will most likely be killed by the cold.

Annual herbs can be cut back drastically, especially those that had an early start. Just don't expect them to grow back quickly. Allow a few weeks or even a month for them to grow enough foliage to start harvesting again.

The Best and the Brightest

When I was a young child, Prof. Price grew tomato plants in his garden at our home in New Jersey. A particular memory of that time was watching him pick the flowers off the tomatoes. When I asked him why he was doing that he patiently explained to me that it would make the plants produce bigger, better tomatoes.

Many fruiting annuals can benefit from the removal of some of the flower buds so that more energy from the plant can go into the remaining flowers and thus into the fruit. Try this not only with tomatoes, but also peppers, eggplants, cucumbers, melons, pumpkins, and squash. By the way, this is one of the tricks some gardeners use to win the blue ribbon for the biggest tomato or pumpkin at the county fair.

Deadheading

No, this has nothing to do with the Grateful Dead! Deadheading is the practice of removing dead blooms from plants. Most deadheading is done on ornamental flowering annuals and perennials and shrubs in order to encourage future bloom production. But some deadheading is appropriate for edibles. You want to do this if the plant flowers but you don't want it to produce fruit or seeds. Use the same technique as you do for pinching out unwanted blooms.

Take Out Your Dead

Death is an inevitable part of the life cycle. With many, if not most edible gardens, death comes every year. We sow our annual plants, they grow, they reproduce and they die. So what do we do with all those dead plants?

After the first heavy frost, just about all the leaves and stems of herbaceous plants will have curled up and died. The annual plants will be dead and the perennials will go into dormancy. You should clean up all the dead plant material (unless you plan to do a tilling; see the next section), and get rid of it. The debris from healthy plants can go on the compost pile. Any with obvious disease problems should be disposed of.

If you have some late harvest plants like turnips or kale, just clean up around them.

Prof. Price's Pointers

Seeds and fruits have the highest priority for a plant's resources. That's why the leaves of heavily fruited plants can sometimes look half dead. It follows that removal of some of the flower buds, blooms, or very young fruits can serve to divert more goodies to the remaining fruits.

Compost Pile

Although it may be tempting to just walk away from the dead garden after a long season of working in it, resist the temptation. Old plant material is a disease and infestation habitat waiting to happen.

Not Dead; Just Asleep

Pulling up all the dead plants is the shortened version of the process of "putting the garden to be bed" for the winter. Fastidious gardeners will do more. For some gardeners, it prolongs the time they get to spend in the garden. For others, it prolongs the time they have to spend in their garden. Either way, the more you do at the end of the season, the less you will have to do at the beginning of the next gardening season.

Here We Go A-Tilling Again

If you have the time and the inclination, you might want to give your garden a good tilling before you close it up for the winter. If you do plan to till, you won't have to pull out dead plants; you'll simply till them under. Just be sure to remove any diseased plants and dispose of them safely.

More Manure

Before you till, you might think about adding a truckload or two of manure. This time you can use fresh manure, because you are putting it on an unplanted bed where it can't burn tender plant parts.

Bedding Down the Perennials

If your garden is in a colder zone, you might want to invest a little time in mulching the perennials. Strawberries, asparagus, and especially artichokes may need that extra protection. The following table will help you determine what type and how much mulch to use, and when to lay it on.

Plant	Type of Mulch	How Much	When to Mulch
Berry	Straw or wood chips	Three to six inches	After first hard frost
Asparagus	Straw, wood shavings, compost, or leaf mold	Four inches	After first hard frost
Artichokes	Straw, leaves, or plastic	Four inches	Before a frost (Artichokes won't survive long, cold winters; this protection is for marginal areas that sometimes experience a cold snap.)

Wrapping Up the Berries

Bramble berries will need some extra protection in cold zones above Zone 6, and you can't very well mulch the canes. But you can wrap them in burlap. (Buy it in long wide sheets rather than in pre-cut sections.) It's not so much the cold that's the problem, though really cold weather can and will kill some varieties. But cold winds can cause terrible damage. To wrap your brambles, drive wood stakes in the ground at convenient intervals around the bramble patch. The stakes should be taller than the canes. Wrap the burlap around the stakes attaching it to the stakes with a staple gun. You can use metal stakes but you'll have to figure out another way to attach the burlap.

Cover Up

Now that you have a beautifully retilled garden bed with nothing in it, why not plant a special crop of plants called a cover crop that will work to improve the soil while you do nothing at all (well, almost nothing). Cover crops, which are sometimes called green manure, help to reduce soil compaction by loosening heavy soils at the root zone, reduce the leaching of nitrogen and other nutrients during winter rains, and, when tilled under, add organic matter to the soil. Legume cover crops add nitrogen to the soil because they fix nitrogen in their roots.

Some of the plants used for cover crops include the following:

- Buckwheat
- Crimson clover (legume)
- Annual ryegrass
- Winter wheat
- Field peas (legume)
- Oats
- Sweet clover (legume)
- Hairy vetch (legume)
- Fava beans

Most cover crops are planted in the later summer or early fall. For more information on how to sow your own, look at one of these websites: www.msue.msu.edu (click on information resources, then home horticulture), www.uri.edu, www.hort.cornell.edu (look for fact sheet #9), or gardening.wsu.edu.

The Least You Need to Know

- Take the time to learn how to prune your bramble berries and grapes to ensure healthy plants and bountiful harvests.
- Pinch back flowers on herb plants to keep them going in hot weather.
- Wrap brambleberries in burlap to help them survive the winter.

- Use mulch to protect artichokes, asparagus, and strawberries in cold weather.
- Plant a legume cover crop to reduce soil compaction and to help return nitrogen to the soil.

Troubleshooting

In This Chapter

- ◆ Become familiar with some of the diseases that could affect your garden
- ◆ Develop a few diagnostic skills
- ◆ Find out why your smoking is bad for your garden
- ◆ Learn to look for disease symptoms

There's a lot that can go wrong in your edible garden. I don't want to sound like an alarmist, but even the most seasoned gardeners have had disappointing seasons or even disasters. It goes with the territory.

But to put your plant problems into perspective, it's important to keep in mind that thousands of plant pathologists, agricultural experts, and farm bureau agents have made plant pathology and the detection of diseases and problems their life's work. For our purposes here, there is only so much we can cover in one chapter. The next few pages are designed to be an overview and a starting point for spotting and diagnosing problems in your garden.

In this chapter, we look at some of the major plant diseases, how you can identify them, and how to handle them. We also look at a few of the more common symptoms of a distressed plant and some of the possible causes of the problems.

Garden Guru Says

If you're having trouble identifying what's wrong with an ailing plant, talk to an expert. But don't expect even the most experienced plant professional to make a diagnosis without seeing the problem first hand. Put the evidence (leaf, stem, fruit, insect, whatever) into an airtight baggie for your own little show and tell. County agents and master gardeners are sometimes available to help. And some garden centers and nurseries have their own garden gurus on staff.

Types of Diseases

Most plant diseases are viral, bacterial, or fungal (not unlike human diseases, for that matter). A few are related to nematodes. Then there are some *abiotic* problems that can occur because of nutrient deficiencies, too much or too little sun, or too much or not enough water.

Prof. Price's Pointers

Abiotic means that the problem is of nonliving or nonbiological origin.

Not every garden plant gets every disease. Some plants seem to get more than their fair share, whereas others are rarely bothered. The following table gives you a quick glance at some of the problems facing a few of your favorite edibles.

Plant	Disease
Tomato	Anthracnose, tomato mosaic virus, curly top virus, blossom end rot, cucumber mosaic virus, root knot, bacterial speck, bacterial spot, bacterial canker, late blight, fusarium crown rot, fusarium foot rot, phytophyhora root rot, tomato powdery mildew, fusarium wilt, verticillium wilt
Lettuce	Downy mildew, leaf drop, turnip mosaic virus, bacterial leaf rot, corky rot, southern blight rust, sow thistle yellow vein virus, anthracnose, lettuce mosaic virus, cucumber mosaic virus, beet western yellow virus, big vein, powdery mildew
Beet	Leaf spot, damping off, pocket rot, root rot, curly top, powdery mildew, downy mildew, cyst nematode
Asparagus	Fusarium root rot, fusarium crown rot, asparagus rust, botrytis blight, Cercospora blight, purple spot, branchlet blight, asparagus virus, tobacco streak virus
Okra	Fusarium wilt, root knot, leaf spot, blossom and fruit blight, cotton root rot, southern blight
Potato	Black dot disease, fusarium dry rot, early blight, late blight, black scurf fungus, silver scurf fungus, powdery scab, pythium seed rot, pythium rubber rot, ring rot, spindle tuber, fusarium wilt, verticillium wilt

As you can see, the lists of diseases are pretty long. Some diseases are peculiar to a specific plant whereas others attack a long list of victims. Don't be totally put off. Your garden isn't likely to be invaded by every disease listed here. But the more you grow, the more likely your chances of learning first hand about these things.

The following sections might help you get to the bottom of what's troubling your plants.

Viral Diseases

As they can with humans, viruses can cause mayhem, turning healthy plants into diseased in a matter of days, if not hours. There are hundreds of viruses that attack plants. Some of the more common ones include the following:

- Beet curly top
- Cucumber mosaic
- Pepper mottle
- Pepper golden mosaic
- Potato virus
- Tobacco mosaic
- Tomato spotted wilt

> **CAUTION**
>
> **Compost Pile** _____
>
> Never put diseased plant material on the compost pile. Dispose of it by bagging it and putting it in the trash, incinerating it (if that's allowed in your area), or burying it far from the garden.

> **CAUTION**
>
> **Compost Pile** _____
>
> The tobacco mosaic, a virus that is deadly for tomatoes, can be spread by smokers. The tobacco in cigarettes can actually carry the virus and the smoker can become the vector (carrier) of the disease. As if you didn't need another reason to give up smoking!

Some symptoms of viral infection include curled or twisted leaves, mottled or mosaic patterns on leaves, brown or yellow spots on leaves, stunted growth, and small flowers that might be brown or otherwise "off."

Many plant viruses are spread by insects with aphids, leafhoppers, mites, and whitefly being the worst offenders. Plant viruses can also be spread by infected tools and equipment, infected mulch, and on a person's hands or even clothing.

Unfortunately, viral infections in plants are not treatable by methods available to home gardeners. The best thing to do if you suspect that a plant has a viral disease is to remove it immediately and dispose of it. Keeping weeds and insects under control will help, too.

Bacterial Diseases

There are lots of bacterial diseases, but the following three are of particular concern to vegetable gardeners.

Bacterial Wilt

Everyone who has ever grown zucchini or pumpkins has probably had experience with this major bacterial plant disease. Bacterial wilt, which is also called *vascular wilt*, causes buildup of the bacteria within the vascular (water carrying) system of plants. When the waterways become completely clogged, they can no longer carry water throughout the plant; it wilts and dies. The disease is systemic, meaning it is carried throughout the plant, rather than localized, or limited to one part of the plant.

Bacterial wilt primarily attacks members of the cucurbit family, especially cucumbers, squash, pumpkins, cantaloupes, and muskmelons. It tends to leave watermelon alone.

Bacterial wilt is spread by cucumber beetles that have the bacteria living in their bodies. When they come up out of the ground in the spring, they start chomping on a healthy plant, making an opening or wound for the disease to enter. The bacteria is in the insects' waste and eventually finds its way into the wound. The plant can be dead in a matter of weeks.

Garden Guru Says

Squash borer produces similar symptoms to bacterial wilt. But with the insect infestation, you might actually find one of the caterpillars inside the plant, or you might find tunnels through the stems.

Food for Thought

One way to help you determine whether your squash or cucumbers have bacterial wilt is to cut a piece of stem from an affected plant. Slowly squeeze the stem and see what comes out. If it is a white, slimy substance that pulls into a string, it is most likely bacterial wilt.

When you first see your cucumbers wilting, you will probably suspect a water shortage. After watering, the plant might perk up a bit, but if it has bacterial wilt it will probably be wilted the next day. Some other symptoms include retarded growth and excessive blooms and branching. You might also see that the veins of pumpkins and squash plants turn yellow. This doesn't happen when cucumbers have bacterial wilt.

The best way to deal with bacterial wilt is to not have it in the first place. Keeping the cucumber beetle population down is key. But the chemicals that kill them also do a number on bees, and they are essential for pollination. Removing infected plants, hand-picking insects, and rotating crops are good natural approaches. If the problem persists after several seasons, consider growing something else instead. Or call your County Extension office to ask for some advice on using chemical controls without endangering bees.

Bacterial Canker

This nasty-sounding disorder is primarily a disease of stone fruit (which we're not interested in here) and tomatoes. It starts out locally with dark spots on the leaves or stems that look wet. The disease can also first appear with an overall wilting. Sometimes the stems split up and down and you might see some dark brown sores (these are the cankers) with necrotic tissue (that's dead plant tissue). The wilting and splitting is evidence that the disease has entered the plant's vascular system and is therefore systemic.

Bacterial canker is caused by a bacteria that lingers in dead or dying tomato plants, or in host plants like eggplant, peppers, and other members of the *Solanaceae* family (the nightshade family). The disease is easily spread by splashing water, by small wounds made during transplanting (just a broken leaf is enough), or when the gardener prunes or removes stems while caging or staking.

To keep the threat of bacterial canker to a minimum, buy certified disease-free seed and seedlings whenever possible, disinfect pruners and snips between each cut, wash your hands before handling tomatoes, stay out of the garden when it's wet, and rotate your crops.

Prof. Price's Pointers

A host plant is one that is susceptible to a certain pathogen (virus, bacteria, and so on). An alternative host is one in which a pathogen has taken up residence at some point in its life cycle. The alternative host might or might not be susceptible to the pathogen.

Garden Guru Says

Some gardeners use a copper-based fungicide to treat a bacterial spot. The fungicide won't cure the plant, but sometimes it will keep the bacteria from spreading to the rest of your tomatoes and peppers.

Bacterial Spot

This disease attacks tomatoes and peppers and affects every part of the plant except the roots, especially during periods of high humidity or rainy, wet conditions. Look for raised yellowish lesions (spots) on green tomatoes and on both ripe and immature peppers. The lesions turn brown or black and start to look like scabs. The leaves will develop spots too and will often drop off. The plant will look absolutely awful and you won't want to eat any of the fruit, even if some of it does ripen.

Bacterial spot spreads pretty much the same way as bacterial canker, and is just as or more difficult to treat. You'll probably wind up just pulling the diseased plants out and discarding them. The best way to deal with this disease is to prevent it in the first place: Use certified seed, stay out of the wet garden, follow strict garden hygiene, and rotate crops.

There's a Fungus Among Us

Fungal diseases are another headache for gardeners. They are insidious, difficult to control, and frequently lethal. Some of the most common are anthracnose, Fusarium wilt, various rusts, and downy and powdery mildew.

Anthracnose

Anthracnose is a pretty ugly plant disease with various forms that attack a number of vegetables including tomatoes, beans, cucumbers, peppers, melons, squash, and pumpkins. It's caused by a fungus that lives in the soil over the winter and is spread by insects, rain, wind, watering, and by infected seeds or seedlings. The symptoms start with large, round, soft spots on the fruits that might become black or brown and develop quickly into rot. The leaves and stems might develop lesions or spots. You might find some relief if you spray with an anti-fungal spray. Other ways to deal with anthracnose include the following:

- Use pretreated seeds.
- Select resistant varieties.
- Practice good garden hygiene.
- Rotate annual crops every year.
- Avoid walking in the garden just after a rain or an overhead watering.
- Keep weeds to a minimum.
- Remove infected plants.

Other plants that can be affected by anthracnose include grapes, raspberries, blackberries, blueberries, strawberries, corn, and lettuce. Infected brambles can be saved by pruning the infected canes and removing them from the patch. Providing good air circulation will also help.

Rust

Rust is another really bad one caused by a parasitic fungus. Rust attacks bramble berries, asparagus, corn, beans, and peas. The first symptom is usually a blemish or lesion on the underside of lower leaves. Eventually it becomes more of a sore which opens and releases the orange to red spores, hence the name. There is no good cure. Commercial growers might use some heavy-duty fungicides, but home gardeners don't want to go there. Instead, cut your losses by digging up the infected plants and disposing of them. In your next attempt, plant in new or different beds and look for resistant varieties.

Fusarium Wilt

Fusarium wilt is tricky because the fusarium fungus can live in the soil for years without showing itself in plants. But when plants it likes (members of the *Cucurbit* family) are planted in the infected soil, it easily enters the plants through their roots.

Plants can be infected at several stages of their development, including just after germination when it results in damping off. Older plants might wilt, then appear to recover, and then wilt again. Later the leaves start to turn yellow or brown, and eventually the whole plant just dies. Sometimes, when conditions are particularly wet and humid, you might see a pale pink powdery residue on the leaves and stems.

There's not much you can do about the disease once the plants are infected. Prevention is the key. The only defense is a good offense—plant resistant varieties. If you have a crop of fusarium-infected plants, don't plant any more *Cucurbits* in that spot for a few years.

Mildew

The two major mildew diseases are caused by different fungal infections. Powdery mildew, which affects cucumbers, squash, onions, and blueberries, tends to hit new growth and particularly blossoms which often dry up, so no fruit is set. The mildew grows on the surface of leaves which will look dark and dirty and will feel kind of sooty.

Downy mildew is actually a parasite that grows inside plants, especially grapes, cucumbers, beans, and onions. It produces purple and black spots on leaves and a gray mold on fruits. Downy mildew weakens plants so they produce less.

Germination Problems

When seeds don't grow, there are a limited number of reasons why, including the following:

> ### Garden Guru Says
>
> A few mildew-killing fungicides on the market are marketed as safe for vegetable gardens. Most contain copper and sulfur. Be sure to read labels carefully before using. And of course, wash any fruit or vegetables that come from treated plants. Both mildew fungi can live in old garden debris, so good garden hygiene is a must.

- ◆ The seed is old.
- ◆ The seed is infected.
- ◆ It is planted too deep.
- ◆ It was washed away in the rain or by heavy irrigation.
- ◆ Birds got it.
- ◆ It was burned by fertilizer.
- ◆ Too much moisture.
- ◆ Not enough moisture.
- ◆ Too cold.
- ◆ Too hot.
- ◆ Residual preemergent herbicide in soil.

Sometimes it's a combination of things that prevents seed from germinating. But if you see a big flock of crows or starlings land in the garden right after you plant, and the seeds don't sprout, I think you'll know what the problem was.

Seedling Situations

So your seeds have all germinated and the little sprouts have gotten off to a fine start and all of a sudden, they are failing to thrive, or even dying. What happened? Following are possibilities for what might have gone wrong:

- Too cold
- Too much water
- Not enough water
- Not enough sunlight
- Too much fertilizer
- Not enough fertilizer
- Insect attacks
- Damping off
- Residual herbicide in the soil

Not all these conditions will result in dead plants. But you will need to correct those things that can be corrected, and quickly, if you want to save your newly planted crops.

Lousy Leaves

The appearance of a plant's leaves will give some pretty clear indications of its overall health. The occasional nibbled edge or a yellow leaf or two is not a sign that the plant is in deep trouble. But if, on the other hand, all the leaves are turning yellow or if more leaves have holes than don't, then you can be pretty sure the plant is in big trouble.

There can be any number of issues that will show themselves in the foliage—disease, insect infestation, lack of nitrogen, or other crucial element. The trick is to make the correct diagnosis.

Yellow Leaves

Yellow leaves are one of the most common symptoms that indicate something is wrong with your plant. And it can be a little tricky. If many of the leaves are yellow, it can mean the plant isn't getting enough nitrogen, the weather is too hot, or there is not enough sunlight.

Food for Thought

Occasionally, too much sunlight can be the culprit that causes leaves to yellow. Though most edible plants want full sun all day, some plants might find themselves suddenly in a sunnier situation than they were used to. This might happen if, for example, you were growing corn next to some kale. But if for some reason the corn had to be removed and the kale was no longer in the shade of the corn, the leaves might turn yellow.

If only the newest leaves are yellow, it might mean that the plant is getting too much fertilizer or it has an iron or manganese deficiency. But when older leaves turn yellow, it could mean there's not enough nitrogen (or iron or manganese), the plant is being watered too often, or it has root rot problems. But sometimes yellow older leaves mean that the leaves are getting ready to drop off anyway. If there are plenty of healthy-looking newer leaves, there probably isn't a problem.

Sticky Leaves

When you find black or brown sticky stuff on your plants' leaves, you know that you'll find some kind of insect infestation. That sticky stuff is called frass or honeydew and it's basically insect poop. Keep your eyes open for the insects that are leaving their calling cards behind. Then refer to Chapter 22 to find out what to do with your insect problems.

Some Other Lousy Leaves to Look For

There are so many things that can go wrong with plants, and much of it will show up in the leaves. Here are a few more symptoms to look for:

Wilted leaves:

- ◆ Too much water
- ◆ Too much fertilizer
- ◆ Root rot
- ◆ Not enough water
- ◆ Too cold (frost damage)

Defoliation:

- ◆ Too much water
- ◆ Too much fertilizer
- ◆ Too cold
- ◆ Not enough water
- ◆ Root rot
- ◆ Exposure to herbicide

Yellow leaves:

- Low nitrogen
- Not enough light
- Too hot
- Sunscald

New leaves are yellow:

- Too much fertilizer
- Iron or manganese deficiency

Older leaves are yellow:

- Nitrogen, manganese, or potassium deficiency
- Too much water
- Root rot
- Normal loss of older leaves

Ends of leaves are necrotic:

- Too much fertilizer
- Damage from pesticides
- Not enough water
- Bacterial wilt

The Least You Need to Know

- Look for disease resistant seeds and seedlings.
- Always buy certified disease-free seeds and seedlings.
- Avoid working in the garden when it's wet.
- Practice good garden hygiene.
- Rotate crops every year to avoid soil-born and insect-spread diseases.
- Consult a garden professional when you can't figure out what's troubling your plants.

Part 6

Reaping the Rewards

This is what it is all about—let's eat! There's nothing like picking crops you have grown yourself. In this part of the book, we look at the end product. You'll learn how to determine when it's time to harvest and how to do it right. There are sections on canning, freezing, and drying food for you homemaker types. You'll also learn strategies to prolong harvest. There's also some information on how to share what you grow with those who are less fortunate. In these last few chapters you learn about seed saving, which has become a near cult with wildly enthusiastic followers. There is also a section on tool care and repair and an admonition to keep good gardening records. Finally, you get a chance to take a guided look back on what you have accomplished; to see what you did right and to figure out what can be done better.

Chapter 24

Harvesting and What to Do with Your Bounty

In This Chapter

- Learn when and how to harvest vegetables and fruits
- Find out how to extend your harvesting season
- Get a basic education in putting foods up
- Discover things to do with too many zucchini

It's finally here. What you've been waiting for all season: the harvest. It's the gardener's big reward. In this chapter, we look at some of the ways you can determine ripeness and some techniques for harvesting. We also talk about how to preserve and store the fruits and vegetables you have grown so that you can enjoy the bounty for weeks and even months after the harvest. And finally, we explore some of the ways you can spread the wealth by sharing the food you have grown yourself.

The Ripeness Test

Many factors contribute to the process of ripening. Plant varieties, soil and air temperature, day length, rainfall or irrigation amounts, stress, even insect infestation or disease can all make a difference on the rate of growth and ultimately ripeness.

> **Prof. Price's Pointers** _____
>
> The ripening of fruit involves many metabolic changes including the conversion of starch to sugars, the breakdown of cell walls and of chlorophyll, and the synthesis of other pigments, such as anthocyanins (red) and carotenoids (yellow and orange). Ripening in many (but not all) fruits is associated with a spectacular rise in the rate of respiration, which goes by the sexy name of *cliacteric*. These metabolic and respiratory changes are very strongly dependent on temperature; as a consequence, refrigerated fruits ripen only very slowly.

Usually, we talk about ripeness with regard to fruiting plants like tomatoes, eggplants, and peppers and for fruits including melons, berries, and grapes. It's actually pretty easy to figure out whether or not they are ripe. Common sense helps. But there are a few rules of thumb to consider before deciding whether something is ready to be picked.

Fruiting Vegetables

Tomatoes, unless they are one of the heirloom or exotic varieties, should be evenly red, with maybe just a little green or yellow at the top where the fruit meets the stem.

Eggplants and peppers should be shiny and firm, but not hard, with well-developed color. You can pick red, orange, or yellow peppers when they are still green. Green green peppers will not change color but will eventually rot if you leave them on the vine too long. If you are growing several varieties of peppers, be sure to place markers so you'll know which plants are which.

> **Garden Guru Says** _____
>
> To harvest fruiting vegetables, use a pair of clean, sharp garden snips or kitchen scissors. Cut just a bit of stem with the fruit. You want to avoid sawing or hacking at the stem (which will happen if you use a dull tool) because that can cause damage, making it easier for insects or disease to enter the wound. Clean your snips with alcohol between each cut, or at least between each plant to minimize the risk of introducing disease.

Fruit

Strawberries should be all red with little or no white at the stem end. Most people pick strawberries with a little thumbnail action. Take all of the berry stem, cutting it off where it meets the main stem. This will help the berries stay fresher longer.

Bramble berries and blueberries should be picked when they are fully ripe but before they become overripe. They should have rich color with no green parts. They should also have a fully sweet flavor with no bitter or tart aftertaste.

Food for Thought _____

Tomatoes can be picked before they are fully ripe. And if the weather turns very hot, you might want to do a thorough harvesting of unripe good-sized tomatoes, and then finish the ripening process on a sunny windowsill. Or you can fry or pickle your green tomatoes, a favorite treat for our copy editor Michael Dietsch.

It's just a little harder to determine the ripeness of grapes. Take the advice of Rosie Lerner, a horticulture specialist at Purdue University who wrote a very useful article on harvesting grapes (the entire article is available at www.hort.purdue.edu/ext/grapes.html).

Look for the following signs that grapes are ripe. They should be or should have the following:

- "Natural bloom," the whitish coating on each grape
- Firm
- Full size
- Brown, not green, seeds
- Just slightly soft
- Sweet-tasting
- The right color (You'll need to know the characteristics of your varieties.)

Did you ever thump a watermelon in the supermarket to determine whether it is ripe? You choose one that "sounds" right only to find that's still hard as a rock inside? Well, even the experts recommend the thump test. But you'll have a better idea if you know more or less how many days the watermelon is supposed to take from seed to harvest and how large it's supposed to be at maturity. Add that information to the fact that ripe watermelons have a little patch of yellow on the skin where the fruit meets the ground, and have that slightly hollow sound when you give them a thump.

For more specific harvesting information on many of the plants we have covered in this book, go to www.urbanext.uiuc.edu and type "harvesting vegetables" in the search box. Or visit www.savvygardener.com/Features/harvesting_vegetables.html.

Size *Does* Count—Bigger Isn't Always Better

When I go to our local Grange Fair, I always visit the vegetable exhibits where area gardeners and 4-H kids get prizes for the biggest tomatoes and pumpkins. Sometimes bigger is better. But often, the smaller veggies have superior flavor. Of course you can grow dwarf varieties or small versions of all kinds of vegetables including cherry and grape tomatoes, carrots, patty pan squash, watermelons, and others.

Some standard-sized vegetables can be harvested when they are still very tiny, yet fully formed. These tasty "baby" vegetables can command high prices in the produce department, but they won't cost you a penny more to grow in your garden. The best vegetables for harvesting young include the following.

Vegetable	Minimum Size to Pick (Estimated)
Beets	Golf ball size
Carrots	Two inches or more
Corn	Fully formed; two to three inches long
Peas	Peas are fully formed; half the size of fully mature peas
Zucchini	Four inches long; one inch across
Summer squash	Four inches long; one inch across
Eggplant	10 inches long
Scallions	As big around as a pencil
Leek	Two inches across
Snap beans	As wide as a pipe cleaner
Cauliflower	Softball size (remember to blanch it)
Potato	Size of a medium egg
Lettuce	The size that appeals to you
Other greens	The size that appeals to you

If you plan to harvest lots of "baby" vegetables, you might want to add extra plants. It takes many more tiny beets or eggplants to fill your dinner plate than normal-size ones.

Late Harvests

As you might have figured out after reading the chapters devoted to how to grow various edibles, some plants have a drawn-out harvest period.

If you have planted in relays (made additional sowings of the same plant over a period of several weeks), or if you have made spring, summer, and fall plantings, you can probably count on a longer harvest period. There are additional methods for giving the home gardener extended and late harvests of some of their favorite edibles, including the following:

◆ Use floating row covers, after the fruit has set, to hold heat in and protect plants from early frosts.

◆ Make mini-greenhouses over your garden rows with wire or wooden frames and plastic sheeting.

◆ Plant a crop of smaller things like lettuce, arugula, tender herbs, mini carrots, and radishes in a cold frame.

◆ Cover individual plants with cloches or bell jars when the temperatures dip. Remove them when it gets warmer.

◆ Bring a few things inside (especially herbs).

◆ Build a greenhouse.

If you do expect an unusually early frost and you don't have the time or inclination to build shelters for your garden, you can improvise. I've used sheets, blankets, beach towels, tablecloths, drop cloths, shower curtains, and even newspapers to throw over plants I was not willing to sacrifice to an early frost. On many occasions, I was able to add several weeks to my gardening season with my eclectic plant covers.

You can also extend your harvest by planting things that you don't mind spending a little time in the cold. You might recall that some vegetables like Brussels sprouts, kale, spinach, and chard can be harvested after the first frost, and some, like rutabagas, turnips, winter squash, and pumpkins actually have a richer flavor after they've been exposed to some cold.

> **Food for Thought**
>
> Garden writers Eliot Coleman and Barbara Damrosch grow organic vegetables year round in their tunnel-style greenhouse using only heat generated by the sun. And they do this in Maine! Coleman has written a book, *Four Season Harvest* (Chelsea Green Publishing Co., 1992) with details on how they have accomplished this amazing feat.

Handle with Care

Some plants—cabbage, cauliflower, carrots, turnips and parsnips, radishes, leeks, onions in particular—are harvested whole. You either cut or pull them right out of the garden and discard the parts you don't want. But many plants—beans, peas, tomatoes, pepper, eggplants, lettuce, zucchini, strawberries, and bramble berries, to name a few—are harvested in stages. Many of these plants produce fruit over the course of several weeks, so the attentive gardener might actually have the opportunity for (or the chore of) daily harvesting.

With this kind of extended harvest period, you must take great care not to damage the plants you pick from. Never yank or tug on a fruit to remove it from the stem. If the fruit doesn't release after a slight twist of the wrist, use your garden snips or kitchen scissors to cut it off. With peas and beans, use your thumbnail to cut through the tiny stem that attaches the fruit to the vine.

Food for Thought

One way to harvest lettuces and other greens such as spinach, kale, chard, beets, and collards is by thinning young seedlings to the desired distances between plants in a row. You can use these tender young thinnings for salad. Later, you can continue to harvest individual leaves from plants without disrupting their growth. Just be sure to only take a few from each plant so that it is left with enough foliage. You should never take more than about ⅛ or so of the leaves of an individual plant until it's time to harvest the whole thing.

Compost Pile

Always wash your hands before entering the garden to harvest, or any time for that matter. It's not a bad idea to wash again between visiting different types of plants. Though this might seem hyper-cautious, it can help to avoid spreading disease in your garden.

While you are harvesting, you should always be on the lookout for signs of disease or infestation. You can examine the undersides of leaves, pick off insects, and remove damaged leaves and fruits. In addition to carrying a basket for your harvest, take along a plastic bag to collect anything yucky. Then dump it in the trash after you've finished your picking.

Try to harvest on dry days and late enough in the day that the dew is gone. Harvesting in the early evening is a good time too, especially right before you start making dinner. You'll have the very freshest produce that way.

Canning, Freezing, and Drying

There is something extraordinarily satisfying about having a pantry full of jams, jellies, relishes, and pickles you have prepared yourself from the bounty of your garden. In the summer of 1977, back when I had my really big garden in New Jersey, I took a course on canning at the Rutgers University Cooperative Extension. It was a half-day affair during which I learned how to "put up" foods.

That summer I made strawberry and cherry jams, mint and apple jellies, bread and butter pickles, and dill pickles, and I put up dozens of jars of tomatoes. It was glorious. I later learned from my mother, who had never in her life made jelly or pickles, that *her* mother had taken the very same kind of course from the Cooperative Extension in Connecticut back in the late 1920s. I felt an incredible sense of connectedness to my roots.

In this section, we talk about some of the options you have for putting food up. Keep in mind that whatever method you try, use only the best and fully ripe fruits and vegetables and those that are free of blemishes and signs of insect damage or disease.

Canning

Canning fresh produce is a great way to preserve the bounty from your garden. And it's not all that difficult. The key is safety. You need to know what you are doing or you could wind up poisoning your family and friends. If you can't take a class at your local County Extension or adult education school, or if you don't have a friend or relative who is willing to teach you, go online for excellent step-by-step instructions. Some of the best sites include www.ext.nodak.edu, www.fcs.uga.edu, www.osu.edu, and www.usu.edu. I found all of them, and many more by just searching Google with the words "home canning."

There are several basic canning methods.

Method	Description
Cold pack	Putting uncooked food into canning jars, then processing
Hot pack	Putting cooked food into canning jars, then processing
Pickling	Combining cooked or uncooked food with a vinegar solution, then processing
Conserving	Combining fruit products with sugar (and sometimes pectin), then processing

The pickling process raises the acid level in the preserving jar to a level that is inconsistent with the growth of bacteria, yeasts, molds, and fungi that cause spoiling, and possibly illness. And because of their naturally high acid content, most tomatoes can be canned without adding anything to them, though some people add a little lemon juice or citric acid. They are usually processed in boiling water for a specific amount of time.

Canning vegetables other than tomatoes will require a different process, one that is done in a pressure canner. And even if you add nothing more than a garlic clove or a sprig of basil to your tomatoes, you'll need to do them in a pressure canner.

CAUTION

Compost Pile

Be aware that some varieties of tomatoes have been bred to have reduced acid levels, which might be kinder on some people's stomachs. However, lower acid levels make these varieties poor candidates for canning. Know your varieties before you can tomatoes.

Freezing

If you plan your garden well, you can freeze enough food to last all year in the freezer. And for those who are just a little afraid of the canning thing, freezing is the way to go.

Just about anything you grow can be frozen. Some things will need to be cooked first, whereas other vegetables can be frozen after a quick blanching in hot water or even raw.

Here's how to freeze some of the vegetables we've covered in this book.

Food	Method
Asparagus	B
Beans	B
Peas	B
Corn	B, C
Broccoli	B
Peppers	R
Cabbage	B
Summer squash	B, C
Winter squash	C
Beets	C
Garlic	R
Eggplant	C
Onion	R
Tomato	R, B, C

Key: B = blanch, C = fully cooked, R = raw

For a complete list, with detailed instructions, go to www.gardenguides.com, www.ext. colostate.edu/pubs, or any other County Extension site you find online.

Garden Guru Says

To learn how to keep your harvest for later consumption in root cellars and cold storage, visit www.extension.umn.edu. This site features a very useful chart on the storage requirements of most of the vegetables we have covered in this book.

Most vegetables are blanched for one to three minutes. To stop the cooking process, put the blanched vegetable in a bowl of ice water, drain, and dry before freezing.

Drying

Humans learned to dry food very early in our collective history. For thousands of years it was the only method they had to preserve food. You probably learned in grade school how Native Americans dried berries, corn, fish, and thin strips of meat to help them survive during difficult times.

Drying food became a lost art until the back-to-nature movement of the late 1960s. Since then more people are trying it. My old neighbor Frank Pinello made sun-dried tomatoes on racks on his terrace one summer, and they were quite delicious.

Tomatoes and various fruits are among the easiest things to dry. But enthusiasts try drying just about any vegetable. It takes a lot of effort, and failure is common. The important elements to success are high heat, low humidity, and adequate air circulation. Open-air drying is the most difficult method and the most prone to failure. Simple solar dryers have more success, while electric dehydrators are probably the best way to go. If you are really interested in trying this method of food preservation, go online to find one the many websites with details on how to do it.

Sharing the Bounty, or What to Do with a Hundred Zucchini

> **CAUTION**
>
> **Compost Pile**
>
> Always keep in mind that no matter how much people like to receive a gift of fresh produce from a gardening friend, no one wants an overweight zucchini. Those huge green hulks that look like caveman clubs are best thrown on the compost pile. Then take a look at them as they rot to remind yourself to harvest early and often.

> **Garden Guru Says**
>
> Plant a Row for the Hungry is a national public service campaign of The Garden Writers Association of America. This program encourages gardeners to grow a little extra each year to share with needy neighbors. To find out more about this organization go to www.gwaa.org.

There are lots of jokes about gardeners searching for ingenious ways to dispose of an overabundance of zucchini or eggplant. That's a success problem that we would all like to enjoy. But sometimes we are blessed with more produce than we can manage to eat, can, freeze, or give to our neighbors and co-workers. So what do we do with it?

If you have given away fresh vegetables and fruits from your garden to everyone you know and you still have too much, think about donating some to a local food bank or homeless shelter. These places are often delighted to be able to offer fresh food to their clients who usually subsist on canned or packaged items.

Some food banks will also accept your fresh food that you have frozen yourself, especially if they know you and you have labeled the item with the contents and the date it was frozen.

There are many such organizations all over the country. Your county extension office might know of some in your community.

If you still have way too much harvest to handle, think about setting up a little roadside stand. Bill and Jane MacDowell, who have an extraordinary garden in my community, put their excess produce on a stand at the end of their driveway with an honor box for people to pay for what they take. Then Bill and Jane donate the proceeds to a local wildflower preserve.

And if your garden produces prolific amounts of gourmet-style vegetables and herbs, you could let some of your local restaurants, caterers, or specialty markets know about it. They might want to give you all kinds of money for your fancy fresh stuff.

The Least You Need to Know

◆ Know your varieties and their approximate maturity times so you can estimate a harvest date.

◆ Use clean, sharp garden snips or kitchen scissors to harvest stem fruits.

◆ Pick when the garden is dry to avoid spreading diseases

◆ Learn how to can and freeze foods so you can enjoy your harvest for months.

◆ Think about sharing your harvest with friends, neighbors, and those who might not have enough to eat.

Chapter 25

Next Year's Garden

In This Chapter

- ◆ Find out about the fascinating world of seed savers
- ◆ Learn how to bring herbs indoors safely
- ◆ Discover the advantages of keeping a record of your gardening activities
- ◆ Get a handle on tool care

If you are an obsessive planner like I am, you'll enjoy thinking about next year's garden and all the wonderful things you might be able to do in it. If you are the out-of-sight-out-of-mind type, you might as well skip this entire chapter.

In the next few pages, we enter the fascinating world of seed savers who might very well have transformed an ancient agricultural practice into a cutting-edge horticultural trend. We also talk a little more about bringing herb plants indoors for winter enjoyment. And we look at why record keeping is not just for tax reasons. You also learn how to take care of your pruners and other tools so they will be ready to go in the spring.

Saving Seeds

Did you know there is a whole culture out there devoted to saving seeds? I'm not kidding. Seed saving is a worldwide phenomenon. There are seed-saving clubs and associations, how-to books and handbooks, newsletters and magazines, websites, legislation, and meetings and conventions. One website starts out with the words "... evolving tool is designed to empower individuals to participate in the creation of tomorrow." It's from an activist network dedicated to "protecting agricultural biodiversity and creating local food security."

Seed saving is a fascinating topic. But what does it have to do with you, you might ask? Well, if you are the thrifty type, you can save money by saving seeds. You can also be assured that you will have seeds of the plants you want, without the risk of disappointment, should the seed company run out of them. Another advantage of seed saving is that you can do your own organic thing. And you could actually develop a new variety with traits that please you.

There are only a few basic things you need to know to start saving seeds. One of the most important is to know the kinds of plants you are planning to collect seeds from. You want to collect seeds from plants that were grown from *open-pollinated* seeds rather than from *hybrids*.

Prof. Price's Pointers

Hybrid plants are those that are the offspring of two plants of different varieties (or species). A hybrid is a new variety with one or more genetic traits different from the parents. **Open-pollinated** seeds come from plants that have been pollinated by nature. Generally they produce offspring that are exactly like the parent plants. It is possible for nature to produce a hybrid.

It's very easy to save seeds from plants that produce seed pods or stalks. You simply allow the seeds to fully ripen on the plant, carefully cut the stalk or pod, place it in a paper bag, and shake it gently. Then you remove the dried stalk and any vegetation, which leaves you with just seeds. Put the seeds in an airtight container like a baby food jar or a plastic zipper bag and store it away from heat and light.

Saving seeds from fruiting vegetables is a little more complicated because you have to deal with the messy insides where the seeds develop.

Garden Guru Says

Be sure to label your seeds as soon as you put them in the storage container. It's really hard to distinguish seeds and you don't want to plant turnips instead of cabbage.

I have read, though I have never tried it, that the way to save seeds from tomatoes is to take the squishy parts that hold the seeds and smear them on a piece of newspaper. Let the newspaper dry, pick the seeds off, and put them in a storage container. As messy a job as it is, I do think it's worthwhile, especially if you've just had a spectacular season with an unusual plant.

Food for Thought

Though I am not a seed saver (I'm way too disorganized), I used to collect seeds from pumpkins every year at Halloween, which is the first stage of seed saving. After my husband cut jack-o'-lanterns with the girls, I would take the big pile of scooped-out pumpkin innards and clean them, removing all the gunk. After that I toasted them, but had I wanted to save them for planting, I would have dried them with paper towels and put them on a drying rack (maybe just some screening attached to a frame) in a cool dry place. After the seeds were completely dried, I would have sorted through them to eliminate any that had any mold or rot, and then put them in an airtight container. Very simple, very easy.

Some gardeners save seeds as a generation-to-generation thing, and they enjoy knowing that the corn or beans they are growing is from the same stock as the ones their grandfathers planted. For other gardeners there is the trading aspect. People swap seeds all over the country. Saving seeds is also a great hands-on science lesson for kids, and they might have fun with it.

Herbs All Year

If you've already had some experience with growing herbs, you know how easy they are to care for. And if you've been using your fresh herbs in your cooking, you'll not want to give them up. Isn't it nice to know that you can keep many of your herbs going all year long, even if you live in a cold climate?

Herbs are relatively easy to bring indoors when the summer growing season is over. And, though they might not grow as well as they did outside, you could still have enough to harvest throughout the winter until it's time to take them outdoors again.

The best herbs for growing indoors are the following:

- Rosemary
- Sage
- Mint
- Parsley
- French tarragon
- Coriander

You'll find more information about growing herbs indoors in Chapter 16. But keep in mind that when you bring plants in from the garden, you'll have to acclimate them to the changes in temperature, light and, most important, humidity. Our homes tend to be a lot less humid than the great outdoors and this can cause major stress on plants. Use a mister to make the plants feel at home.

It's a good idea to use fresh potting soil when you bring plants indoors. Never bring in soil from the garden; that's just asking for trouble. And be sure to inspect the plants for insects. Even if you don't see any, they might be there. One way to deal with that possibility is to spray the plants with an insecticidal soap before bringing them in.

You can suffocate insects on outdoor plants that are making the transition to indoors by putting the plants in a plastic bag, closing it with a twist tie, and putting the bagged plant inside another sealed plastic bag. Leave the shrouded plant in the bags for a few days. The plant must be dry when you do this or it can rot. But the lack of oxygen might be enough to kill any lingering insects.

Keeping Records

I think the human race is divided into two basic groups: those who keep records and those who don't. The record-keepers always write down their ATM withdrawals; the nons don't. Record-keepers remember birthdays and anniversaries; the nons forget more often than not. I'm a non, and I keep lousy garden records—but that doesn't mean I'm not a good gardener, and it doesn't mean you aren't a good gardener either.

Keeping a record (or at least good notes) provides gardeners with all kinds of valuable information that not only helps in planning future gardening efforts, but also allows you to improve your gardening skills. When you keep a record of your efforts, you'll see patterns of success and failures so that you can change what you are doing when necessary or increase other activities that are going well.

Take notes on what interests you. These are some of the things you might keep records of, but don't limit yourself to the ones I have thought of:

- Plants, including the varieties and numbers you have planted
- Sowing dates
- Weather details (temperature, rainfall, frosts, conditions; include dates)
- Germination times and success rates
- Set-out dates
- Flowering dates
- Fruit-set dates
- Maturity dates
- Harvest quantities and dates
- Insect information and dates they appear
- Disease problems and dates they appear
- Fertilizer use (types, quantities, dates)
- Expenses
- Tool purchases and repairs

Food for Thought

Some of my favorite garden books are the elaborate written records of their years of experience. Thomas Jefferson's phenomenal garden notes have been published in a book (a copy of which my parents gave me) that is more than three inches thick. It provides readers with a fascinating glimpse of the history of gardening in America.

It's actually fun to go back through your notes from previous years to compare this year's weather or harvest details. And when you get old, you can impress your grandchildren with your ability to "remember" that, on March 17, 2003, you planted five rows of peas and on August 1 of the same year, there was a huge storm with hail.

There are lots of pretty garden journals on the market. More often than not they are given to gardeners as holiday or birthday gifts; I don't think gardeners tend to buy them for themselves. You can use a ledger book, like Thomas Jefferson did. Some people like to keep their journals on wall calendars (although it's hard to find one with large enough squares), or in day planners. Having the dates right there makes it easier to keep track.

On my few attempts at keeping notes, I used a spiral-bound notebook. I liked the large pages, which gave me plenty of room to paste in seed packets, photos, and articles cut from magazines or newspapers. I like those notebooks with little pockets built into the front cover. That makes it easier to keep handouts from the County Extension or receipts from garden centers.

Planning for Next Year

For passionate gardeners, planning next year's garden usually starts about the time the last seeds and seedlings have been planted this year. That's when they wish they had ordered more arugula seeds or had planted five different types of eggplant instead of just two.

Thinking about next year's garden is actually one of my favorite off-season pastimes. I always have a stack of gardening books and catalogs beside my bed along with note cards and a pen so I can make lists (although I am a poor record-keeper, I am a world class list-maker).

Here are some resources for planning and reading up on next year's garden:

- Stock up on gardening books (you can find lots of them at the library, but I think most gardeners like to own them; perhaps that's the garden writer in me telling you to buy more books!).
- Read and cut out magazine articles on garden topics that interest you.
- Send for gardening catalogs.
- Make lists of things you want to grow next year.
- Take classes and attend lectures (see the list of gardens open to the public in Appendix C, many of which offer educational programs; community colleges, adult schools, and County Extension offices also offer courses and talks).
- Visit garden centers, nurseries, public gardens, and even friends' gardens to look for ideas and gather information.

You can also take time during the off-season to go through the copious notes you took in your garden book. This will refresh your memory and give you a little shot of reality before you place your seed orders in December or January.

Tool Care and Repair

You probably have a bit of investment in your garden tools, so you should take good care of them. We will assume that during the gardening season you have been reasonably careful with your tools, taking care to clean off the soil and debris after each use. And you've always put them away at the end of the day. Right? Well, even if you've been a little slipshod, you make up for it by giving all your tools a good cleaning and servicing before you hang them up for the winter.

Sharp as a Tack

Keeping pruning tools sharp is an essential task. You can have it done by a professional, which isn't usually very expensive. Or you can do it yourself.

My good friend Steve Cooper, who managed one of my favorite nurseries, used to sharpen my pruners for me when I would stop by for a visit during the off-season. He would take out an ancient whetstone and, with just a few strokes, he would make them razor sharp. It's a very old-fashioned skill, and one worth having.

Here's how to take care of your of your pruners:

1. Clean the blades with a solvent like paint thinner, turpentine, or nail polish remover.

2. Rub the blades with steel wool or emery cloth to remove any rust or plant residue.

3. Sharpen the blade with a sharpening stone (also called whetstone or honing stone) at the same angle as the blade and always going in one direction (away from the blade).

4. Lubricate the hinges and springs with WD-40 or other lubricating oil.

5. Rub all the metal parts with mineral or vegetable oil or some other lubricating oil.

6. Wipe clean.

7. Return them to their proper storage space.

Food for Thought

I've seen classes on tool sharpening offered at large garden centers, adult schools, and County Extension offices. If there's one scheduled near you, go for it. Take all your pruners along and get them done while you learn the tricks of the trade.

Some experts suggest taking pruners apart to clean them thoroughly, but I'm not convinced. It would be just my luck to drop a screw or misplace a spring, and I would never be able to get the pruners back together again.

Other Tools

We will assume that you have cleaned all the soil off your spades, shovels, rakes, cultivators, and hand tools. That's a given. The last cleaning of the season should include a thorough buffing with steel wool or emery cloth on the metal parts, followed by a rub down with some kind of oil.

Pay attention to any wood handles too. Sand wooden handles that might have developed rough spots, chips, or splinters. If the tools are old, the wood might be dried out. You can use some liquid or spray furniture polish or linseed oil to put some moisture back in.

Hoses and Stuff

If you live in an area that gets really cold, you should put all your hoses away. First drain them thoroughly, especially if you store them in a place that isn't heated. Then roll them up. It's simple, and it will save you money if you don't have to replace hoses that have split open because they froze with water in them. Also be sure to drain any outside faucets that aren't protected.

Machinery

Of course you will need to clean off any power equipment like a tractor or tiller. And you might want to think about having them serviced. But don't do it now. Instead, make an appointment now to have the servicing done a month before you usually open your garden. That way it will be taken care of when you want to be out there digging. If you put off taking your equipment, you'll have to wait along with all the other gardeners who weren't smart enough to plan ahead.

Garden Miscellany

Gardeners always have lots of other things besides tools that need to be taken care of at the end of the season. Here are a few to keep in mind:

- ◆ Clean and stack tomato cages.
- ◆ Untangle, roll, and store bird and pea netting.
- ◆ Gather and bundle stakes (throw away any broken ones).
- ◆ Pull up, clean, and put away row markers.
- ◆ Empty watering cans and put them away.
- ◆ Check irrigation timers for any needed repairs or replacements, clean, and store.
- ◆ Clean wheelbarrow or garden cart, and check for needed repairs. Don't put it at the back of the shed because you might need it during the winter.

◆ Clean and disinfect pots and containers. Stack and store terracotta pots where they won't get wet (they absorb water, which when it freezes will cause cracks or disintegration).

◆ Review any containers of herbicides, pesticides, and fertilizers to see if they should be kept or disposed of. (Check with your local waste management people to find out the proper methods of disposal.)

Let's Rethink This

Did you make some really big mistakes this year? If you did, you are not the only gardener who needs to make changes in next year's effort. The biggest mistake many new gardeners make is that they started off with too much garden, and it just got away from them.

Other mistakes include growing too much of one thing and not enough of something else. Some gardeners vow at the start of the season that everything will be done organically and naturally, but then they run into problems with severe infestations or diseases, or find out that the nitrogen deficiency isn't helped enough by the application of a natural fertilizer.

The important thing to remember when you realize that you've made a mistake is that all gardens are living things; that they grow and change every season and every year. You can always learn from your mistakes, make changes and adjustments, try new plants, look for new solutions.

The Least You Need to Know

◆ Keep good records of your gardening activities.

◆ Use fresh potting soil and check for insects when bringing herbs indoors.

◆ Take advantage of your off-season time to attend gardening classes and lectures, to visit garden centers and botanical centers, and to read gardening books.

◆ Use your down time to repair your tools, to replace those that are beyond repair, and to add new ones that will make gardening easier or more fun.

◆ Don't be afraid to change the size of your garden or the way you work in it.

Appendix A

Gardening Resources

This short list of manufacturers and companies is just a starting point for finding gardening equipment, tools, seeds, and plants. Spend a few minutes online and you are likely to find plenty of sources of your own.

Cyndi's Catalog of Garden Catalogs
www.qnet.com/~johnsonj/

This site lists hundreds of well-known and obscure gardening catalogs including dozens of catalogs featuring vegetable seeds and plants. It originates in Canada and has that orientation but is a great site for all gardeners.

GardenGuides
www.gardenguides.com

This website calls itself "a growing resource for gardeners." You'll find links to hundreds of mail order resources including seed, tool, and equipment companies; newsletters, books, and magazines; and much more.

Tools

Smith & Hawken
Mill Valley, CA
1-800-940-1170
www.smith-hawken.com

Gorgeous catalog and wonderful assortment of tools. This is where my favorite poacher's spade came from.

Kinsman Company
Point Pleasant, PA
1-800-733-4146
kinsmangarden.com

Michelle and Graham Graham (who live just up the river from my house) have assembled a terrific collection of tools and garden equipment, many imported from England. Nice garden decor items, too.

Mantis Tiller/Cultivator
Southampton, PA
1-800-366-6268
www.mantisgardentools.com

This company makes the tiny tiller.

Lagenbach Fine Garden Tools
Galesburg, IL
1-800-362-1991
www.langenbach.com

Large selection of tools, including lots of pruning equipment.

Seeds and Seedlings

Seeds of Change
Santa Fe, NM
1-888-762-7333
store.yahoo.com/seedsofchange

Seeds of Change is biodiversity-oriented with gourmet greens, cover crops, and interesting veggie varieties. Check out the nice photos at its website.

Sand Hill Preservation Center
Calamus, IA
563-246-2299
sandhill@netins.net

Sand Hill offers more than 350 tomato varieties, 50 sweet potatoes, rare poultry breeds, and more!

Irish Eyes—Garden City Seeds
Thorp, WA
509-964-7000
www.irish-eyes.com

The Irish Eyes specializes in unusual potatoes (more than 80 varieties), onions (a few dozen), shallots, garlic, and other veggies. It also provides some great online growers guides.

Johnny's Selected Seeds
Albion, ME
207-437-9294
www.johnnyseeds.com

This is one of the best-known seed companies that specializes in short season crops. It offers a broad selection of everyday seeds to exotics, cover crops, lots of melons, peppers, tomatoes, and potatoes.

Native Seeds/SEARCH
Tucson, AZ
560-622-5561
www.nativeseeds.org

This group offers seeds of Southwest Native Americans.

Heirloom Seed Project
Lancaster, PA
717-569-0401
www.landisvalleymuseum.org

The Heirloom Project offers 200 heirlooms, including many vegetables and herbs (you can also visit the farm museum).

Colonial Williamsburg Colonial Nursery Seed List
Williamsburg, VA
757-565-870
www.history.org/History/CWLand/nursery3.cfm

You guessed it. This organization offers seeds from colonial America.

Abundant Life Seed Foundation
360-385-5660
www.abundantlifeseed.org

If you want to find heirloom and rare seeds for vegetables, herbs, and grains, the Abundant Life has something to offer you.

W. Atlee Burpee and Company
Warminster, PA
1-800-333-5808
www.burpee.com

Burpee is one of the grand old seed companies with extensive offerings and specialty catalogs.

Evergreen Y. H. Enterprises
Anaheim, CA
www.evergreenseeds.com

Asian vegetable seeds are this group's specialty.

The Cook's Garden
Londonderry, VT
1-800-475-9703
www.cooksgarden.com

The Cook's Garden has culinary plants and seeds, especially large collection of herbs.

Park Seed Co., Inc.
Greenwood, SC
1-800-213-0076
www.parkseed.com

This company has a huge inventory with dozens of varieties of your favorite vegetables. Look for their Whopper hybrids of super-size vegetables.

Thomas and Morgan
Jackson, NJ

This is the famous English seed company that features a vast collection of seeds. I counted 36 varieties of beans and 28 types of lettuce alone!

Fruit Plants

W. Atlee Burpee and Company
Warminster, PA
1-800-333-5808
www.burpee.com

You'll find all kinds of fruit plants through the Burpee company including grapes, brambles, blueberries, rhubarb, and strawberries.

Equipment and Supplies

Benner's Gardens
Conshohocken, PA
1-800-753-4660
www.BennersGardens.com

This is my friend's family's company. They sell the mesh deer fencing and cattle grates that really do keep deer out. Also look for their simple compost bins. If you call, tell them I sent you!

Natural Insect Control

Ontario, Canada

www.natural-insect-control.com

I like this company's earth-friendly tone. They sell beneficial insects, insecticidal soaps, organic fertilizers, and some great bird houses (birds eat insects, get it?).

Gardens Alive!

Lawrenceburg, IN

812-537-8650

www.gardensalive.com

This company boasts "environmentally responsible products that work." They have organic fertilizers and insecticides, floating row covers, soil test kits, and a zillion other things organically minded folks will appreciate.

Books, Magazines, and Websites

Books and Magazines

Creasy, Rosalind. *The Complete Book of Edible Landscaping*. London: Periplus Publishing, 1982.

Rosalind Creasy also has a series of books on specific edible gardens including: *Mexican* (2000); *Asian* (2000); *Italian* (2001); *Edible Flowers* (1999); *French* (1999); and *Edible Herbs* (1999).

Sunset Books Editors. *Vegetable Gardening Illustrated*. Palo Alto, CA: Lane Publishing Company, 1987.

Basic how-to information for growing vegetables and small fruits with good sections on raised beds and container gardening.

Editors of *Organic Gardening. Best Methods for Growing Fruits and Berries*. Emmaus, PA: Rodale Press Inc., 1981.

A nuts-and-bolts guide.

Nick, Jean, M.A., and Fern Marshall Bradley. *Growing Fruits and Vegetables Organically*. Emmaus, PA: Rodale Press, 1994.

This small book covers all the basic techniques you will need to grow fruits using organic methods. It covers tree fruits as well as the fruits we talk about in this book.

Lovejoy, Sharon. *Sunflower Houses*. Loveland, CO: Interweave Press, Inc., 1991.

Whimsical and wonderful garden projects for children. (I heard the author speak at a children's gardening convention many years ago, and she was inspirational.) Find tee-pee plans, how to grow a zucchini in a bottle, and a personalized pumpkin in this book, along with a lot of other great ideas.

Bagust, Harold. *The Gardener's Dictionary of Horticultural Terms*. London: Cassell Publishers Limited, 1992.

A thorough dictionary with an English (as in England) focus, so you'll find some words we don't use in the United States.

U.S. Department of Agriculture. *USDA's Complete Guide to Home Canning*. Mineola, NY: Dover Publications, 1999.

This is a no-nonsense guide to putting food up. If you take a course at your local County Extension, chances are you'll follow directions from this guide.

Brenzel, Kathleen Norris, ed. *Sunset Western Garden Book*. Palo Alto, CA: Sunset Publishing Group, 2001.

Prof. Price consults this book when he has questions related to his San Diego garden.

Waters, Marjorie. *The Victory Garden Kids' Book*. Boston: Houghton Mifflin, 1988.

This charming book has been around for a few years, but its approach to gardening with children couldn't be more with it. My friend Alison Kennedy, who is the art director for the book, gave it to me when my kids were little. The simple, step-by-step approach is just as helpful for grown-ups as it is for children.

Websites

Besides the various websites referenced in the chapters, here are others that will be useful as you plan, plant, and harvest your edible garden.

Historic

www.monticello.org/shop
Thomas Jefferson Center for Historic Plants (at Monticello). Go to Twinleaf Online to find fascinating article on Thomas Jefferson's gardens.

www.gardendigest.com/timegl.htm
Timeline of gardening from ancient times to 1600.

www.gti.net/mocolib1/kid/food.html
Amazing timeline; includes when many foods were first introduced.

horizon.nmsu.edu/garden/history/welcome.html
Where food crops originated.

General

www.reeusda.gov/1700/statepartners/usa.htm
Links to many of the extension offices at land grant universities around the country.

www.doityourself.com
Search for "gardening" for a lot of do-it-yourself gardening tips.

www.gardeninglaunchpad.com
Four thousand gardening links.

The Best Extension Office Websites

ohioline.osu.edu
From Ohio State University, click on "yard and garden," and you'll find very detailed articles on individual fruits and vegetables.

www.clemson.edu/extension
From Clemson University, click on Subject Matter; then Home and Garden Center; then Landscape, Garden, and Indoor Plants; then Vegetables, Fruits, and Nuts to find great info on specific plants.

oregonstate.edu/extension
Click Gardening information, then on vegetable gardening, which is highlighted in the text, then you can select a topic.

www.rce.rutgers.edu/pubs
Click on Gardening and Landscaping; excellent articles, especially on insects and pests and soil stuff.

Kids

www.kidsgardening.com
Ideas, projects, and products designed to get kids into the garden. A project of the National Gardening Association.

www.cln.org/themes/gardening.html
Directed toward teachers, but parents might find something they'd like to do with their kids.

aggie-horticulture.tamu.edu/county/smith/kids.html
From Texas A&M, lots of links for kid-related gardening topics.

Associations and Organizations

The Garden Club of America
New York, NY
www.gcamerica.org

This organization is dedicated to stimulating "the knowledge and love of garden." You will find a list of all the member clubs from around the country on their website.

Herb Society of America, Inc.
Mentor, OH
www.herbsociety.org

This organization promotes the knowledge and use of herbs. There are member clubs across the country.

The American Horticultural Society
Alexandria, VA
www.ahs.org

This is the oldest gardening organization in the United States. It offers educational programs, seminars, special events and reciprocal admissions for members to arboreta, gardens, and conservatories all over the country.

The National Gardening Association
South Burlington, VT
www.nationalGardening.com

This organization focuses on promoting youth and community gardening projects. It also does extensive market research for the lawn and garden industries.

Gardens to Visit

All the gardens listed here are open to the public. Some charge an admission fee, whereas others are free. Call or visit their websites to determine open hours before visiting.

New York Botanical Garden
Bronx, NY
www.nybg.org

Herb and kitchen gardens.

Cornell Plantations
Ithaca, NY
www.plantations.cornell.edu

Heritage vegetable including World War II Victory Garden; herb garden.

Harmony Demonstration Gardens
Marinette, WI
715-732-7570

Heritage Hill
Green Bay, WI
1-800-721-5150

Theme gardens.

Sandhills Horticultural Gardens
Pinehurst, NC
www.sandhills.cc.nc.us

Vegetable garden and vineyard.

**Cleveland Botanical Garden
Hershey Children's Garden**
Cleveland, OH
www.cbgarden.org

A fanciful place for children to learn about the wonder of plants.

Hovander Homestead Park
Ferndale, WA
360-348-3444

Historic vegetable garden.

Philipsburg Manor
North Tarrytown, NY
914-631-3992

Heirloom vegetables and herbs.

McDowell House Apothecary and Gardens
Danville, KY
606-236-2804

Medicinal herb garden.

Shaker Village of Pleasant Hill
Harrodsburg, KY
1-800-734-5611

Nineteenth-century-style herb and vegetable gardens.

Ballard Garden
Haddam, CT
203-345-2400

Herbs and vegetables.

Bellamy-Ferriday House and Garden
Bethlehem, CT
203-266-7596

Colonial-style parterre.

Community Gardens
Portland, ME

Vegetable gardens run by local gardeners.

Johnny's Selected Seeds Trial Gardens
Albion, ME
207-437-9294

One of the largest vegetable trial gardens in United States.

Hancock Shaker Village
Pittsfield, MA
www.hancockshakervillage.org

Heirloom gardens.

Harlow Old Fort House
Plymouth, MA

Raised bed gardens.

Old Manse
Concord, MA
978-369-3909

Nineteenth-century-style organically grown vegetable garden.

Plimoth Plantation
Plymouth, MA
www.plimoth.org

Seventeenth-century reproduction gardens (one of my favorites).

Sandy Point Discovery Center
Stratham, NH
603-675-2175

Native American vegetable gardens.

Shelburne Museum
Shelburne, VT
www.shelburnemuseum.org

Vegetable gardens.

The Stone House
Freeport, ME
207-865-3429

Demonstration garden for organic gardening.

Grandmother's Garden
Westfield, MA
413-562-2022

Community garden.

Caprilands Herb Farm
Coventry, CT
www.caprilands.com

Herb display gardens.

Ogden House Museum and Garden
Fairfield, CT

Medicinal and culinary plants from the eighteenth century.

Michigan 4-H Children's Garden
East Lansing, MI
www.4hgarden.msu.edu

Another garden devoted to kids.

Urban Garden Center—Oahu Cooperative Extension
Pearl City, HA
808-453-6050

Vegetable idea garden.

Dwight Miller Orchards
Dummerston, VT
www.strollingoftheheifers.com/
farms.html

Largest organic fruit farm in eastern United States.

Elm Lea Farm
Putney, VT
www.putney.com

Extensive vegetable gardens on grounds of private school.

Old Salem Gardens
Old Salem, NC

Church community garden.

The Rutgers Gardens
New Brunswick, NJ
aesop.rutgers.edu

Display gardens of All America Selections winners. (Prof. Price taught at Rutgers; Daria is a Rutgers College graduate.)

Penn State Trial Gardens
University Park, PA
www.psu.edu/research/trial
814-863-7725

All America selections.

Stonecrop Gardens
Cold Spring, NY

Vegetable parterre at center of English-style flower garden.

Billings Farm and Museum
Woodstock, VT
www.billingsfarm.org

Kitchen garden with heirloom vegetables.

Tennessee Agricultural Museum
Nashville, TN
www.picktnproducts.org/agmuseum

Kitchen and herb gardens.

Rio Grande Botanic Garden
Albuquerque, NM
www.cabq.gov/biopark

Children's vegetable garden exhibits.

Belttown P-Patch
Seattle, WA
www.speakeasy.org/ppatch

Community garden.

Quad City Botanical Center
Rock Island, IL
www.qcgardens.com

Exotic vegetable display gardens.

Fort Vancouver National Historic Site
Vancouver, WA

Heirloom vegetables, herbs, and berries.

Colonial Williamsburg
Williamsburg, VA
geninfo@cwf.org

Colonial-style kitchen and herb gardens.

Mount Vernon
Mount Vernon, VA
mvinfo@mountvernon.org

George Washington's kitchen gardens
with heirloom vegetables.

Monticello
Charlottesville, VA
www.twinleaf.org

One of the best vegetable gardens in the
country and my personal favorite.

Gateway Greening
St. Louis, MO
314-577-9484

Community gardens.

Glossary

abiotic Nonliving or nonbiological origin of condition such as sunscald or injury. [Greek: *a* = not + *bios* = life]

aggregates Clusters of soil particles, the shapes of which determine the structure of the soil.

alkaline A pH greater than 7 or a substance that raises pH. [Arabic: *al-gili* = ashes]

alternate host A different host plant to a pathogen that may or may not develop the disease or condition caused by the pathogen.

annual A plant that completes its lifecycle in a year and does not survive into a second season.

anthracnose Diseases caused by certain fungi that produce ulcerlike symptoms. [Greek: *anthrax* = carbuncle + *nosos* = disease]

bare root Certain plants, particularly fruits, are sold with bare roots, that is without any soil around the roots.

bell jar A bell-shaped glass jar, often placed over a delicate seedling to protect it from cold.

biannual (biennial) A plant that develops roots, leaves, and stems its first year, but does not flower and produce fruit or seed until the second season. [Latin: *bis* = twice + *annus* = year]

biological control Control of a disease by a biological agent, such as the bacterium *Bacillus thuringiensis* (BT) that is effective in controlling some insects.

blight　A disease symptom characterized by the death of a specific organ (for example, leaf blight).

bloom　The production of flowers.

bolt　The rapid growth of a stem for a rosette stage, usually resulting in flowering and seed production.

bone meal　A fertilizer prepared from ground-up bones that is rich in phosphate.

bramble　A prickly shrub; also raspberry and blackberry shrubs.

broadcast　A method of planting seed by throwing it uniformly over cultivated soil.

canker　A lesion of decay in the bark of a tree or shrub or on the stem of a herbaceous plant.

chelate　Combination of a metal ion with an organic compound that renders the metal ion water soluble. [Greek: *chele* = claw]

chlorophyll　The green pigment in plants that absorbs light in the process of photosynthesis. [Greek: *chloros* = green + *phyllon* = leaf]

chlorosis　Yellowing of leaves. [Greek: *chloros* = green]

cloche　French for bell jar.

cold frame　A box with a removable glass cover that can be used for an early start for seedlings, for hardening off young seedlings, or for prolonging the growing season.

compost　Organic material collected from kitchen, yard, garden, and barnyard that has been decomposed by microorganisms into small bit of organic matter for use as soil enhancer, fertilizer, or mulch.

cover crop　Planting a crop in the off season to minimize soil erosion and, when legumes are planted, to help add nitrogen to the soil. *See also* green manure.

crop rotation　The practice of growing different crops on a piece of land in alternate years, especially the practice of alternating legumes (which fix nitrogen) with other crops.

crown　The upper portion of a plant with the newest leaves and buds.

cultivar　A variety of a species, typically one that has been bred for agriculture.

damping off　The death of seedlings from excessive moisture (rot); the pathological agent is typically a fungus.

dead heading　The practice of removing dead flowers to limit the amount of the plant's resources that would otherwise be put into making seeds.

determinate   A trait in which all of the buds on a stem become, after a certain state, flower buds, resulting in no future vegetative growth, but instead the production of flowers and seeds.

dioecious   Plants with male and female flowers on separate plants. In certain species (less than 5 percent of all species, including asparagus and spinach), some individual plants produce only male flowers, while other produce only female flowers.

dormancy   In some species, seeds or mature plants remain inactive, producing no new growth; active growth does not begin until they receive a certain environment signal (heat, cold, light, and so on).

double digging   A system of bed preparing that moves enriched topsoil to subsoil level and brings subsoil to surface where it is improved with amendments.

downy mildew   Infection by a certain class of fungi.

drainage   The way water passes through soil.

fibrous root   A root that branches out in many directions.

floret   Many inflorescences, such as those of broccoli, are composed of numerous individual flowers; these are florets.

flower   The earliest structure in sexual reproduction is the flower, composed of carpels (the female part) and stamens (the male part), plus petals, sepals, and so on.

frass   Insect excrement. *See also* honeydew.

friable   Crumbles readily, referring to soil.

fruit   The organ that encloses the seed or seeds; when ripe, the fruit attracts animals, such as ourselves, to eat the fruit and spread the seed.

fungicide   An agent that kills fungi.

germination   The earliest stage in the development of a seed into a plant; seeds typically germinate only after they have been exposed to moisture.

green manure   A cover crop such as annual rye grass or field beans grown to improve soil during the off season. Usually plowed under before it sets seed.

hardening off   The process of increasing the ability of plants to withstand cold or dryness, typically of seeds started indoors, and often by withholding nitrogen fertilizer and progressively decreasing the supply of water while exposing the plant to an outdoor environment.

hardscape   The structural elements in a landscape including walls, fences, paths, buildings, gates, and arbors.

herb   A nonwoody vascular plant; or a plant valued for its aromatic, savory, or medicinal properties.

herbaceous   Soft, succulent plants that develop little or no woody stems.

honeydew   Insect excrement. *See also* frass.

humus   The remaining part of organic matter in the soil after it has completely decomposed.

hybrid   The results of a cross between different varieties within a species, between different species (interspecific hybrid), or between different genera (intergeneric hybrid).

insecticide   A substance that kills insects. [Latin: *insectum* = insect + *cida* = to kill]

leaf mold   The remains of leaves that have been decomposed by microorganisms.

loam   A soil that is a mixture of clay, sand, and organic matter, typically the ideal mixture for agriculture.

micro-climate   In many parts of the country, the climate can vary greatly depending on exactly where you are: the north or south side of a hill, how far from a body of water, or the direction of prevailing winds.

microorganism   An organism that can only be seen as an individual with a microscope; for example, a bacterium and many fungi.

monoecious   Plants in which male and female flowers are produced separately on the same plant; examples are members of the squash family, in which the first flowers to be produced are only male, with female flowers produced further along the vine. *See also* dioecious. [Greek: *mono* = one + *oikos* = house]

necrotic   Dead or dying. Dead spots on a leaf are frequently referred to as necrotic lesions. [Greek: *necros* = dead body]

nematode   A class of tiny worms, most nematodes do not attack plants but instead help to break down dead organic matter; some nematodes, however, attack plant roots and are serious pests.

neutral soil   Soil that is very near pH 7.

nitrogen fixation   The process of converting the nitrogen in the air to ammonium nitrogen. Nitrogen fixation is carried out by three groups of soil bacteria, some in collaboration with legumes.

node   The place on the stem where there is a bud or a branch.

parasite   An organism that lives in or on another organism to the detriment of the host. [Greek: *parasitos* = eating beside another]

parterre   Garden bed intersected by paths and walkways often with a formal, geometric pattern.

pathogen An organism or virus that produces disease in a host. [Greek: *pathos* = disease + *genesis* = to be born]

perennial A plant that lives for multiple years.

pH The measure of the hydrogen ion activity in soil. Simply put, the pH shows how acidic or alkaline the soil is.

photosynthesis The conversion of light energy into the energy that makes plants grow.

potager French for kitchen garden.

rhizome Underground stems. [Greek: *rhizo* = root]

rot Decomposition of plant parts brought on by microorganisms; specific diseases.

rust Fungal disease, so called because of the color of the fungi as they appear on leaves and stems.

sterile Incapable of reproducing. Male sterile, where the plant produces normal carpels but no pollen, is a useful character in plant breeding.

stomata Tiny openings in leaves through which water evaporates.

taproot Long root, typically fleshy and thick with few branching roots, as in carrots or parsnips.

tender Plants that are particularly sensitive to cold; typically plants that can not withstand a hard frost.

thin To remove young seedlings from a row, bed, or planter in order to have proper spacing between plants.

thinnings The small plants removed during the thinning process. Sometimes used in salads.

transpiration The movement of water from the roots, through the plant, and exiting by evaporation through the stomata of the leaves.

tuber Enlarged rhizomes (underground stems) that typically serve as storage organs; for example, potato tubers.

variety A member of a species with a distinguishing set of characteristics; a variety developed for agriculture is called a cultivar.

vermiculite A micalike mineral that is added to soils, especially in container gardening, to increase the water-holding capacity of the soil.

wilt A disease symptom in which the leaves droop, cause by interference in the uptake or retention of water; a specific disease caused by bacteria or virus.

Index

D

Q-R

T

U–V

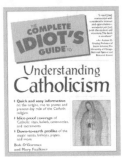

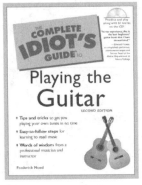

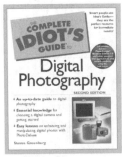
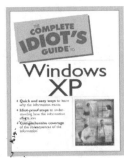